THE COMPLETE IDIOT'S GUIDE® TO

Beading

Illustrated

by Georgene Lockwood

ALPHA

A member of Penguin Group (USA) Inc.

To all the "beady buddies" who have helped me along the way and with this book.
And to my special buddy Bobbi Wicks for her patience, attention to detail, and love.
Thanks from the bottom of my heart.

ALPHA BOOKS

Published by the Penguin Group

Penguin Group (USA) Inc., 375 Hudson Street, New York, New York 10014, U.S.A.

Penguin Group (Canada), 10 Alcorn Avenue, Toronto, Ontario, Canada M4V 3B2 (a division of Pearson Penguin Canada Inc.)

Penguin Books Ltd, 80 Strand, London WC2R 0RL, England

Penguin Ireland, 25 St Stephen's Green, Dublin 2, Ireland (a division of Penguin Books Ltd)

Penguin Group (Australia), 250 Camberwell Road, Camberwell, Victoria 3124, Australia (a division of Pearson Australia Group Pty Ltd)

Penguin Books India Pvt Ltd, 11 Community Centre, Panchsheel Park, New Delhi—110 017, India

Penguin Group (NZ), Cnr Airborne and Rosedale Roads, Albany, Auckland #1310, New Zealand (a division of Pearson New Zealand Ltd)

Penguin Books (South Africa) (Pty) Ltd, 24 Sturdee Avenue, Rosebank, Johannesburg 2196, South Africa

Penguin Books Ltd, Registered Offices: 80 Strand, London WC2R 0RL, England

International Standard Book Number: 1-59257-256-1
Library of Congress Catalog Card Number: 2004111434

06 05 04   8 7 6 5 4 3 2 1

Interpretation of the printing code: The rightmost number of the first series of numbers is the year of the book's printing; the rightmost number of the second series of numbers is the number of the book's printing. For example, a printing code of 04-1 shows that the first printing occurred in 2004.

Printed in the United States of America

Note: This publication contains the opinions and ideas of its author. It is intended to provide helpful and informative material on the subject matter covered. It is sold with the understanding that the author and publisher are not engaged in rendering professional services in the book. If the reader requires personal assistance or advice, a competent professional should be consulted.

The author and publisher specifically disclaim any responsibility for any liability, loss, or risk, personal or otherwise, which is incurred as a consequence, directly or indirectly, of the use and application of any of the contents of this book.

Most Alpha books are available at special quantity discounts for bulk purchases for sales promotions, premiums, fund-raising, or educational use. Special books, or book excerpts, can also be created to fit specific needs.

For details, write: Special Markets, Alpha Books, 375 Hudson Street, New York, NY 10014.

Publisher: *Marie Butler-Knight*
Product Manager: *Phil Kitchel*
Senior Managing Editor: *Jennifer Chisholm*
Senior Acquisitions Editor: *Randy Ladenheim-Gil*
Development Editor: *Christy Wagner*
Production Editor: *Janette Lynn*
Copy Editor: *Nancy Wagner*

Cartoonist: *Richard King*
Cover/Book Designer: *Trina Wurst*
Indexer: *Heather McNeill*
Layout: *Becky Harmon*
Proofreading: *Mary Hunt*
Graphics: *Tammy Graham, Laura Robbins*
Photography: *Georgene Lockwood, Jim Lockwood*

Contents at a Glance

Appendixes

Contents

Foreword

Not long ago, archaeologists in South Africa discovered shell beads dating back more than 70,000 years and designated them as the world's oldest known jewelry. Throughout history and in virtually every corner of the world, people created and wore beads not simply for adornment, but as symbols of power, magic, wealth, and status. Beads were also a long-standing form of currency, fueling European trade for hundreds of years.

Our current revival of beading as an art, craft, and hobby has its roots in the late 1980s. Bead shops were few and far between in those days—some remained from the crafty era of the 1960s and 1970s, others served the garment industry's need for beaded embellishment. By the early 1990s, a few brave entrepreneurs were opening shops, and curious fiber guilds began sponsoring classes by a handful of teachers knowledgeable in what were then newly revived beading techniques. In 1994, with the launch of *Bead&Button*, beaders got their first magazine dedicated to this pursuit.

Interest in beading gained momentum in the mid-1990s, and its continued growth has been breathtaking. The fashion industry can take some credit for its recent popularity. As soon as beaded jewelry debuted as a must-have accessory in department stores and boutiques, savvy beaders began to make their own necklaces, bracelets, and earrings at a fraction of the retail cost. Their nonbeading friends noticed, signed up for classes, and started making jewelry, too. And beading took off.

Once an obscure niche among craft trends, beading has blossomed into one of today's leading hobby categories among women (and a few men) in all age groups. Bead supplies are everywhere and not just in bead shops. You'll find them in the aisles of craft chains and giant retailers; in catalogs as thick as phone books; on eBay and at hundreds of other Internet sites; and at multivendor bead sales held across the country. At no time in history has there been such a wealth of materials available for the art/craft/hobby of beading.

If you're ready to get started in beading, it makes sense to get familiar with the basics. Don't let unfamiliar terminology, supplies, or techniques send you running for cover. (I've heard stories from people who've gone into bead shops, been mesmerized by the inventory, and walked out dazed and empty-handed.) That's not likely to happen if you spend a little time with this excellent book. Georgene Lockwood provides her readers with careful explanations of bead choices, stitching and stringing materials, findings, and techniques in a thoughtfully organized and well-illustrated volume. She beads, and it's clear that she knows what she's talking about.

Don't be fooled by the book's title. *The Complete Idiot's Guide to Beading Illustrated* may indeed contain information that every beginner should know, but Georgene covers much more than the basics. By including wirework, loom work, and bead stitches, Georgene gives her readers enough ideas for a lifetime of enjoyment. I like to think that Georgene wrote this book not just to initiate a flirtation among her readers, but to ignite a full-fledged affair.

Mindy Brooks
Editor, *Bead&Button* magazine; founding editor, *BeadStyle* magazine

Introduction

The bead is a powerful object. It is imbued with history. It is a compact record of human ingenuity and creativity. Beads are, quite simply, beautiful. When we learn how to create with them, their beauty and power are limitless.

One of the great things about beading is that it can be extremely easy or very complicated, depending on how much time or patience you're willing to give. Stringing some lovely beads on a cord and wearing your creation—what could be easier? But if you want a challenge, well, there's more than enough of that to lead you down the beading path.

The Complete Idiot's Guide to Beading Illustrated will give you all the skills you need to do many of the different kinds of beadwork made all over the world. I have given you step-by-step instructions and simple samples to make for each technique, then I've provided you with a few more advanced projects to go to the next level, and finally I've given you the resources you need to take your work as far as you want to go.

The world of beading is an ever-inspiring and challenging world for me, and it is my sincere hope that this book will introduce its pleasures to you. Happy beading!

How to Use This Book

Beading has so many applications it would be difficult to cover them all in one book. Here you will find the basics of the most common forms of beadwork, from simple stringing to weaving to wire work and beyond.

Part 1, "The Venerable, Adaptable Bead," gives you a context for the world of beadwork. You'll learn a little about the history of beads, places to get them, guidelines for buying some of the more expensive ones, instructions for making your own, and other things you need to work with them effectively. There's also a discussion of some design basics, so you'll quickly learn how to adapt patterns and instructions to your own liking.

Part 2, "Bead Spaghetti: Stringing and Weaving Techniques," will teach you everything you need to know about beads on string, cord, or flexible wire, including the most commonly used off-loom weaving techniques. Then I'll introduce you to the bead loom—how to choose one, how to set up one, and how to do loomed beadwork.

Part 3, "Getting Wired!" covers the basics of wirework for jewelry-making. You'll learn how to select the proper wire for the job, as well as how to make French and Victorian beaded wire flowers.

Part 4, "Beads on Fabric and Fiber," is all about bead embroidery, needle weaving, and macramé.

Part 5, "Bead Potpourri," will deal with a variety of topics every beader should know about safety, taking care of beaded objects, and using beads to make decorative things for your home and/or to give as gifts.

Part 6, "Let's Bead It! Additional Projects for Beginning Beaders," will take the skills you learned in the first five parts of this book and give you additional projects to complete with your newfound skills.

At the end of this book, you can turn to a comprehensive glossary, an extensive list of helpful resources, and some additional bead references for adding a personal touch to your beadwork.

Extras

This book features a number of valuable sidebars with additional information about beading: definitions, hints and shortcuts to make things easier, cautions to keep you from making common mistakes, and notes to boost your creativity.

Knots!

Warning! Here are some things to look out for. Avoid common errors and difficulties by heeding these signposts.

A-Bead-C's

When you need to understand a term as you read, look to this sidebar. There's a more extensive glossary in Appendix A, when you need to refresh your memory.

Findings

Why not benefit from experienced beaders? Here are tips, hints, and shortcuts to make your road to bead mastery a smoother one.

Put On Your Beadin' Cap

You'll get ideas for ways to enhance your beading creativity in this sidebar. We'll also be doing a small patch or sample for each major technique. If you choose to work along with this book from beginning to end, you'll have a unique "beading cap" sampler of your journey through the world of beading and this book. Look for more information on this at the end of Chapter 2!

Special Thanks to the Technical Reviewer

The Complete Idiot's Guide to Beading Illustrated was reviewed by an expert who double-checked the accuracy of what you'll learn here, to help us ensure that this book gives you everything you need to know about crafting beautiful works with beads. Special thanks are extended to Bobbi Wicks.

Acknowledgments

Extra special thanks go to Bobbi Wicks, my beadin' buddy, who served as my technical editor and helped test many of the projects in this book. She made sure my instructions were clear, let me wake her many times very early in the morning, and held my hand when the going got tough. May all your bead dreams be happy ones!

Always a huge debt of gratitude goes to my husband, who now knows the routine when it comes to writing a book and always gives me the space, time, and support to make it happen. Thanks for not complaining all those nights I was too tired to cook.

Thanks, too, to the many folks who helped along the way with ideas, tips, copy review, and sharing their work. To name just a few:

Rosemary Topol, for her great video that helped so much to learn how to make French beaded flowers.

Barbara Grainger, who shared her two-needle peyote start and other tips.

Mindy Brooks of *Bead&Button* magazine, for her enthusiasm and encouragement.

Marian Ward, for her fabulous class on PMC.

Mike Frazier at Gigagraphica and Mark Ramsey at Virtual Bead Works, for sharing their bead design programs with us.

Claudia Chase at Mirrix Looms, for everything.

Katharina Saghi of The Bead Shop in Palo Alto, California, for providing us with their super videos.

Dianne Lehmann, for making wirework fun and easy those many moons ago.

Rowena Tank, Wendy Blair, Bobbi Wicks, and Lana Ante, for sharing their beautiful work for this book.

Macy and the Orchard Ranch beading group and all the ladies of the Beady Babes bead group of Chino Valley, Arizona, for sharing their work and beady-eyed excitement.

George Koldoff and his staff at Arizona Gems and Minerals, for their expertise.

Rachel Griffiths, for her support.

Amanda Tolman, for her way with words and encouragement.

Gail Devoid and the many, many other members of the beading community, both off- and online, who answered my many questions and guided me in the right direction.

Thank you, all!

Trademarks

In This Part

The Venerable, Adaptable Bead

Those little things with holes will launch you into worlds of fun and imagination. But first you might like to know more about them. Where do they come from? Why have people throughout time and across the world valued these little nuggets? Where can you find them, and how do you choose from so many?

I'll answer these questions and more in Part 1. You'll learn about the history of the bead, ways to choose the right ones, some easy steps to make some of your own, what tools and accessories you'll need to work with them, and some basic principles of design and style.

When you're done with these four chapters, you'll have all the background you need to start down the beading path.

In This Chapter

- ◆ A brief history of beads and their uses
- ◆ Common bead materials
- ◆ Bead types and styles
- ◆ Some helpful measurements
- ◆ Sources for finding beads

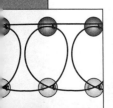 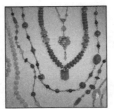   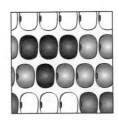 

Beads, Beads, Everywhere!

Beading is one of the fastest-growing hobbies today. What gets so many people started playing with beads? Many times it's the desire to repair a treasured piece of jewelry, or sometimes it's not being able to find just the right accessory for a special outfit.

I started beading when I decided I was spending too much for simple earrings. I like having a lot of choices and often couldn't find exactly what I wanted at a price I wanted to pay. I took a beginning wirework class at a local bead shop and I was hooked.

What makes a bead a bead? If I asked you for a definition of the word *bead*, you'd probably reply with something such as "A bead is a small object with a hole in it for stringing." That sounds like a pretty good definition to me. Beads are most commonly round, but they can also be a tube, barrel, disk, or some other unusual shape. Even buttons can be used as beads. If it has a hole through it and is not too big or heavy, you most likely can use it as a bead!

But beads are so much more than just pretty pieces of glass you string together and wrap around your wrist or stitch on a sweater. Let's take a look at some of the various roles beads have held through the years.

Beads Throughout History

Of course you'll find beads used in jewelry from necklaces to earrings to bracelets to anklets, as decoration, or as part of changing fashion. But they're also found throughout the world in head decorations, on garments, and even on furniture coverings. And that's not all …

The history of beads is the story of man's ingenuity. In times past, many cultures used beads to pay for goods and services, express social status, embody religious beliefs, and ward off envy or malice. A bead is a symbol of culture and tradition, and it's an object of awe and respect—that's a lot to pack into a little bead!

Findings

Walk into any bead shop, and hold on because you're about to take a mini-trip around the world. You'll travel to China, India, Germany, Bali, the Czech Republic, Italy, Africa, and many other exotic places. Vintage and antique beads will even add time travel to your journey.

In primitive cultures, beads set people apart and also showed where or to whom they belonged. Certain bead patterns showed which tribe an individual belonged to, and slight variations within that pattern indicated a person's position within that tribe.

Beads have been used as currency and even mathematical tools. String together beads of a uniform size, and you've got an abacus. In Africa, for example, beads were brought by Venetian merchants mostly to trade for gold in the thirteenth century, hence the name African trade beads or money beads. Wampum, beads made from various seashells by Native American tribes, were used more specifically to seal treaties and agreements.

Beads have been used as ritual offerings, worn for their healing powers, and offered as part of prayer and religious worship. The religions of nearly two-thirds of the world's population use some type of prayer beads, the rosaries of the Catholic Church being a common example.

A-Bead-C's

The word **bead** is derived from the Anglo-Saxon *bidden*, which means "to pray," and *bede*, which means "prayer."

The smooth, pleasing shape and texture of some beads can be calming to the touch. "Worry" beads are still used in Greece and Turkey, and even some Westerners have discovered worry beads as a means to relieve stress and aid in meditation.

Many cultures thought beads became charged with the essence of the person who wore them, and particular materials were believed to have special magical powers. Beads were often buried with the person who owned them, which is why so many beads from antiquity have survived today. It was believed that these personal possessions had some supernatural power to help the owner on his or her way to the afterlife and offer comfort when he or she got there. The rarer the material and the more complex the artistry, the more valuable the beads and the more helpful in the hereafter.

Findings

There are two great bead museums in the United States. If you're lucky enough to live in the western or northeastern United States, take a trip to one of them for a fascinating history of beads:

The Bead Museum
5754 W. Glenn Drive
Glendale, AZ 85301
623-931-2737
www.thebeadmuseum.com

The Bead Museum of
Washington, D.C.
400 Seventh Street Northwest
Washington, DC 20004
202-624-4500
www.beadmuseumdc.org

Precious and Everyday: What Beads Are Made Of

Some of the first beads were "found objects," stumbled upon by our ancestors as they traveled over the landscape in the course of their daily quest for survival. One can almost imagine the first time someone took a stone or shell with a hole worn through it, threaded it on a piece of dried sinew or cordage, and tied a knot.

Among the first natural materials used as beads were stones with worn holes, seeds, berries, corn kernels, nuts, fossilized shells and sea animals with natural holes, cloves, porcupine quills, grasses, tortoise shells, hard beetle shells, claws, bones, snake vertebrae and rattles, tusks, beans, husks, horn, bamboo, bark, stems, cork, eggshells, and whole eggs.

Knots!

Some natural materials can be toxic if ingested. Certain berries and beans are of particular concern. Most adults would be unlikely to put such things in their mouths, but children are known to put everything in theirs! Be careful if you use such objects in your beadwork.

Throughout history, when new technologies came into being, beads were often one of the first items produced. Bronze and iron were first used to make weapons, tools, and—that's right—beads! When glass was invented, it was used right away to make beads.

Let's take a closer look at materials used for beads past and present—and the endless possibilities you have to enhance your beadwork!

Mother Nature's Handiwork

Coral   Coral is formed from the skeletons of small marine polyps that can grow on each other to make what look like branches and twigs. Bright-red coral is the most prized, followed by pink coral. Black coral is a very rare and protected form. Many coral reefs have been overfished, so divers have to go deeper to find good coral, which has driven up the cost. Pollution is also a problem, destroying or even killing coral in some areas. Inferior coral can sometimes be enhanced artificially, so be aware of that when you buy.

Coral can be used whole or cut into branched sections and drilled or made into beads. Coral lookalikes include carnelian, jasper, bauxite, glass, porcelain, dyed bone, shell or ivory, carved plastic, and polymer clay. To spot real coral, look through a magnifying glass for a woodlike grain. If you think a piece has been dyed, rub it with acetone and a clean cloth to see if any color will come off.

Knots!

Because some natural materials can be expensive, simulated forms are usually available. Recognizing real from fake can be a real challenge.

Amber   Although technically not a stone, amber does sometimes look like one. Amber dates back to 50 million years B.C.E. and is fossilized resin from a type of pine tree found in the Baltic region, Sicily, and some parts of South America. Linked to the sun in ancient symbolism because of its color, amber can vary from yellow to deep brown and can be transparent or opaque. Amber is also very lightweight.

Animals that became trapped in the pine resin as it hardened made these pieces highly prized in ancient times. Amber also becomes electrically charged when rubbed, giving it a magical quality.

Be careful not to confuse amber with other lightweight materials such as copal resin, ambroid (melted pieces of amber), horn, or plastic.

Jet This black, shiny fossilized coal was once used extensively in Victorian mourning jewelry and to embellish nineteenth-century mourning attire. The best jet comes from Whitby, on the Yorkshire coast of England.

Ebony and "bog oak" are sometimes mistaken for jet. If you see a grain, you've got bog oak, not jet. Small black faceted beads are usually glass.

All That Glitters ...

Pearls Linked to the moon in ancient symbolism, pearls form naturally inside the pearl oyster. They can also be "cultured" on a pearl farm in a controlled environment to assure uniformity. Pearls can be dyed, but natural pearls come in colors ranging from creamy-white to pinkish, gold, blue-gray, and even black. Irregularly shaped natural pearls are called "baroque."

Simulated pearls vary in quality; the best are made of glass with a pearl-like coating. To tell the difference between natural and simulated pearls, rub the pearl on a tooth. A real pearl will make a grating sound; an imitation pearl is completely smooth.

Findings

For an amazing source of more than you ever wanted to know (or maybe not) about minerals, check out the alphabetical listings at webmineral.com.

Semi-precious stones Also known as gemstones, semi-precious stones are widely used in beadwork. There are too many to list here, but do become aware of them as you get into beadwork. Studying precious and semi-precious stones and minerals is fascinating! They are full of lore and symbolism, not to mention beauty.

Gemstones come in round beads, ovals, drops, briolettes, cabochons, chips, plus some specialty and novelty shapes. Gemstones are often quite expensive, so you might want to string them using the individually knotted method (see Chapter 6). If the thread should break, you won't lose many beads. Flexible wire or closed-circuit wirework are other options, because they're stronger and less likely to break than a continuous strand of thread.

Findings

As you learn about beads and gemstones, it's helpful to find either a good bead store or a comprehensive and easy-to-understand guidebook until you feel comfortable identifying specific stones or distinguishing between good quality and just so-so. Get to know your local bead store owner or manager, and ask a lot of questions. If you don't have a knowledgeable person to ask, one of the best guidebooks I know of is *Gemstones of the World, Revised Edition*, by Walter Schumann (Sterling, 2000). If you don't know your stones, you risk making some costly mistakes.

Keep these things in mind when you're choosing semi-precious stones:

◆ **Check the color.** Gemstones can be dyed to enhance color, but these "enhanced" stones should be less expensive than those in their natural state. If the color is too uniform, suspect a "dye job." To test if a bead has been dyed, dip a cotton swab in alcohol and run it over the bead surface. If color comes off, the bead has been dyed.

◆ **Consider the temperature.** In normal settings, stone is usually cold, glass is warmer, and plastic is warm.

◆ **Check the weight.** If a bead is very light, it's probably plastic (although real amber is quite light). Stone is usually heavier than glass, and both are heavier than plastic.

◆ **Test its sound.** If you tap it lightly against a hard object, does it sound like the high, crisp pitch of glass, or does it have a deeper, heavier sound like stone? Plastic has a flat sound.

◆ **Look at it more closely.** If you look at a stone under magnification (I keep a small magnifying glass called a loupe with me most of the time), you should be able to see various striations and imperfections. Compare what you see to pictures in your gemstone guidebook.

The more you look and the more you learn, the better able you'll be to distinguish one stone from another and the real thing from an imitation.

More of Mother Nature's Handiwork

Wood   Beads made of woods are among the simplest beads you can find, and turned wood beads are classic. They can be carved, painted, dyed, or stained and varnished. Wood beads are also used as the base for some beaded beads (see Chapter 2) and for making tassels.

Wood beads are versatile, and you can find novelty wood beads of all kinds, including bright, whimsical painted animals and flowers. Japan and China export some exquisitely carved wooden beads. The most common woods used for making beads are ebony, beech, rosewood, laburnum, pine, yew, holly, oak, walnut, boxwood, mahogany, and tulipwood. Sandalwood beads are also available; these have a lovely fragrance and are often used for prayer beads.

Metal   Many kinds of metal are used for beads. You'll find stamped, hammered, embossed, granulated, enameled, cloisonné, gilt, silver-plated, gold-plated, dipped, cast, and filigree choices, to name a few. Tubular silver- and gold-colored beads called "liquid" gold and silver make nice filler beads or can stand on their own.

Many base metal and plastic beads on the market look like metal. These might be fine for something quick that isn't going to take a lot of time and effort to put together, but the finish of these beads rubs off in time, and you'll be disappointed if you use them in something you've worked hard on. I very rarely use them. I prefer to use sterling silver, gold- or silver-plated, or brass beads in my work.

Very popular today are sterling-silver beads from Bali. These come in many different shapes, styles, and patterns and are loaded with fine detail. Bali beads work well as spacers or focal beads, depending on their size and shape.

Ceramic   Clay and dried mud were among the earliest materials used to make beads, and today, ceramic beads come in many different styles and colors. Look for colorful ceramic beads from Peru, China, and Greece.

Faience   Also called "Egyptian paste," faience is a type of ceramic developed by the Egyptians and is made with quartz sand and a colored glaze. Faience is thought to be the forerunner of true glass. You can still buy faience beads today in Cairo and on the Internet (if you can't make it to Cairo).

All About Glass

Glass One of the most versatile materials used in making beads is glass. Glass beads commonly come from India, Italy, and central Europe. Bohemian beads are especially desirable.

> **Findings**
>
> The first glass factory in America was in Virginia and primarily was used to make beads to trade with the Native Americans. It was destroyed in 1622 during the Jamestown Colony massacre.

The Venetian glassworks at Murano, Italy, was a major center for glass-making during the Renaissance, and Venetian glass beads are still a favorite. Sometimes you'll see them referred to as "wedding cake" beads because, like a fancy cake, they're ornately decorated in raised fashion.

A few kinds of glass beads are worth special mention so that when you encounter them on your bead hunting trips, you'll know what they are:

◆ **Swarovski crystal** In 1895, Austrian Daniel Swarovski invented a way to cut large amounts of quality glass beads. His method is still a secret. Swarovski Austrian crystal beads have a high lead content and lots of sparkle. They come in a variety of shapes, sizes, colors, and finishes.

◆ **Recycled materials** African tribes, particularly in Ghana and Nigeria, have specialized in making ground glass beads from recycled medicine, soda, and beer bottles. These are opaque, often have two or three colors, and are quite pretty.

◆ **Millefiori** These are glass beads with a very ornate pattern resembling bouquets of flowers (*millefiori* literally means "1,000 flowers" in Italian). These beads originated at the Venetian glassworks in Murano, Italy. They are made from slices of multicolored glass rods called canes that are laid over a glass core and smoothed to the surface while still hot.

Here's an example of millefiori beads and the cane used to form them.

Glass beads come in more finishes and styles than I could ever list here; however, here are a few basic types you should be familiar with:

◆ **Aurora Borealis** Written *AB* when labeling beads, this finish gives glass beads an iridescent look. Sometimes the finish is only on one side of the bead. Beads can be finished more than once, so sometimes you'll see 2XAB or 3XAB referring to the number of times they've gone through the finish, especially on Austrian crystal beads. Compare these finishes in good light to see the difference.

◆ **Bugle** These are tube-shape and are generally available in four sizes ranging from 2mm to 35mm in length. They also come in a variety of finishes, many of the same ones available for seed beads, so they can be combined nicely or used as spacer beads. Bugles can be straight, hex-cut, or twisted. Most bugles are made to be compatible with a size 11° diameter seed bead.

Bugle beads.

♦ **Ceylon** A ceylon finish is a pearl-like finish on an opaque bead.

♦ **Charlotte** These are basically seed beads but are cut, or faceted, on one side only. The size available is usually 13°, and the holes tend to be smaller than in other seed beads, which can make them a little harder to work with (I use a magnifier).

♦ **Color-lined** These beads have a solid-color core with a transparent overlay either in the same color family or two different colors.

♦ **Dichroic** This prismatic glass made of layered oxides is usually used for cabochons.

♦ **Dyed** A surface dye can be used on almost all types of beads. The color might rub off or fade over time, so you'll want to ask about this.

♦ **Faceted** Faceted glass beads can be hand cut, polished, or molded. They can have one or more flat surfaces, giving them sparkle and shine.

♦ **Fire polished** This is glass that has been heated at an extremely high temperature and treated to give it a very clean glossy surface. The fire polish sometimes smoothes out the bead's faceted edges.

♦ **Fringe** Fringe beads look like tiny holiday ornaments. The bead looks like a tiny droplet with the hole going sideways through the smaller top of the bead.

♦ **Galvanized metallic** This is a shiny metallic-coated bead.

Knots!

Do not use galvanized metallic glass beads or metallic coated beads in a project that will see a lot of wear such as a bracelet. The coating on the bead will wear away, and you'll be disappointed with the results. To help prevent this from happening, you can coat your finished project with clear fingernail polish or spray with Krylon, but there's no guarantee there won't still be some wear over time.

♦ **Greasy** The surface of this semi-opaque glass (which allows light in but you can't see through the bead) appears "greasy."

♦ **Hex cut (or hexagonal cut)** This is the common cut in Japanese cylinder beads.

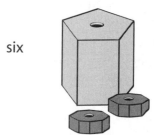
six

Hex-cut beads.

♦ **Iridescent** These beads have been given a special finish to make them look as if they were dipped in oil. They almost have a rainbow glow to them, depending on the light.

♦ **Iris** This bead has a rainbow iridescent coating, usually on dark, opaque beads.

♦ **Japanese cylinder beads** This seed or rocaille bead is typically made in Japan. The two most widely known manufacturers are Miyuki Shoji (Delica) and Toho (Aida, Antiques). These beads have larger holes than typical seed beads and come in two sizes—1.5mm, or the same as a size

12° seed bead, and 3.3mm, or equal to a size 8°. The color range for these beads is enormous, and they are very uniform in shape, which makes them useful for off- and on-loom weaving techniques. Japanese cylinder beads give your finished product a uniform, blocked look.

◆ **Lampwork**   These are individually crafted beads made by winding molten glass around a metal rod. The glass is heated using a small torch. "Art" beads are often lampwork beads, and one bead can be very expensive. These one-of-a-kind beads are usually used as a focal bead and surrounded by less-expensive beads. Lampwork beads from Venice have been highly prized throughout history. Some lampwork beads from Czechoslovakia and India are made by craftsmen who have apprenticed and learned to make beads nearly exactly alike and in larger quantities.

◆ **Luster**   A luster bead has a semi-transparent, high-gloss coating with a pearl-like appearance.

◆ **Matte**   A matte bead has a nonshiny matte finish that is accomplished by tumbling or etching a bead until it appears dull or frosted. Matte beads don't show wear as easily as shiny beads and offer a nice contrast in many beadwork projects.

◆ **Opaque**   Opaque beads are solid-color beads you can't see through nor can light flow through them. Opaque seed beads are used traditionally in Native American beadwork. Gemstones are also either opaque or transparent. Quartz is transparent, for example, because light can pass through it, but jade is opaque.

Put On Your Beadin' Cap

Once you've got a variety of beads in different finishes, lay them out on a light background and play with them. What happens when you put matte beads next to transparent beads? Iridescent next to faceted? Do some beads seem to "come forward" while others seem to "recede"? You can do this with whole hanks of beads (strands of beads tied together), arranging them beside each other and observing how they look and feel. Play!

◆ **Pressed glass**   Glass is pressed into a mold while it's still soft to create a bead. These come in a wide variety of shapes and sizes.

◆ **Rocaille**   This type of seed bead has a silver lining and usually a square hole.

◆ **Satin**   A satin finish on a bead is reminiscent of satin fabric, hence the name. This sheen is created by pulling bubbles through the glass as it's formed into a bead.

◆ **Seed**   These beads are also called "pound" beads and are generally available in a variety of sizes and finishes. Some have off-center holes and are irregularly shaped. Irregularity is part of the design element, but you might want to sort them for various projects. Seed beads come on *hanks* in sizes from the very small 24°, used in antique beadwork and for miniatures, to size 6°, mostly used in bead knitting and crochet.

A-Bead-C's

> Confused by all the **24°** and **6°** numbers? These indicate the size of the bead. The higher the number, the smaller the bead. Seed beads come in **hanks,** which are usually 12 (18- to 20-inch) strands of beads tied together or packaged in bags or tubes. Beads are also sometimes sold by weight. See the charts I've provided for you in Appendix C for some helpful information on seed beads.

Seed beads.

◆ **Silver-lined** You can get a metallic look by using silver- or gold-lined beads in your projects. The metallic finish is on the inside of the bead and is covered with a layer of transparent glass.

◆ **Square cut** Any bead can be cut into a square. Usually square beads are called cubes, but small, square seed beads are called square cuts.

Square bead.

◆ **Three cuts** These highly reflective hand-cut beads with three surfaces showing at one time were popular in the 1920s and 1930s and are now being made again in the Czech Republic.

◆ **Translucent** These smoky beads allow some light to enter but are not clear.

◆ **Transparent** You can see through a transparent bead. They are crystal clear.

◆ **Triangle** Beads large and small can be cut into triangle shapes. Even some seed beads are triangle-cut.

Triangle bead.

◆ **Two cuts** These cylinder-shape beads are cut on each end. A bugle bead is a two-cut bead. Two-cut beads can be as small as 1mm, as are the Czech "micro" tubes.

◆ **White heart** These two-layer beads have color (usually red or orange) on the outside and a white "heart" on the inside.

Man Made

Plastic And last but not least, plastic can be made to simulate just about anything. Some plastic beads are very convincing and look astonishingly like coral, pearl, metal, or glass. In my opinion, the best plastic beads are the ones that don't pretend to be something else. There are some great plastic novelty beads, especially in the shapes of flowers and leaves. Otherwise, I'd rather have the real thing!

Shapes of Things to Come: Bead Types and Styles

The shapes of beads in the past were limited by the technology of a particular culture. It's easier to make a tube-shape bead, for instance, than a uniform sphere. But sphere-shape beads appealed to almost every culture, and the circle is a powerful symbol in many belief systems, so round beads were—and still are—held in high esteem.

To help you recognize common bead shapes, I've listed them here:

Bicone or lantern cut beads.

Briolette bead.

Cabochons.

Cameo.

Chevron.

Corrugated bead.

Crow, pony, or "E" beads.

Disk beads.

Donut beads.

Double-drilled bead.

Drops or teardrops.

Druk or round bead.

Eye beads.

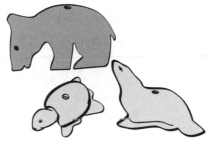

Fetishes.

Heishi beads.

Lantern bead.

Melon beads.

Oval bead.

Rice beads.

Rondelle beads.

Side-drilled bead.

Slant-drilled beads.

Tube beads.

A Little Math

Don't panic! I was never good at math, either, but it does help to know a few things about measurements and scale when you learn to bead. One shortcut is to do the math ahead of time and create a chart or list of often-used measurements that will save time and aggravation. If you're still cringing and wondering where your calculator is, relax. I'm going to make it easy for you. I've already created the charts you'll need (see Appendix C).

Findings ____

You might want to copy the various charts I've given you in this book, assemble them on separate sheets of paper, then put them in a beading notebook or on the wall near where you work. You can also purchase a helpful 11×17-inch laminated wall chart from www.beadedphoenix.com. It was put together, along with a booklet, by Rosanne Andreas.

So how do you measure a bead? Bead sizes are given in millimeters (mm)—even in the United States. Usually this measurement is the diameter of the bead or the distance through the hole.

Some bead measurements are given as diameter by length, both in millimeters, as in, for example, 4×10mm.

Cabochons and cameos are measured in either diameter if they're round or in width by height at the widest points (for example, 18×13mm).

Where to Find Beads

Now that you know what mind-boggling varieties beads come in, you know you just *have* to have some, right? My motto is "You can never have too many beads!"

So where can you get 'em? I've included some of my favorite sources in Appendix B, but here are some other ideas, too:

◆ **Bead stores** When you're first learning how to bead, it's hard to order beads and findings from a catalog sight unseen. You need to touch and see the beads to get familiar with them. As you progress in your beadwork and know you'll be using a lot of the same beads or findings, you can order in larger quantities and use online and mail-order catalogs effectively.

Don't forget to look for bead stores when you travel! When I visit a new town, one of the first things I do is pull out the local phone book and look up "beads" in the Yellow Pages!

Many bead stores have a "make and take" policy. You can pick out your beads and components, keeping track as you go along, make your item at the store with help from the staff, and pay only for what you use.

Also, don't overlook kits because they are another good way to begin beading. You're only paying for exactly what you need; you already know what the finished product will look like; plus the instructions are all there. Just be sure the kit is appropriate for your experience level.

◆ **Thrift stores, consignment stores, or yard sales**   One of the best ways to become acquainted with various kinds of beads and not invest a lot of money at first is to reuse beads from existing jewelry. You can use a piece you already have or something you find at a yard sale or thrift store. The great thing is, it doesn't matter if it's broken!

Findings

If you make or buy a piece of jewelry or other beadwork and tire of it, don't toss it. Instead, cut it apart and reuse the beads and components in a new way!

◆ **Nature**   Don't overlook natural materials. Start looking around in the great outdoors for found items you could use. What a great excuse to become a beachcomber!

◆ **Mail-order catalogs**   These often have a greater selection and can be less expensive and more convenient than bead stores, but as a beginner, it's difficult to assess color, texture, and size without being able to see and touch the beads. As you become more familiar with beads, you'll find catalogs more and more useful, and you'll know better what to look for. I have a list of my favorite and most trusted sources in Appendix B. I would recommend that you begin to gather some of the major catalogs anyway, even if you don't order from them at first. They're a wealth of information, and they're simply fun to drool over!

◆ **Online**   My comments on mail-order catalogs apply to online sources as well. Some websites have wonderful glossaries with photos or illustrations, lots of fact sheets, charts, and other information. I've given you a collection of websites to explore in Appendix B.

◆ **Bead shows**   Where else can you see so many different beads all in one place at the same time? Bead shows are a great place to become aware of the possibilities. Look. Touch. Ask questions. But bead shows are also a good place to empty your wallet! They can be a bit overwhelming, even for an advanced beader, so be prepared. Choose a smaller show to start.

In the beginning, you might just want to browse. Keep a list of questions and get business cards from the vendors you are most drawn to. You might come back to them when you become a more experienced beader. See Appendix B for a list of exciting bead shows throughout the country.

◆ **Hand-me-downs** I especially like to collect vintage and handmade beads and findings. They make me wonder, *Who wore these? What was the person like who made them?* I find these mostly in thrift and antique stores, at bead shows, and on the Internet (eBay can be a dangerous place!), but some have come to me through family and friends. Once people know about your bead passion, they often help you indulge it.

◆ **Make your own** I'll be talking more about this in Chapter 2. There are materials you can use to make your own inexpensive and totally unique beads. A whole other world awaits you there!

◆ **Crafts stores** Chain stores such as Ben Franklin and Michael's do stock some beads. They don't have the great variety or quality of most bead stores, but you can still find the basics if you're just getting started.

◆ **Bead magazines** Read the ads when you look at bead magazines (I've given you a list in Appendix B). Certain companies specialize in certain things, so you might want to make a note of those that most intrigue you in your beading notebook.

◆ **Collectors** If you want to create a unique piece of jewelry, you can sometimes buy very special beads from a collector. Or you might want to become a collector yourself! There is at least one

bead collector's e-mail list on Yahoo!, so you might be able to make some connections there. Another good place to start is beadcollector.net. You also might be able to locate collectors through museums and local bead societies or guilds.

You'll undoubtedly find your own special haunts as you start looking. Add these to your beading notebook along with comments about what kinds of beads you found especially plentiful there, what classes they offer, and any other impressions you might have had of the store, owner, manager, selection, etc.

As you start to amass some beads, you'll find yourself needing to sort them and looking for ways to store them. Many systems are on the market, plus the old standbys such as baby food jars and small plastic resealable bags. You'll find your own best ways as you go along and I give you some more ideas in Chapter 16, but if you start organizing early, you'll be ahead of the game.

Findings

As you buy beads, you might want to label the containers. Note where you got them, how many you bought, and how much you paid for them (I actually figure out a cost per bead as I go along). This gives you an idea of how much something you make is costing you, and if you run out of a particular bead, you'll know where to get more.

You're on your way to creating your first bead project. Soon you'll be able to make jewelry and accessories for yourself and your friends. In the chapters that follow, you'll learn all about the few tools and materials you need to begin beading.

The Least You Need to Know

- The history of beads is full and rich—and worth learning about.
- Beads are made from a wide variety of materials, from wood to glass to metal—and nearly everything in between.
- The many shapes, sizes, and styles of beads give you unlimited options and variety for your beadwork.
- You can learn reliable ways to tell quality materials from imitations.
- A little math can help the beginning beader, although having some prefigured charts will save time.
- The sources for finding beads are almost endless!

In This Chapter

- ◆ Making simple paper beads
- ◆ Creating polymer clay beads
- ◆ Decorating wooden beads
- ◆ Aromatic beads made from flowers and spices
- ◆ Beaded beads and more

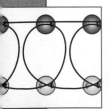
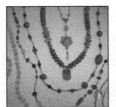

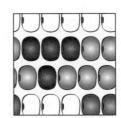

Chapter **2**

Making Your Own Beads

I hope by now you're as sold on beads as I am. But wait! There's more: Not only can you make amazing things *with* beads, but you can also actually make your *own* unique and beautiful beads. I don't want to discourage you from shopping, but just know that there are more bead choices available to you than what's in your local bead store or on the Internet. If you can't find that perfect bead, you might be able to make it yourself, which will make your work that much more unique.

Remember, if you can put a hole through it and thread it onto something you can hang or wear, it's a bead! As you make your way through the world of beading, being aware of the many ways you can make your own beads and findings will make the adventure that much more enjoyable.

Let's put on our beading caps again and take this whole bead thing one creative step further.

Embellish It!

One of the easiest and quickest ways of making your own beads is to start with a simple base bead and cover it, decorate it, or otherwise embellish it using any one of a variety of techniques and materials.

Try any one of a variety of prefabricated materials as your base bead. Use wood, plastic, or Styrofoam as a form to build on. You can even cover a bead with other beads!

The simplest way to do this is to coat the base bead with glue and roll it in seed beads. Voilà! Now you have a pretty bead-covered bead!

Findings

Why should you consider making your own beads? First, it's fun and easy. The materials and techniques are ones you'll remember from grade-school art class. Be a kid again or grab a kid! You'll both have a blast.

Another slightly more elegant method of embellishing beads is to simply string an anchor bead slightly larger than the hole of your base bead on a length of thread with a needle at the end and tie it on using an overhand knot. This will keep everything from sliding off. Next, thread the needle through the hole of the base bead and then thread on lots of seed beads. Gluing as you go, wind the strand of beads around the base bead in an increasing spiral, starting around the hole and working outward, then graduating down until you reach the other end.

You can also embellish base beads with decoupage, foil, and gold or silver leaf. Let your imagination run wild!

It's Only a Paper Bead

If you still can't find beads you like or you just want to try your hand at making beads yourself, why not make some paper beads? Paper is one of the simplest and least-expensive materials you can use for making beads. The more interesting in color, pattern, and texture the paper is, the more interesting the bead will be. This is a great project to do with even the youngest kids, but the results can be exciting enough to satisfy any adult.

Rolling Paper Beads

Rolled paper beads are simple to do and look nice strung together with accent beads or you can make one as a focal bead. If you want to try your hand at this kind of beadmaking, follow these easy steps:

1. Assemble a variety of papers, including old magazines, junk mail, scraps of gift wrap, homemade paper, origami paper, and wallpaper. Whatever you choose, just be sure it's substantial enough to hold up when saturated with glue.

2. To form the beads, you'll need long triangles of paper. An efficient way to cut these triangles and create uniform and elegant beads is to start with a square piece of paper and mark 1½-inch increments across the top edge with a pencil. On the bottom edge, mark ¾ inch from the right side and ¾ inch from the left side. Then mark 1½-inch increments between these two ¾-inch markings as you did on the opposite edge of the paper. Then, with a ruler connecting the base of the triangle at the bottom of the paper to the tip at the top, mark the triangles to cut.

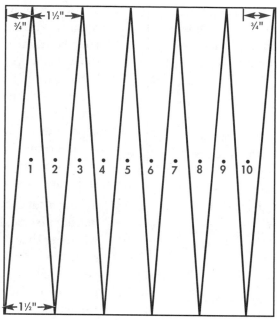

Diagram for cutting paper bead triangles.

You can try other cutting patterns as well. The longer and thinner you cut the strips of paper, the smaller and fatter your finished bead will be. The wider your strip, the more tubular your bead will be. Experiment with different-size strips and see what variations you get.

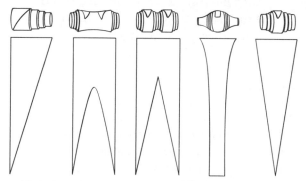

Variations you can use to get different paper bead shapes.

3. Once you have a size of paper strip you like, use a small paintbrush and coat the top side with glue (Elmer's is fine). Then it's time to roll! Starting with the widest end of the paper, roll it tightly around a skewer, drinking straw, or toothpick, depending on the size hole you want. Roll until you get the size of bead you like, then cut off any leftover paper.

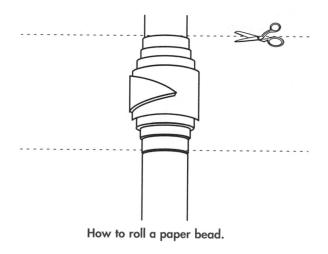

How to roll a paper bead.

4. If you're using a straw as the base of the bead, just cut off the straw at both ends of the bead. It can remain inside and strengthen the hole. If you're using a skewer or toothpick, gently pull it out.

5. Let the bead dry for several hours or until completely dry, then seal it. You can "glaze" the bead by painting it with a thin layer of glue that's been diluted with a little water. Or you can use several coats of varnish for a different look. Be sure to test a scrap of paper with either sealer to be sure it doesn't cause the color or print to run.

Findings

You can vary the length and width of the triangle or cut the paper in a more rectangular shape to get different sizes and shapes of beads. I've also seen similar beads made with strips of fabric saturated in thinned glue and wound around a toothpick or a skewer in a similar manner. Experiment and see what you can come up with!

Papier-Mâché

Another versatile material you might remember from childhood activity time can take on a grown-up look—or not! Papier-mâché is a great way to use those old newspapers you might have stacking up.

Many recipes are available for papier-mâché, and you might have a favorite of your own. Here's the recipe I use:

1. Mix 3 parts water with 1 part flour or wallpaper paste.

2. Tear old newspapers into about 1-inch squares. Make enough scraps to mix with your flour-and-water solution so it's not too wet and not too dry. Using your hands, squeeze a small amount of paste into the paper pieces and work it in until it feels like clay. Start with a few pieces of newspaper and add a little at a time until you get the right consistency. If it gets too dry, you can always mix up a little more flour-and-water paste to add.

3. Taking a small amount of the papier-mâché mixture, form your beads into whatever shape you like. You can roll some papier-mâché between your hands to get a tubular or round bead, or free form the papier-mâché into other shapes. Remember to poke a hole in the bead with a toothpick or skewer, depending on the size of hole you want.

4. Put your beads on a cookie sheet and let them air dry for a day or two. You can also put them in a 150°F oven for 2 to 3 hours to speed things up.

5. When the beads have hardened (and cooled if you hardened them in the oven), you can paint your beads with acrylic paints. After the painted beads are dry, seal them with acrylic spray sealer. Let them dry again, then get stringing!

Origami

Anything you can make using origami you can make in miniature and hang as a pendant bead. Small paper cranes make beautiful pendant earrings, or try folded stars made of shiny metallic papers for Christmas. These might not last for generations, but if handled carefully, they can survive quite a while. If they get a bit shabby, just fold yourself another pair!

For an inexpensive and easy-to-follow guide to beginning origami, I would suggest John Montroll's book *Easy Origami*, published by Dover Publications. Dover is also a good source for lots of other origami books and also beautiful origami papers that could do double-duty for making paper beads. Or you could go online and try some of the free instructions available at www.origami.com or www.opane.com/origami.html. Try making the project in full-size first, then reduce the paper size to make a miniature version.

Beads of Clay

Clay opens an exciting world for the beader. You can use the simple self-hardening, air-dry clay you probably used in grammar school to make beads that stand by themselves or can become the bases for embellished beads. The newer polymer and precious metal clays are especially fun to work with!

Let's take a look at some of the basic types of clay.

Air-Dry, Self-Hardening Clays

These clays are easy to work with and don't require baking in an oven or firing in a kiln. Once beads made with these clays are thoroughly dry, you can decorate them with school paints, acrylics, temperas, liquid crayons, or whatever else you can think of. They are not waterproof, however, so you will need to coat them with shellac or varnish to seal and make them water-resistant. I have made beads from these clays that have a nice, rustic look, but they are somewhat fragile and can break if rapped sharply on something hard. Some easy-to-find brand names for this clay are Amaco Marblex and Crayola Model Magic.

Bread-Dough Clay

Remember the clay you made from bread dough as a kid? You can also use this "clay" to make beads. Lots of different recipes are around, and you might even have a favorite of your own. In case you don't, here's a simple recipe.

Bread-Dough Clay Recipe

2 cups salt
2½ cups boiling water
4 cups flour

1. Add salt to boiling water, then stir salt-water mixture into flour in a big bowl. Stir until mixed.

2. Turn out dough onto floured board and knead. Shape into beads, make holes with a toothpick or a wooden skewer depending on how big you want the holes, and bake for 2 to 3 hours in a 250°F oven or until just slightly golden, checking often after 2 hours.

3. Remove from the oven and cool thoroughly, then paint with acrylic paints. When your beads have dried, seal them with an acrylic spray sealer. When they're dry, they're ready to string.

Polymer Clays

Polymer clay is probably the most versatile type of clay out there for bead making. It is actually a plastic called polyvinyl chloride (PVC) mixed with a plasticizer for flexibility and any number of pigments for color, from pearlized and muted tones to a vibrant palette of every color of the rainbow.

You can shape and mold the clay by hand prior to baking it in a typical home oven at temperatures from 215 to 275°F, depending on the manufacturer. Once hardened, you'll have a hard, durable bead that can be embellished in myriad ways including wet-sanded, drilled, carved, buffed, glued, and painted.

Common brand names of polymer clay you'll see are Sculpey and Fimo. Each has its own characteristics. Try them and see which you prefer.

Polymer clays are basically all handled the same way:

1. First, thoroughly knead the clay to make it soft and pliable. The heat from your hands is all it takes. Work on a flat, smooth surface such as marble, glass, or Plexiglas.

2. Either roll the dough into an even sausage shape or make an even flat pancake using a rolling pin. You can then cut the clay into even increments or cut out shapes using a canapé cutter or craft knife.

3. Poke a hole into your bead, then emboss, carve, or embellish the bead as you wish.

4. Bake according to the manufacturer's directions.

Knots!

Polymer clay is certified to be nontoxic, but it's still a good idea to keep the tools you use for working with clay separate from those you use with food. Also, wash your hands after working with clay, and be sure you have adequate ventilation when the clay is baking—after all, it is a petroleum-based product. If you're sanding or drilling hardened pieces, be sure to wear a mask and eye protection as well. Finally, do not work with polymer clay on unprotected wood surfaces. Contact with the clay can hurt the finish. It can also react with some plastics.

Try mixing together different colors of polymer clay to create a marbleized effect. You can knead various additives into the clay to change or enhance a particular color as well. Because of the low baking temperature required, you can often embed found objects into the clay, and they won't be harmed by the baking process.

You can also use polymer clay to create millefiori beads similar to the ones I talked about in Chapter 1 that were made from glass. In this case, the "canes" are made from long snakes of different-colored clay put together and wrapped in still more clay, then sliced. This is an advanced technique but one that can produce amazing results.

Molds that make you an artist in an instant are also available for polymer clay. They are incredibly detailed and easy to use, and when you're done using them in clay, you can use with other craft materials as well.

Another valuable tool for working with polymer clay looks like a big hypodermic needle. Clay can be extruded from it using an assortment of different discs to make all sorts of textured clay embellishments.

And speaking of texture … Anything with a texture you like can be used to emboss the surface of the clay. Have a piece of lace you love? Press it into the surface of the clay to decorate the clay. You can also layer the clay with different colors and shapes for raised designs—elegant or fantastic.

The finishes for polymer clay are almost endless. You can brush on metallic powders or use matte or glossy acrylic paints. Want a bead that looks like porcelain, glass, stone, or leather? There's a way to do it in polymer clay. Go to town!

Put On Your Beadin' Cap

You can make polymer clay look like almost any material though various painting and finishing techniques. To see all the creative possibilities, check out Sue Heaser's book *Making Polymer Clay Jewellry* [sic] and Leslie Dierks's *Creative Clay Jewelry*.

Precious Metals Clay (PMC)

This is a relatively new clay. Invented by a Japanese company for the semi-conductor industry, it has opened up a fabulous new world for the craft hobbyist and professional alike. The only way to describe it is *alchemy!* You work with PMC much the same way you work with any other clay, place it in a kiln, and fire it. But what comes out of the kiln is *real metal!*

Findings

Although this material is expensive and you have to have access to a kiln, it's worth mentioning here just so you know it's out there. It's a tremendous medium for the beader. You can make metal beads and findings using PMC without the tools and know-how of a metal worker. I recommend taking a class or getting a video before attempting to work with PMC to save yourself both aggravation and money.

One easy and economical way to work with PMC is to make your item in polymer clay, bake it, then make a mold of the bead or pendant using mold-making material you can get from any number of hobby or crafts stores. Simply push the PMC into the mold, release it, and you're ready to fire. (To make the pieces lighter and less costly, you might want to hollow out the backs before removing from the mold.) PMC dries quickly, so any method that helps you work fast is good!

Although PMC is perhaps not a beginner material, it's something a beginner should at least know about because as you learn about beading, you'll very likely be prompted more and more to want to make your own beads and findings.

Findings

One tool clay workers often like to have is a hand-crank pasta maker for rolling out thin sheets of clay. Also look for little canapé or aspic cutters at cooking stores or even yard sales. Ask your dentist if he or she has any old tools they're planning on discarding, too!

Clay is one of the most versatile materials available to the beader for creating unique hand-crafted beads. Once you begin playing with clay, you'll be hooked!

Out of the Woods

Wood is one of the oldest materials used to make beads. Premade wooden beads are inexpensive, and you'll find them in any craft or hobby store. They can be carved, painted, burned, and treated with various finishes.

Findings

To hold any bead while you're trying to apply a finish, push it over a small craft paintbrush handle. The graduated-size handle will hold the bead secure while you work with it—and you won't finish your fingertips!

Try using permanent markers, acrylic paints, and various wood stains on a raw wooden bead, or even carve simple designs using basic wood-carving tools. A wood-burning tool will give yet a different effect. Finally, seal your wooden beads with varnish or other finish coat.

Here again, your imagination is your passport to anywhere your creative mind wants to go.

Found Beads

Anything you can see as a bead—a shell, a seed, a washer, a nut—can be made into a bead! If it has a hole in it or if you can make one, it can be a bead.

Some found objects are soft enough that you can just push a needle through—instant bead! Seeds, nuts, acorns, beans, rose hips, and dried berries would most likely fit this category. Others might just need to be soaked in water to soften them before a needle can be pushed through easily. Experiment and you'll find the best method.

In some cases, however, to go from found object to bead you might very well need to drill a hole.

Also, be sure you match the size of the hole to whatever you plan to thread the bead onto, be it cord, beading thread, or wire.

Knots!

If you're going to be drilling anything to create a bead, be safe! Make sure you use the correct drill (a Dremel is best for most small applications) and appropriate drill bit for the material. You might need a small vice or other device to hold the object as you drill. Sometimes you can temporarily affix the object to a piece of wood with some clay or secure it with a pair of pliers. You might need to lubricate the drill frequently with water. Be sure you have more than one of what you're trying to drill in case it breaks. And always wear safety glasses!

Flower Petal Beads

Rosaries were originally made out of beads composed of dried rose petals and were made by hand. That's where the name *rosary* comes from. You can still buy these rose-petal-bead rosaries if you look for them, although today most are made from glass or wooden beads.

The Victorians made beads out of all sorts of flowers and spices, and it's likely this practice dates back to medieval times or earlier. These beads were both aromatic and rustic in their beauty.

Numerous recipes exist for flower petal and spice beads. You'll sometimes find them in old herb books. One of my herb teachers, Jeanne Rose, has recipes for various rose and spice beads in her book, *Herbs and Things*. You might also want to check out www.mindspring.com/ ~maclain/southdowns/phoenix/Articles/ rosebeads.html. Mary Maguire's book on making beads, *Beadmaker: Projects for Creating Hand-Crafted Beads* (see Appendix B), also has several. Have a *scent*sational time making your own beads from botanicals!

Findings

If the beads you have made begin to lose their scent, add some essential oils to bring them back to life. Essential oils are natural plant essences, as opposed to fragrance oils, which are synthetic. You can use both, but the essential oils will have a more pleasing scent that lasts longer and will smell more like the original spice or flower.

Wired for Beads

You can use wire not only to connect beads (as you'll learn more about in Part 4), but also to *make* beads.

You can make a very simple wire bead by coiling wire around a piece of dowel or metal rod. Just cut some 24-gauge art wire to approximately 12 inches in length and coil it around a ¼-inch dowel, keeping the wire tightly wound together. You'll get a modern "bead" that looks great with clay beads or simple round plastic, wooden, or lightweight glass beads. Pony or crow beads would work well with this wire bead, too.

You can make far more elaborate beads and connectors by using a wire jig or coiling device. We'll get into these tools later. Wire can also be used to enhance a bead. If you can't wait until the wirework chapters, log on to www.thewirewizard.com/blgallery.htm to see some exciting examples!

Other Beads You Can Make

Still don't have enough ideas for making your own beads? Here are some more for you to explore.

Temari

Temari is a form of intricate Japanese woven embroidery and is believed to date back over a thousand years. It was first used to make toy balls for children's play, and temari balls are traditionally given as gifts in Japan to this day. They have found favor in the West as colorful Christmas ornaments. You can create a spectacular focal bead by using a large wooden bead with a fairly large hole as a base and covering it with batting, then wrapping the entire bead surface at random with crewel or tapestry thread to hold the batting in place. What happens next is too involved to go into here, but if you'd like to explore temari as a bead-making possibility, check out the resources I've given you here and in Appendix B.

Findings

Check out Diana Vandervoort's website at www.temari.com and her temari bead project on Home and Garden Television's *Carol Duvall Show* (www.hgtv.com, episode CDS-1028). She has books and videos available, too. They're gorgeous.

Chinese Knotting

You can make some great pendants and even spacer beads with Chinese knotting techniques. This is believed to be an ancient art, although there is little documentation except in painting and sculpture of its early use. In the late nineteenth and early twentieth centuries, Chinese knotting appeared on many everyday objects, then nearly disappeared by the 1950s with the establishment of the People's Republic of China. It saw a renaissance around the same time as the re-emergence of macramé as an art form in the 1960s and 1970s.

There are 12 basic knots, and with a little practice you can learn them pretty quickly. Imagine a necklace or a lamp pull made with some Chinese or Japanese porcelain beads finished off with a Chinese knot, another spectacular bead and a tassel!

What other materials or techniques can you come up with that you can use to make a bead?

Findings

Yvonne Chang, who studied with a master of Chinese knotting will tell you all about it at www.knottingartist.com. There are books to help you get started as well. Check them out in Appendix B.

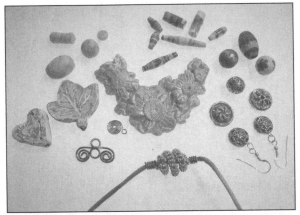

An assortment of beads you can make yourself with simple materials.

Put On Your Beadin' Cap!

Now that you've made a few of your own beads, you'll need to have a place to put them! Let's make a special place where you can put samples of your work and add to them as you work along in this book.

Buy or make yourself a cap. Perhaps you have one already gathering dust in your closet. I got a plain baseball cap at JoAnn's Fabric and Crafts. You can also try a beret, cloche, or whatever you like. If you'd like to make your own, check out Simplicity, McCalls, or Butterick patterns for a cap you like. If you make your own cap, be sure to make it in a material thin enough to sew through easily.

As we work through each technique in this book, you'll end up with a small sample you can either sew or glue onto your cap. When you're done, you'll have your very own beading cap. Whenever you put it on, I guarantee your creativity will soar!

From now on, you'll be reminded to put your sample onto your very own "beadin' cap." Like magic—you're a bead artist!

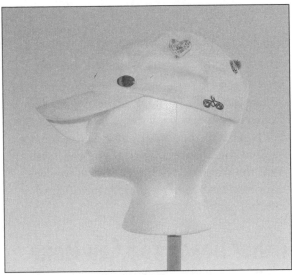

With your own beadin' cap, the sky's the limit.

The world of beads is so full of creativity, it can literally take you around the world, back to the past worlds of your childhood and ancient civilizations, or into whole new worlds of space-age materials and innovative modern techniques. You might not want to explore them all at once, but they'll be waiting for you whenever you're ready! With all the different materials and techniques out there, your work will be unique to you and not look like *anyone* else's!

The Least You Need to Know

◆ Making your own beads gives you unlimited ways to express your creativity and adds a personal, one-of-a-kind dimension to your beading.

◆ Paper is an inexpensive material that you can use to make a variety of attractive beads with minimum effort.

◆ Clay, especially polymer clay, is one of the most versatile materials for bead making. There's even a new precious metals clay that enables you to make metal beads and findings without learning metalworking.

◆ Use a wood or plastic bead as a base for many techniques that can be worked over it, such as gluing, embroidery, gold leaf, or decoupage.

◆ Making or buying your own beading cap will allow you to display samples of your work and enhance your creativity every time you wear it.

In This Chapter

- ◆ What findings are and how to use them
- ◆ The essential contents of every beader's toolbox
- ◆ Glues, conditioners, and other gooey substances
- ◆ How to be an organized beginning beader

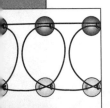

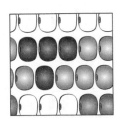

It's More Than Beads

In Chapters 1 and 2, you learned all about beads—what they're made of, where to find them, and how to make your own. Now that you've got a bunch of beads, how do you put them together? You're going to learn about that in this chapter.

To put together beads into a finished project, you'll need a variety of connectors and other mostly metal findings, some basic tools, and possibly some different types of glues and "goos." And to help you keep all those tiny things handy and easy to find, we'll examine a few of the containers, trays, and other organizing tools you might want at the beginning to pick up to stay organized. I'll cover this more in depth in Chapter 16.

What's a Finding?

A *finding* is any various piece besides a bead that you can use in making jewelry and other beaded items. Connectors, clasps, finishings, and embellishments are all considered findings, and most findings are made of metal. If it's not a bead, it's probably called a finding.

You'll use many different findings for making jewelry and personal accessories, and you might need special ones for creating certain decorative beaded items for your home. Each beading technique will have its own findings, tools, and materials. You'll become familiar with what's needed for each as you learn that particular technique. However, you'll need some basic items for most beadwork, and that's what you'll learn about in this chapter.

I recommend you always buy the best-quality findings and materials you can afford. You'll be making too great an investment of time and creative effort to have your project fall apart after it's made or to see the look tarnished by inferior materials.

Findings come in sterling silver, gold-filled, silver- or gold-plate, or base metals such as brass, iron, steel, copper, nickel, lead, or tin. Niobium, titanium, and pewter are also used, and some metals can be given a color coating.

Bead findings fall into a few basic categories:

◆ Connectors
◆ Clasps
◆ Finishings
◆ Specialty items
◆ Embellishments

Let's examine each.

Connectors

You can join beads together with a variety of methods. The most obvious way is to put them together on a string, either with or without knots between them. But they can also be joined with wire, including special wire "pins" made for connecting and hanging, along with various premade wire loops and rings.

Here is a brief list of the connectors you'll most likely encounter as a beginner and can find in any good bead store:

Bails   These are used to create a loop to attach a drop or pendant. Some bails have to be glued, and some have prongs that fit into a hole drilled at the top of the pendant.

Chain   Chain is available in many different styles, link sizes, and types. Some chain is fine enough to pass through a bead, and some chain is made specifically to suspend charms, so the links are bigger to hold the charm connector. Certain types of chain are not suitable for beading, however, because they are too tightly woven to insert any hanging pendants, connectors, or charms into the links.

Some common patterns of chain you can use in beading are cable, charm, curb, figaro, long and short cable, rollo, mariner, and krinkle link. I've given you a chart of the most common chain patterns suitable for beading in Appendix C.

Head pins   Head pins are basically straight lengths of wire with a flat pinhead on one end, much like a sewing pin except that the end opposite the head isn't sharp. They are used for connecting dangles and come in lengths from ½ inch to 4 inches and thicknesses from .020 to .029 inch.

Eye pins   Similar to head pins, eye pins have a round loop at the end instead of a head. By making a loop at the other end, you create a connector. Eye pins are available in the same lengths and thickness sizes as head pins.

Jump rings   Jump rings are round or oval wire rings used to join and attach. They come soldered or nonsoldered (connected or not connected) and in sizes from 2mm to 12mm in diameter. You can also make your own jump rings quite easily.

Knots!

Never open an unsoldered jump ring by pulling it apart. Use two pairs of pliers to twist it open, turning the pliers in opposing directions. Repeat in the opposite direction to close a jump ring.

Split rings   Split rings are like jump rings only doubled, which makes them stronger than jump rings. They come in sizes 5mm to 28mm. A special pair of split ring pliers is helpful when working with split rings.

Cord coil   This coiled wire with a loop at the end is for attaching a clasp to a cord. It is applied to the end of the cord; then the coil farthest away from the loop is crimped, locking it onto the cord.

Crimp beads   These soft metal "beads" are used instead of knots to secure ends and make secured loops on beading wires. They come in 2mm, 3mm, and 4mm sizes. These can't be used on thread or cord, however, as they might fray or cut it.

Crimp tubes   These are used the same way crimp beads are used, only instead of being round, they're tubular.

"Y" connectors   This special connector is used most often in making necklaces. It is made in the shape of a Y—hence the name—and has a loop or hole at the end of each "leg" of the Y. Y connectors enable you to create a necklace with a drop while the Y finding becomes part of the design.

3-to-1 connectors   Decorative findings with three loops or holes on one end and one loop or hole on the other, these are used to go from a multi-strand design to a single strand for design purposes or for attaching to clasps. They are also used for making earrings with multiple dangles.

Clasps

Whatever you make, you'll need a way to fasten it. If you're making a bracelet and it's long enough or if you use elastic, you can simply knot the string and just pull it on and off your wrist. But what if it's not long enough or you don't use elastic? In this case, you'll need a clasp.

Let's take a look at some of the clasps you can use:

Spring ring clasps   These clasps are circular with a spring mechanism that opens when you push on a small protruding tab and closes when you let go. A spring ring clasp needs a chain tab, a jump ring, or a split ring at the other end of the strand to hook on to.

Fishhook clasps These clasps consist of one end that is shaped like a long hook, similar to a fishhook, and another end that is shaped like an oval with an opening and a small bar across the opening. The hook is placed over the bar and then inserted into the clasp.

The advantage of a fishhook clasp is that it has two ways of clasping to prevent it from coming apart. If the clasp pops open, the necklace or bracelet is still held together by the hook and the bar. It can be difficult to maneuver, however, especially behind your neck.

Fold-over clasps Fold-over clasps look like a little box with a hinge. It folds over itself and "locks" after a ring is inserted from the other end.

Insert clasps These clasps are comprised of two halves, one, a small, hollow square, rectangular, or circular box with a little notch at the opening and the other half, a piece of metal folded in half with some "spring" to it. The folded side fits into the little box, and a tab on the folded side snaps into the notch on the box side. You open the clasp by pushing down on the tab on the folded side and pulling it out.

Toggle clasps Some truly lovely and interesting toggle clasps, which can be an important design element in a beaded piece, are available. They consist of one half that's a large ring and a second half that's a bar made slightly larger than the diameter of the ring. The bar is held vertically and slipped into the ring, then released to turn horizontal and hold secure.

They are not quite as secure as some of the other kinds of clasps, though, so they are best used on items that have some weight, as the weight keeps the clasp from coming undone.

Barrel clasps When these clasps are closed, they look like a little barrel. Each half of the barrel has a loop at the top for joining to the necklace or bracelet, and the loop rotates inside the barrel. One half has a threaded piece, and the other half accepts the threaded half. To close the clasp, you thread one half into the other, letting the loops rotate as you do, so the necklace or bracelet doesn't get twisted. The barrel clasp holds pretty securely.

Torpedo clasps These clasps are basically the same as barrel clasps, but are just longer and skinnier.

Magnetic clasps Magnetic clasps are essentially two small metal pieces that both look like a little bell with a loop at the top. One is magnetized; the other is not. Simply pull the two apart to take off the jewelry, and put them close together to fasten.

These are very effective with fairly light pieces of jewelry. However, heavy pieces might have sufficient weight to pull the magnets apart.

Findings

Certain fasteners can be difficult to operate for people with arthritis or other conditions that affect dexterity. I often use toggle clasps when I make jewelry, because they are extremely easy to connect and disconnect. The barrel clasp is another fairly easy clasp to open and close. Magnetic clasps are also good for people with arthritis, hand, or eye problems.

Lobster claws   I like to use lobster claw clasps because they are secure and look very streamlined. They come in different sizes and metals and have a spring action for opening and closing, much like the spring ring clasp. You'll also need a chain tab or ring at the other end of your piece to hook the lobster claw clasp to.

"S" hooks   One of the simplest clasps to use, you can easily make them yourself using wire (I'll show you how later). Again, weight keeps this clasp from coming apart, so S hooks work best on heavier pieces and are not recommended for a bracelet, where the action of your hands and wrists might cause it to come undone.

These are just some of the most common clasps you'll find. You'll likely see others when you start to shop for findings. Look at the jewelry you already own and see how many different kinds of clasps you can identify.

A collection of various clasps and connectors. Can you identify them from the descriptions I've given you?

Finishings

Sometimes your projects will require a particular finding to finish or end it off. Here are two you're likely to encounter:

Bead tips (or knot covers)   Bead tips hide knots at the ends of necklaces and bracelets and have a loop at one end to attach the clasp to. These are basically of three types: the standard, the side clamp-on, and bottom clamp on (clamshell).

***Bullion* or French wire**   Bullion is very thin wire wound in a tight coil and is used to finish and reinforce the thread that goes through a clasp when stringing beads. It comes in long lengths and is cut to size. Bullion is often used in finishing fine pearl or stone necklaces.

Specialty Findings

As you get more into your beadwork and want to expand your horizons, you'll need special findings for special applications. There are things available for just about anything you can think of, from barrettes to lampshades and purses!

Barrette backs   Wire beads or glue a piece of woven beadwork onto a barrette finding for a new look.

Cones   Use cones when making multi-strand jewelry to hide the ends. They have a wide opening on one end and a smaller opening on the other.

Cord caps   Cord caps are like cones and are used to hide knots in multiple-strand jewelry. Unlike cones, they're not completely open on the large end. They are more like cups with holes in the middle.

Earring findings   When making earrings, you'll need one of several types of findings to attach it to the ear. For pierced ears, use ear wires (French, kidney, and closing), posts, and hoops. For nonpierced ears, choose from clips and screw-type findings. These come in a variety of metals and styles.

Eyeglass chain findings   Eyeglass holders are very popular these days, and in addition to being a practical way to keep from misplacing your glasses, they are also worn as jewelry. An eyeglass chain is basically a necklace with an adjustable loop at both ends. A special finding creates that loop.

Hair combs and tiaras   Whether plastic or wire, premade hair combs and tiara bases can be used to create hair accessories with any number of techniques.

Hatpins   Hatpins are generally long, thick head pins with a sharp point. The hatpins sold in many bead stores and catalogs are just too flimsy and bend when you try to poke them through a hat with any thickness. Search until you find one that's heavy and stiff with a very sharp point. You'll also need an end cap to avoid sticking yourself.

Lampshade frames   There are several different types of frames on the market for making beaded lampshades. I give you some sources in Appendix B.

Neck wires   Neck wires are rigid rings that fit around your neck with threaded screw clasps. They are used for wearing larger beads, are usually 16 inches in diameter or more, and look very modern.

Perforated disks   These are special domed or flat perforated disks you can use to weave beads onto with thread or wire for earrings or pins.

Pin backs   To turn your beadwork into a pin, you'll need a pin back. These come with various types of clasps, and you either glue or wire your beadwork onto it.

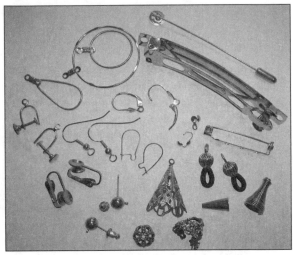

An assortment of specialty findings to enhance your beadwork.

Purse frames   Beaded purses bring back a bygone era. To make one, you'll need a purse frame with a handle. These come in many different styles and sizes, and quality varies widely. Beaders also look for vintage and antique purse frames on online auction sites and in antique stores.

Embellishments

Yet other findings have been created to add pizzazz or elegance to your finished products. They can make all the difference between "just okay" and "wow!" A plain and simple bead can become a dazzler just by adding a set of bead caps. A pretty bracelet can be personalized by the addition of some meaningful charms. Look for some of these "add-ons" when you visit your favorite bead sources.

Bead caps   A plain or fancy little cup with a hole in the center, this finding can turn a so-so bead into something spectacular. Caps can be used singly or in twos to surround a bead.

Bell caps   These are similar to bead caps, only they have a loop at the top. They are glued in place and make an object that doesn't have a hole into a bead.

Charms   These small cast or stamped objects in a multitude of shapes are used to embellish bracelets, wine glass markers, watch bands, earrings, or whatever you like!

Pendants   Pendants are free-hanging objects that dangle from a string of beads or a beaded chain. They usually provide a focal point in a piece of jewelry.

Spacer bars   Bars with varying numbers of holes are used at intervals on multi-strand necklaces or bracelets to keep the strands equidistant from one another. They come in designs from very plain to very fancy.

> **Findings**
>
> Take this book with you to a large bead store and look for as many of these findings and tools as you can find. You don't have to buy anything; just look, touch, and ask questions. This way, when you *do* need to buy some supplies, you'll already have some familiarity with them.

Thread, Needles, Cord, and Wire

You'll learn more about thread, cord, flexible wire, and needles when you get ready to do stringing and bead weaving, both off-loom and on-loom. In Part 4, you'll learn all about the different gauges and types of wires and the tools you need to work with them. However, let's take a brief look now at those items you're most likely to need right away.

Thread

We'll look more at thread in Chapter 5, but for now, the least you need to know about beading thread is that it comes in silk and synthetics and can be purchased on spools or in smaller quantities usually wound around a small card. You'll want to choose a thread that's small enough to go through your bead several times yet is strong enough to support its weight.

The most popular synthetics right now are nylon, polyester, and Kevlar, and people like them because they're generally stronger and more enduring. Some people like to work with various fishing lines as well. However, silk is easier to knot and doesn't stretch as much as nylon does, for example, plus for some beading jobs like pearl stringing, nothing else lays quite like it.

For your beginner's beading box, I'd recommend your getting some Nymo nylon beading thread in sizes 0, B, and D. As you progress as a beader, you'll be adding other threads to your box.

Needles

You'll need needles to do stringing with thread. I'll tell you all about them in detail in Chapter 5. For now, though, you need to know there are three basic kinds—big eye, twisted, and regular—and each has its particular uses and benefits.

I recommend John James English beading needles. Most good bead stores will stock them. A good beginning assortment would contain some needles of size 10, 12, and 13. You'll be adding different sizes and types as you progress with your stringing, bead weaving, and bead embroidery skills.

Cord

Cord comes in various diameters, colors, and materials. You'll usually see leather, waxed linen, silk, hemp, and elastics. I'll discuss cord at length in Chapter 5, but because they're relatively inexpensive and versatile, you might want to experiment with some different types right away and have them handy. A pretty cord threaded with a special bead and knotted at the ends can make a very attractive necklace in no time!

Wire

I'll discuss wire in great detail in Part 4, but for now, you should at least have on hand some 20- and 22-gauge wire for making earrings.

Be aware that there are also some flexible beading wires used for stringing on the market. I'll discuss these at length in Chapter 5. When you make your first trip to the bead store, you might want to look and feel, but hold off buying these until you need them for the techniques and projects I'll be teaching you later.

Findings

When you find broken jewelry, save the findings and the beads! You'll save money and have some unusual pieces to choose from down the road.

The Beader's Toolbox

One of the great things about beading is that you don't need to invest a lot of money in tools or equipment to start. You can actually make many, many items with just a few beads, some string, two or three findings, and a couple of simple tools. As you get more involved, you can slowly acquire some of the more specialized tools and equipment you'll need for specific tasks.

Tools for the Beginner

These tools should be in your toolbox or at your work area as you begin:

Chain-nose pliers   These are long, tapered, half-round pliers. They are used for gripping, crimping, wrapping, opening and closing rings, and squeezing bead tips closed. Choose pliers that have a smooth inside edge so they don't make marks on wire or findings.

Round-nose pliers   These have long, full-round, tapered points and are used for making loops in wire, head pins, or eye pins and for closing the loops on bead tips.

Side wire cutters   These are cutters with the cutting blades on the inside of the jaws. They are good for cutting wire or tigertail (see Chapter 5).

Flush wire cutters   The blades on these cutters are on the tip, which makes them good for cutting things flush or close.

Scissors   If you don't already have a pair, get yourself some good-quality scissors. I have two pair in my bead box—one very small pair of embroidery scissors and a larger pair of Fiskars scissors.

Ruler   You'll find a ruler with both inches and millimeters absolutely essential.

Adequate lighting   Light is something that's easy to overlook, yet it's terribly important. It can make all the difference between beading with ease and struggling, with the added hazard of damaging your eyes. I like a combination of natural and artificial light. An Ott Light is an interesting light on the market; it simulates natural light, and there is a new bulb available called Reveal by General Electric that also makes it much easier on the eyes when you're working with beads. Check these out for yourself and see what works best for you.

Magnifier I have four different kinds of magnifiers, and I use them all at different times for different things. I have one type that is suspended from a band that fits around my head, a magnifying lamp, and a pair of extra-strength glasses. I also have a loupe that I keep with me when I'm on shopping trips for closely examining beads and findings. Have some form of magnification handy, even if only to aid in threading beading needles. And get glasses if you need them! If your prescription needs updating, you'll be doing yourself a favor by doing it now, before you get started beading.

Beading surface A piece of velvet, velour, or felt; a scrap of carpet; or a towel can all be used to set beads and findings on while you're working. Whatever you decide to use, make sure it's got some texture and your work pieces won't slide off easily.

"Extra" Tools

You can make a lot of wonderful beaded items with no more than the tools and equipment I've given you earlier in this section. However, in addition to the essentials I've given you, you're likely to want some other tools and gadgets at some point. You don't need them right away, but if people are looking for small gifts to give you, they make great stocking stuffers!

You might want to add these extras to your toolbox:

Flat-nose pliers As the name suggests, these are flat and straight and don't taper. The inside surface is smooth so they don't make marks on wire or findings. Use this tool to bend wire, open and close jump rings, and squeeze bead tips closed.

Crimping pliers You'll need these if you ever want to use crimp beads. They have two indented places along the inner edge. The indentation closest to the handle makes the first dimple in the crimp bead, and the one closest to the tip finishes the crimp, folding it over and making it round.

Put On Your Beadin' Cap

If you want to see all the creative possibilities and boggle your mind, get a couple of major bead catalogs. I recommend *Fire Mountain Gems and Beads* catalog (www.firemountaingems.com). For a complete mind-blowing experience, order a couple of *Rio Grande* catalogs (www.riogrande.com). *Gems and Findings* and *Tools and Equipment* are good choices.

Split-ring pliers Before I got these, I hardly ever used split rings, even though I knew they were much stronger than jump rings. I just couldn't get them open easily, but these pliers make it a snap!

Bead reamer set Reamers are used for enlarging holes in beads or making them smooth. They usually come as a set so you can pick the right size for your bead. Add a drop of oil to the bead hole, then turn the reamer back and forth to grind away the extra material.

Bead-picking tweezers These are something of a luxury, but they're nice to have. They have little cups at the end that are just perfect for picking up exactly the bead you want.

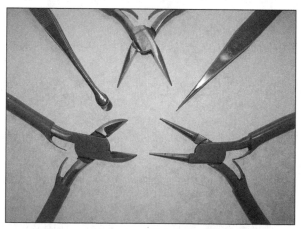

Here's an assortment of basic tools, plus some "extras" that are nice to have. Can you name them from the descriptions I've given you?

Glues and Goos

Occasionally you'll need various potions to help you with your beading. You'll find this brief list of glues and goos handy to have when starting:

Thread conditioner You'll definitely want to have some beeswax or Thread Heaven thread conditioner in your bead box. These products help keep thread from knotting or tangling, and you might find you have a preference for one or the other. I use both, depending on what I'm working with.

Glue Hundreds of glues have been formulated for different purposes by the hobby and crafts industries. You will definitely need at least a couple in your toolbox for securing knots and bonding stones or cabochons.

I recommend the following glues to start:

◆ **E-6000** This clear, waterproof glue is used for just about everything except securing knots. It should not be used on foil-backed beads as it might damage them.

◆ **Vigor Super Glue** Used for gluing knots, this glue dries almost instantly.

There are lots of specialty glues. I once bought a small tube of everything my bead store carried, then tried them all. I read the directions on the containers to see what their setting times and applications were. Some were "quick set." Some allowed me to move something around and hold, then set. Some are superpermanent. You need to know what you want to do and find the appropriate glue or cement for the job. Ask. Don't buy a large container at first until you see what you end up doing most and which glue you need and like.

Clear nail polish You can use this to set knots, strengthen frayed thread, and stiffen beadwork. One caution: Clear nail polish contains acetone, so check it on an extra bead first. It might remove color on some beads.

Organizing and Sorting

If you start out organized, you'll stay organized—at least that's the plan! Beads and findings have a way of multiplying pretty quickly, so be prepared with storage solutions from the start.

Bead board Although it's not completely necessary, this is a very handy thing to have. I have one large one and one smaller portable one. The main reason? Because I have cats! The grooves in the board keep my work pretty safe in spite of the occasional padding paw. A bead board allows you to measure your strands as you design and lay out your work. They are usually made of wood, plastic, or flocked plastic and have inch markings along the grooves for laying your beads. Some have U-shape grooves and have several grooves side by side, so you can design a multi-strand necklace easily.

Bead sorting trays   These come in all shapes and sizes and configurations. They allow you to see all your choices at once, sorted by color, size, or however you wish. Helpful for any kind of beading, these are almost essential for seed beadwork. The compartments need to be fairly shallow so you can retrieve beads easily. I use a divided glass dish that was originally made for olives and pickles, proof that your bead container doesn't have to be made especially for beading.

Findings

Your bead containers don't have to cost a fortune. Look in hardware and discount stores for good choices. They don't have to be designed specifically for holding beads, either. They just need to have lots of compartments and a secure lid.

Here are some helpers you might want to have to help you keep things straight when you first start to bead.

The "Nice to Haves"

This last group of items certainly won't make or break your beading hobby, but they're simply nice to have around. In fact, you might already have them!

Hand vacuum   A small portable hand vacuum is a real boon when you dump a bunch of seed beads on the floor—which you will inevitably do. Be sure it's empty and clean, then vacuum up the beads and dump them out in your container. You're done!

Dremel tool   The more I bead, the more I find myself stealing my husband's Dremel! I use it to drill holes in found objects I want to be beads. The polishing and grinding attachments are useful for removing burrs or imperfections. And I know I haven't even begun to tap the possibilities.

The Least You Need to Know

◆ In addition to beads, you'll need certain metal findings to complete your beading projects.

◆ Investing in good tools will make your beading more enjoyable from the start.

◆ You can make many different items with only a few essential tools and supplies.

◆ Getting organized at the beginning will save you time and aggravation as you progress in your beading hobby.

In This Chapter

- ◆ Getting ideas for designing your own beadwork
- ◆ Using simple concepts from the art world in your designs
- ◆ Considering classic styles from past and present
- ◆ Learning to work with color

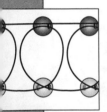    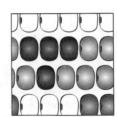 

Chapter 4

Beading With a Plan: Design Basics

One of the terrific things about doing your own beadwork is that you can have exactly what you want. See something you like but don't like the colors? No problem! You can make it yourself in different beads. Or perhaps you find an inexpensive piece made with plastic components but would like to have it in elegant glass and sterling silver. You can have that, too!

One way to design a piece of jewelry for yourself or an accessory for your home is to use an existing design as a starting point. I have bought things just to see how they're made and then have duplicated or improved on the design using beads and findings of my own choosing.

Another way to create your own beaded items is to follow a "recipe" or set of instructions a bead artist has devised so you can duplicate her design. Here, again, you can copy the design exactly or substitute beads of the same size or general composition, but of your own choice. All these ideas are ways of training your "design sense."

Sooner or later, however, you'll probably want to start designing some of your own pieces from scratch. Some people even start off that way! Maybe you have an outfit you'd like to make beaded accessories to complement or you've bought one spectacular bead you'd like to "do something with." Your choices can be overwhelming. However, having a plan in mind will help you narrow down the choices, and knowing a few design principles will hold you in good stead.

Finding the Artist Inside

You don't have to be an artist to do beadwork, but you'll be employing some of the basic principles of art when you design your own pieces.

Any craft has several parts—the tools and materials, the individual skills, and those mystical ingredients that only you can bring in your unique way: imagination, color sense, creativity, flair, and a feeling for design.

Put On Your Beadin' Cap

Creativity is like a muscle; it gets stronger with exercise. With practice, you learn to trust yourself. The great thing about beading is, if you don't like the results, you can cut it apart and start over!

The more beadwork you do, the more you'll develop your own special flair. Luckily, you have lots of resources around you to draw on to spark your creativity and imagination. Sometimes all it takes is to think about them or to look around you.

Where to Get Design Ideas

Inspiration is everywhere around you. Seeing it is just a matter of training your eyes. My sources of inspiration might not be the same as yours, but I'll share them with you to give you some ideas.

Lately I've noticed that female television news anchors are wearing a lot of beaded jewelry. Because they are viewed mostly from the waist up and even as just a "talking head" most of the time, their jewelry has to be attractive but not so overwhelming that it's distracting from what they have to say. Some of the pieces I've seen are quite lovely, and so I've begun sketching what I can see and adapting them to my own designs.

Another place to look is movies, including period movies or fantasies, and television shows. You might not be able to duplicate a piece exactly, but the overall look is something you can possibly use for inspiration. Again, you'll need to do a quick sketch (or tape the movie or show) so you can remember what you've seen. I'm no artist, but I can draw lines and circles!

Look in these other places for creative ideas as well:

◆ **Fashion magazines.** Next time you look at a magazine, rather than looking at the clothing, pay attention to what jewelry and accessories the models are wearing.

◆ **Department stores and boutiques.** Look at how things are made and what beads and components have been chosen. When you're attracted to something, analyze why. You don't have to buy. Just look. You'll be making your own versions before you know it.

◆ **Mail-order catalogs.** Certain catalogs consistently have jewelry and accessories that suit my tastes. I clip out those examples that especially catch my eye and keep them in a design folder.

Put On Your Beadin' Cap

Start your own design folder and fill it with your sketches and pictures that inspire you.

◆ **Online stores, galleries, and auction sites.** I often look at sites such as eBay for antique pieces or things that other people are making. There are also some wonderful sources for findings and beads online, some of which I've listed in Appendix B.

- ◆ **Galleries.** You might be lucky enough to have some galleries in your neighborhood or find them when you travel. Often they feature bead artists and can give you some great ideas.

- ◆ **Craft shows.** Our town has several large crafts shows on the downtown square. Craftspeople from all over the country come to sell their wares, and many are beaded jewelry and accessories makers.

- ◆ **Art books and museum catalogs.** I especially like Victorian and medieval styles, and I drool over books on antique jewelry and catalogs from museum exhibits. I've found some wonderful ones at very reasonable prices through online used book services that have inspired me.

- ◆ **Reprints of old jewelry catalogs.** Occasionally you'll find a publisher such as Dover Publications that reprints old mail-order catalogs. You can get a lot of ideas from the past. Dover's contact information is in Appendix B.

- ◆ **Bead catalogs and magazines.** Again, Appendix B contains major bead suppliers and magazines. They also have websites, and several have free patterns and instructions you can copy or adapt.

Shape and Line

In Chapter 1, I discussed the different shapes of beads. But beads and findings aren't the only shapes you should take note of when designing your beadwork. When you combine them in sequences or patterns, they take on an additional shape or "line."

Consider the necklace. A single bead hanging in the center of a cord or chain creates a V shape when it hangs from the neck. Make that bead a long, tube-shape bead or series of beads, and you have more of a U. A dangling pendant creates a different line. Place three larger beads with either smaller beads in between or knots on either side of each and produce a diamond. Another placement gives you a rectangular shape. A two-to-one connector and a dangle create a Y, and a tassel gives yet another line.

What you like, what looks best with your body type, and what you're making a particular necklace to accompany will determine the line you choose.

Some examples of necklace illustrating shape and line. Can you pick out the ones I've discussed in this chapter.

Symmetrical, Asymmetrical, Repeating, and Random Design

Almost all jewelry pieces fall into one of four basic design categories:

◆ Symmetrical

◆ Asymmetrical

◆ Repeating

◆ Random

Symmetrical means that a design is balanced on both sides of a central point or line. If, for instance, you were creating a Y necklace, you would have the exact same arrangement of beads on both the right and left sides of the upper part of the Y.

Asymmetrical design is not balanced because the focal point is placed to the right or left of center. This type of design has a more "modern" feel to it.

A-Bead-C's

Symmetrical design is arranged so that parts on opposite sides of a line or point are equally or regularly proportioned and often identical. Asymmetrical design is not identical on both sides of a central line and looks off center.

A repeating pattern, although it might not be totally symmetrical, gives a kind of balance to a piece. You can create a single design "unit" and repeat it or repeat several different units, alternating them throughout the piece.

You can also use a random design, perhaps all in the same color family, perhaps not. I find this works best with beads that are similar in size and weight, so they are unified by something else other than pattern.

Start looking at your own jewelry collection or what you see in stores or catalogs. Can you identify the design? What is the effect?

Knots!

Asymmetrical design poses some technical problems with a hanging piece such as a necklace. A larger, heavier bead placed off center will want to slide down to the middle, so you have to account for that in your design.

The four types of jewelry design.

Common Necklace Lines

When it comes to making jewelry, particularly necklaces, there are some classic forms to look for.

We've already talked about the Y necklace. You can create the apex of the Y by using a connector finding or simply a jump or split ring.

The simple circle is probably the most common necklace form. Various lengths of circle necklaces even have names. A circle of 12 to 13 inches is called a *collar* and is worn tight around the neck. Often this will be made up of 3 or more strands of the same length. A necklace 14 to 16 inches long is a called a *choker* and falls just above the collarbone. A necklace 17 to 19 inches long is a *princess* length. *Matinee* length is 20 to 24 inches long. *Opera* length is 28 to 34 inches long and can be worn as a single strand, or, doubled around the neck, it becomes a two-strand choker. A *rope* necklace is usually 45 inches or more and can be doubled over itself or possibly even wrapped three times for versatility.

The lariat style is even longer than a rope and is not connected as a circle. It's simply a long strand that's loosely tied or wrapped around the neck.

Multi-strand necklaces can be made in a variety of styles as well. A common one is the *bib* necklace, where each strand is longer than the one before. The strands can also be all the same length, which looks best if a variety of shapes and sizes of beads are used to add interest. Or for a nice effect, several strands of similar beads can be twisted together and caught at the ends into a single strand.

Size and Proportion

When designing a piece, often you will want to use either a single focal bead or pendant or perhaps three or so special beads. These will usually be the largest beads in the piece. Here's where your bead board will come in handy. You can lay out your beads and play with the different sizes and their placement.

When you are designing a piece, also consider the size of the person you're designing for. A very small person might not look well in a very large, chunky necklace or earrings. Also consider the size and shape of the face when designing earrings.

Findings

Something else to consider—and I'm not being indelicate here, just practical—is the bust size. A woman who is fairly large-busted might need a necklace to be longer or shorter to hang right. Perhaps you can have an existing necklace that the recipient already wears as a guide, or you can use a piece of string or cord cut to the proper length to help you.

A person's height, weight, the length of his or her neck, and the length and style of his or her hair are also issues to take note of when designing a piece of jewelry.

Weight

I can't stand to have heavy jewelry hanging from my neck or earlobes for very long. I also find that chunky bracelets get in my way when I'm typing. I usually end up taking off these things after a short while, so they're really not practical for me. I prefer lighter, more delicate jewelry both for comfort and style.

However, I know people who have no problem carrying off massive pieces with lots of heavy stone and metal beads, and they don't seem to have any discomfort at all.

Know your own preferences or those of the person you're making a piece for, and consider the weight and size of the materials you use.

> **Knots!**
> Be sure to match the thread or wire and findings you use with the weight of your beads. A light clasp, for instance, may not hold up to a heavy string of beads.

Size can be deceiving when it comes to weight. A large bead made of stone obviously has a different weight than a large bead made of polymer clay, hollow metal, or plastic. Even natural materials vastly differ in weight. Amber, for instance, is deceivingly light for its size.

Texture

What is *texture?* It's how a surface looks and especially *feels* to the touch. Texture can be rough or smooth, regular or irregular, matte or shiny. Sticking with similar textures or mixing them can give completely different looks to beaded pieces. When you go bead shopping, don't just look—*feel* the beads as well! If you're going to

be wearing something around your bare neck, the texture of the beads that will touch your skin need special consideration. Rough or sharp beads might irritate, so keep this in mind when creating your designs.

> **A-Bead-C's**
> **Texture** is the visual and especially the tactile quality of a surface.

You sometimes enhance the more dramatic beads in your piece by combining different textures. The sum is more than the parts. Matte beads will make glass beads shine even more. Metal beads mixed with stones or pearls will often enhance the colors. This, again, is where your bead board comes in handy. Try pairing different combinations on the board, and note the effects.

A Word About Color

Most of us are somewhat timid about using color. We are afraid to shout too loudly or make a mismatch. So we play it safe, imitating catalogs or fashion magazines that play it safe. But one of the advantages of learning a craft is that you can have it your way!

Remember the color wheel from elementary school art class? Well, if you don't, now might be the time to revisit it. First, you have your three primary colors: red, yellow, and blue. Then you have the secondary colors, which you get by combining equal parts of any two of the primary colors. These secondary colors are orange, green, and violet.

Last are the tertiary colors. These are created by combining primary colors and secondary colors. There are six tertiary colors: red-orange, yellow-orange, yellow-green, blue-green, blue-violet, and red-violet.

When you look at the color wheel, you can see that the color directly opposite the one you've chosen is "complementary," meaning the two will look well together. And the colors on both sides of the color you've chosen are analogous or similar to each other and will also look well together.

Findings

Get yourself a color wheel. We've even given you one in this book! Flip to the color insert, and you can see the color relationships I've discussed here at a glance.

You can also look at color in terms of families. There are neutrals, pastels, and vibrant colors, and each gives a different effect when used within its family.

Often you will choose a dominant color, say, red, and then a subdominant color that can either "cool" or "warm" that dominant color. Use silver or brown with red to tone it down. Use gold or even white with red to make it stand out. Play with different combinations on your bead board and see what mixing various subdominant colors with your dominant color beads will do.

You might also want to take into account special meanings associated with color or a particular stone such as the signs of the Zodiac, the chakras, healing properties, birthstones, colors of the season, and anything else that has meaning for you or the person you're making a piece for. I've given you several suggestions in Appendix C.

Put On Your Beadin' Cap

Get some paint chips from your local paint or home improvement store, cut them up, and play with them. Look for primary, secondary, and tertiary colors. Take a bright color and see what effect different neutrals have when placed beside it.

If you're making a piece for someone in particular, keep in mind his or her personal coloring. What is the individual's hair color? Skin tone? Eye color? What colors does she usually like to wear? What might look great on you may not necessarily be attractive on someone else.

Classic Styles

Some jewelry and home decorating styles are simply classic. They never go out-of-date and seem to reappear every so often as the "latest" in fashion. Depending on your personal tastes or the mood you're trying to create, you might want to choose one of these styles and design accordingly. Here are a few for you to play with.

Primitive or Ethnic

The basic elements of this style are rough textures, natural materials, and either neutral colors or bright, happy colors. Popular in this category are African, Native American, and various Central American styles.

Put On Your Beadin' Cap

The Bead Museum in Glendale, Arizona, and The Bead Museum of Washington, D.C. (mentioned in Chapter 1), are both good places for inspiration when you are looking for beadwork from primitive cultures.

Contemporary

Sleek, uncomplicated lines; modern materials; and asymmetrical design are characteristic of this style. Look in jewelry design magazines such as *Lapidary Journal* and high-end galleries to see contemporary pieces.

Victorian or Romantic

If you like feminine, elegant, intricate jewelry, then this is the style for you. Filigree findings and beads, pearls, faceted beads, fancy pendants, and lots of intricate chains are commonly found in vintage pieces from the 1800s through the 1920s. This style especially lends itself to evening and bridal wear—or maybe you want to dress romantic all the time!

Glitzy

I like to call this style "Hollywood" or "drippy." It utilizes lots of big, sparkly findings and beads—think rhinestones and pearls and anything with lots of shine. If you like sequins, faux fur, and lamé, this is the style for you!

Whimsical

If you like primary colors and "little kid" charm, your style may be whimsical. Cute beads in animal, fruit, or bold geometric shapes together with charms and other playful findings round out this look. The 1960s kind of personified this style.

You have many other styles to choose from. Just keep your eyes open. Whatever you can think of, you can bring to your beaded designs.

The Least You Need to Know

- Use resources all around you to inspire your imagination when creating your own beaded designs.
- You need to match the size and proportion of the beaded piece with the person you're designing it for.

- Keep in mind the weight of a piece when choosing your thread and findings. They need to be strong enough to hold the beads and components.
- A person's comfort and style is important when choosing materials for your designs.

In This Part

Part 2

Bead Spaghetti: Stringing and Weaving Techniques

Many cultures have developed stringing techniques both on and off looms. In some cases, it doesn't get any simpler than putting beads on string, thread, or cord. But you can also loom beadwork to create a beaded "fabric" that's both beautiful and durable.

In Part 2, you'll get a comprehensive overview of stringing materials and the basic techniques as well as some basic off-loom weaving stitches. Then I'll guide you through choosing a loom (or choosing to make your own), setting it up, and making your first beaded project on a loom.

In This Chapter

◆ Choosing the right beading thread for stringing and weaving

◆ Everything you need to know about flexible beading wires and when to use them

◆ Beading cords and their special uses

◆ Picking the right needle for the job

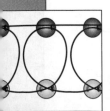 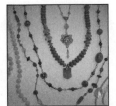   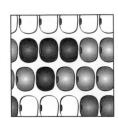 

Chapter 5

Threads and More: What You Need to String a Bead

Bead stringing is the most basic beading technique there is. What could be simpler than taking a piece of string, threading it through holes in beads until you fill up the string, then fastening the two ends together to make a beaded circle?

But that's just the simplest kind of stringing. Most strung beads are joined together with a clasp of some kind. And once you get a bunch of beads on a string, you can weave them, either on a loom or without one.

Stringing is just the beginning. There's so much more you can do. So let's get to it!

Puttin' It On! Bead Stringing and Weaving Materials

You can use many different kinds of materials to string or weave beads. The most common are thread, cord, flexible wire, and fishing line. I'll take these one at a time and discuss the advantages and disadvantages of each. I have my personal favorites, but you'll need to find out for yourself which you like best.

The major qualities you'll want to know about for any bead stringing or weaving material are as follows:

◆ Strength

◆ Resistance to abrasion and fraying

◆ Flexibility

◆ How well it takes and holds a knot

◆ How it holds up to sweat, wet, and sun (or dryness, if you live in the Southwest like I do!)

◆ Whether it stretches when you don't want it to (or does when you do)

◆ How it looks when it goes through a bead

◆ Colorfastness (in the case of colored threads or cords)

If you're using smooth, lightweight beads and just want to string one strand with a clasp, you should use a different stringing medium than if you were making something with sharp, heavy beads and wanted knots in between. Think about your project's requirements, and then choose the stringing medium that suits it best.

Beading Threads

Thread is the most common bead-stringing medium because it's completely flexible and knot-worthy. And beads strung on thread lay softly and have a fluid look to them. The disadvantage of some threads is that they can stretch, fray, or break, especially when used with heavy or sharp beads.

Of course, not all threads are created equal. Some are stronger than others and have different properties that make them better suited for one particular project or another.

Findings

Beaders take their threads seriously, let me tell you! Get on any online beading list or talk to a room full of beaders, and you'll get a passionate discussion about which is the best beading thread.

I'll give you the major threads that seem to engender the most loyalty and passion in this section. Try them and decide for yourself.

Beading thread is basically divided into two categories: nylon and silk.

Knots!

When selecting a thread, you don't want the thread so thin that it's "sloppy" in the bead hole because that will increase friction. Some people recommend choosing a size that allows you to double it to increase strength and fill the bead hole; however, if you have to take your work out for some reason, that gives you extra strands to contend with. It's best to choose a thread size that will fit through the bead at least twice but isn't so thin that it leaves a lot of space.

Silk   Silk beading thread is essential for beading light, soft gemstones such as pearls, especially if you're planning on knotting in between the beads. It drapes like nothing else.

Silk comes in many different colors, which can be used as part of your design when working with clear beads. It is available in sizes 00 (the thinnest) to FFF (the thickest), and you'll work most often with sizes D through FFF.

You will need to condition silk thread before you use it, or it will tend to knot and kink. Silk stretches less than linen or cotton thread, but it still does stretch. You can help avoid this by prestretching it as you work.

Silk thread does not hold up well to repeated exposure to moisture, so it's not good for use in jewelry that will be worn on a daily basis or while swimming. You'll want to restring valuable pearls and gemstones periodically. Still, I prefer silk for stringing pearls and lightweight gemstones. An excellent brand name to look for is Gudebrod.

Nylon   Many different nylon threads are designed (or in some cases borrowed from other crafts) for various applications. When you first begin stringing or bead weaving, you might want to ask your teacher or bead store owner for advice. You'll probably get a recommendation for one of these threads:

◆ **Nymo**   The name Nymo stands for "nylon monofilament." It's a waxed nylon thread recommended specifically for working with seed beads, especially for bead weaving and Native American–style beadwork.

Nymo is available in bobbins or on bulk spools and is sized from 00 to FF, with 00 being the thinnest. You'll most often see 00 to D in bead stores and catalogs because these are the sizes used most often for bead weaving, including weaving on a loom. All sizes are available in black and white, and most are available in a variety of colors. Many bead artists consider Nymo the thread of choice for bead weaving. It can stretch a bit, so you might want to pre-stretch it as you work.

Knots!

Keep in mind that colored thread can completely alter the look of a transparent bead. You might want to use a transparent, neutral white, or off-white thread, or you might want the effect a particular colored thread gives. Creating a small sample might be your best bet to avoid any unpleasant surprises. Just thread all the different color beads you intend to use on the thread and see how they look.

◆ **Silamide**   This two-ply twisted nylon thread was originally used in the hand-tailoring industry. It is available in 24 colors and comes prewaxed. Silamide is used like Nymo and is even preferred over it by many beaders. Although Silamide is not as stiff as Nymo, it doesn't fray as easily and is stronger. It comes in size A only, which is probably its greatest disadvantage. It can also be used for on-loom weaving.

◆ **C-Lon**   A relatively new beading thread, C-Lon is drawing praise from beaders. It doesn't stretch, is quite strong, and frays less than some other threads. It comes in 36 colors, so if color is important, this might be the thread for you. It's one disadvantage: It only comes in size D.

◆ **"Silkon" bonded nylon**   This thread is made especially for stringing hard or sharp beads that might fray softer threads or cords. You would use this for stones such as garnet, amethyst, and crystal as well as for metal beads. This thread comes in many colors and takes a knot well. It is sold in 20- and 100-yard spools in three sizes: #1 (smallest), #2 (medium), and #3 (largest). Silkon comes in 12 colors.

◆ **Kevlar** Made from the same material used to make bulletproof vests, Kevlar is extremely strong. It doesn't knot well, however, and only comes in black or its "natural" yellow, which takes a fabric dye relatively well. Some people have reported that Kevlar disintegrates over time and may wear through when it rubs on itself.

Findings

If you're not sure what stringing material to use for a project and the instructions don't specify, put together a small sample before you actually start your project for keeps. This might take a little extra time, but you'll find that it will save you either having to start over because you don't like the way your choice is turning out or having to repair a piece later because your choice didn't hold up. Pull on your sample, move it, drape it, and see how it lays!

Beading Cords

You can use many cords on the market for beading. Some are made specifically for beading, and some are borrowed from other crafts. Here's a brief summary of the cords you might encounter:

Satin cord I really like the look of satin cord for the simple presentation of one or just a few larger, special beads. It's rich and elegant-looking and is easy to knot. Satin cord is colorfast, comes in at least 8 colors, and comes in three sizes:

◆ **Rattail** Thickest at 2mm, used for large beads and Chinese knotting

◆ **Mousetail** Medium, 1.5mm

◆ **Bugtail** Thinnest, 1mm

C-Thru "thread" This woven, clear nylon cord is used for stringing clear beads when you want little or no color from the thread or cord to show through. Similar to fishing line, it has multiple strands instead of just a single strand. It knots well and can be used with bead tips.

Elastic cord This is generally sold by the spool and has a diameter of .045 inch or 1mm. Especially great for bracelets and anklets, you can make the elastic fit your wrist or ankle exactly, and the elastic allows you to slip it on and off. You don't need a clasp although you can add one with a cord cap or coil. Your beads need to have holes 1mm or larger to fit on this cord. It comes in 11 colors.

Powercord Also a stretch cord, this has a good "memory" and knots easily. It comes in 10 colors as well as clear, which is nice to use with transparent beads. The clear cord is available in five diameter widths from .5mm to 2.0mm, and the colors are available in two diameter widths: .5mm and .8mm.

Imitation sinew Actually made from a continuous-filament of waxed polyester cord, this comes in white, brown, black, and sometimes other colors and is quite durable. Use this cord for heavy glass and ceramic beads such as trade beads. Favored by reenactors for primitive "mountain man" designs, it can be split to make thinner cord.

Leather cord Real leather cord comes in .5mm, 1mm, and 2mm sizes and is good for large-holed beads and pendants. It is available in lots of colors (I've seen at least 13), and the dye used is permanent and colorfast. You can also dye leather whatever color you desire.

Suede leather cord is also available. Imitation leather cords made from woven biodegradable cotton are available. Although these imitation leather cords are stronger than real leather, they're not colorfast, so choose accordingly!

Natural waxed cotton cord   This cord comes waxed to make it easier to bead with. It knots easily and holds well, is tightly woven, and is colorfast.

Crinkled silk cord   Made from real silk, this is actually a silk fabric tube sewn along its length. It has a luxurious feel, but at 4mm, it is very thick, which makes it best for use with a beaded pendant or braided together with a beaded strand.

Hemp cord   Hemp is the cord of choice for doing macramé with beads. You can also buy jute cord, but it's rough and not as strong. You can buy hemp "natural" or in a polished version, which makes it more uniform and fray-resistant but gives it a different look. I've seen hemp cord available in at least 8 different colors. Just be sure whatever you choose is colorfast.

Invisible beading cord   This is clear and almost, as the name implies, "invisible." It works great for "illusion" necklaces where you want the beads to appear to be "floating" around your neck. It comes in .25mm and is generally sold in 50m spools.

"Parachute" cord   This high-tech cord made from "spectra fibers" gives it less stretch than some other monofilaments, and it is highly resistant to sun damage and moisture. It comes in black and white in 18-pound (.004 inch), 30-pound (.006 inch), and 50-pound (.012 inch) test.

Flexible Wire

Flexible wires for bead stringing have many advantages. First, they're strong. You can use heavy beads and know the wire won't break. They are relatively flexible, although not as flexible as thread or cord. They're also durable and don't stretch.

Findings

If you're very active and like to wear your jewelry while swimming or doing other sports, you should probably consider one of the flexible wires.

The main disadvantage of flexible wire is that it tends to kink when you're working with it. Don't squash or bunch it up as you're working. Flexible wire often is not suitable for knotting, although some of the new, very fine flexible wires both resist kinking and can be knotted.

Another small problem is that lightweight beads tend not to hang well on flexible wire. It's best used with beads and findings that have some weight.

Here's a short summary of the types of flexible wires you are most likely to encounter:

Tigertail   Tigertail is a thin, braided steel cable that's been coated with nylon. It's very tough and good for heavy beads and beads that have sharp edges that might cut through thread. Tigertail doesn't drape very well, it can't be knotted, and if you put a kink in it, it will be weakened at that point. Tigertail comes in sizes .012 to .026, with .012 thinnest.

Soft Flex wire   Soft Flex wire is constructed of either 21 or 49 micro-woven, stainless-steel wires that have been braided together and then nylon coated. This wire is my personal choice when a flexible wire is called for. I particularly like the new Soft Touch wire, which can be knotted, although the manufacturer recommends a specific knot be used for best results. See its website at www.softflexcompany.com for instructions on how to do the "eight-knot" and lots of other helpful hints. I generally just use crimp beads when I work with flexible wire.

Soft Flex is marine quality, so it can be worn in and out of salt and fresh water. Regular Soft Flex comes in .014, .019, and .024 diameter. Soft Touch comes in these sizes plus .010 and is even more soft and flexible.

Soft Flex now also has a Gold Flex wire that is 24k gold over stainless steel (21 strands). It is knottable, nylon coated, and great for designs where you want gold flexible beading wire.

Other good brands of flexible wire are on the market. Try them for yourself and decide which ones you like best.

Foxtail   Foxtail is actually a fine, strong chain, rather than a wire. It's usually made of nickel but is also available in sterling silver. Foxtail is used for stringing metal and glass beads with rough drill holes that would fray regular bead cord. You'll want a special crimp hook and eye clasp to finish the ends.

Memory Wire   Memory Wire is wire that "remembers" its shape. You don't need a clasp to finish a piece made with memory wire. It can be adjusted to fit almost anyone.

Fishing Line

Many beginning beaders like to use nylon monofilament fishing line for their projects. It's strong, and it's cheap! However, it has a reputation among beaders for breaking down over time. It breaks with exposure to heat and sunlight; it tends to stretch when used with heavier beads; and besides, it's just plain stiff!

But some of the newer fishing lines are made out of something called Dynema, a gel-spun polyethylene (GSP). This extremely strong fiber is just about indestructible, plus it has a softer drape and can be knotted. Dynema fishing line is sold under the brand names Spiderline, PowerPro, and FireLine. You'll want to use a 6- or 8-pound test for beading. There aren't a whole lot of choices when it comes to colors, but you can't have everything!

Get It On! Needles for Beading

I talked briefly about beading needles in Chapter 3, but let's just revisit them for a moment and fill in a little more detail as they relate to bead stringing and weaving.

You can use several different kinds of needles with thread for stringing. I prefer the twisted-wire needles or big-eye needles because the larger needle eyes are easier for my older eyes to see to thread. With the twisted-wire needles, the eye is forced closed when you pull the needle through the bead, but if you need to open it again, it's easy to do with a pin or other sharp object.

If you're working with beads that have very small holes, sometimes you'll need to use English beading needles. The larger the size number, the thinner the needle. Size numbers are meant to match up with seed bead numbers, but you may want to choose a needle one size smaller (the next largest number), because you'll probably be needing to go through the bead more than once.

But, you ask, what needle should I use with what thread? The best explanation I've seen is from an article called "What Should I Use?" by beading divas Virginia Blakelock and Carol Perrenoud (*Bead&Button* magazine, December 2003, the article is available to download in PDF format at www.beadandbutton.com).

Findings

Need help threading beading needles? You can use the same needle-threader you might remember from your mom's sewing basket. Or use a magnifier. Always make sure you have good light! And a tip I learned from a quilter—hold the thread steady and move the needle eye to the thread end. Don't try to put the thread through the needle. Also try Fray Check or a light coat of glue at the end of the thread to make it easier to thread through the eye of a needle.

To summarize what these experienced ladies had to say, here's what to use when:

Seed Bead Size	Needle Size	Thread Size
6°, 8°, or 10°	#10	FF, F, EE, or E Nymo
11° or 12°	#11 or #12	D Nymo
13°, 14°, or 15°	#13	B, A, or 0 Nymo
16° to 24°	#15 or #16	00 or 000 Nymo

If you're using something other than Nymo, you'll have to relate this information to that particular thread. For example, with C-Lon, because it comes in size D, you'd use a #11 or #12 needle.

The best needles for loom work are #12 that are 3 inches or more long. You might want to have some sharps on hand for loom work and bead embroidery. Sharps are not actually any sharper than other needles; they're just shorter and usually stiffer than other needles.

Besides bead size, personal preference is usually the reason most beaders choose a particular beading needle. Needles are cheap, so buy an assortment and try different ones to see what works best for you.

Smoothing It Over: Thread Conditioners and Waxes

No matter what thread you use, you will probably have some problems with tangling, knotting, and fraying. Thread conditioners keep these "thread monsters" at bay.

There are basically two types of thread conditioners: beeswax and a synthetic conditioner called Thread Heaven. Both help reduce fraying and tangling; which you use is really a matter of personal preference.

Beeswax is, of course, a natural material. It tends to put a heavier, stiffer coating on thread and can coat somewhat unevenly. It smells wonderful, by the way.

Thread Heaven is a silicon-based thread conditioner that is lighter than beeswax and comes in a convenient easy-to-transport plastic container. The Thread Heaven website (www.threadheaven.com) gives tips on how to use it and answers frequently asked questions.

I've used both conditioners and continue to do so depending on what seems to work best with a particular thread. I've even used both on the same thread! In most books or instructions I've seen, beeswax and Thread Heaven are used interchangeably. I'd suggest having both on hand so you can see for yourself.

All these threads, cords, flexible wires, and fishing lines can be used to make a gazillion different necklaces, bracelets, anklets, earrings, pulls, key chains, beaded curtains, and whatever else you can think of! In the next chapter, you'll learn how to make your first bead stringing projects.

The Least You Need to Know

- There are two basic kinds of threads for bead stringing and weaving: nylon and silk. Each has particular uses and advantages and disadvantages.

- Flexible wires are another very strong stringing medium that produce good results.

- Beading cords are generally used for larger beads for a more "chunky" look and can be knotted easily.

- Fishing line is generally not recommended, unless you use one of the new, stronger GSP types.

- The right needles and thread conditioner will ensure successful results with your bead stringing or weaving project.

In This Chapter

- ◆ Beading three bracelets using different stringing techniques and materials
- ◆ Making a continuous-loop necklace
- ◆ Learning and using knotted stringing
- ◆ Adding clasps and findings

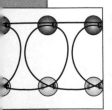

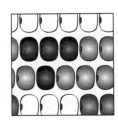

Chapter 6

All Strung Out: The Basics of Bead Stringing

Now that you have all your tools and supplies (beads, findings, clasps, etc.), it's time to start cookin' with beads! The first thing we're going to make is spaghetti! Well, what else would you call strings of beads?

In this chapter, you're going to learn how to make three kinds of bracelets and a continuous necklace, plus I'll teach you the basics of knotted bead stringing.

It's All in the Wrist

The first kind of bracelet I'll teach you to make is on flexible wire. Two brands of flexible wire you'll most likely see in bead stores are Soft Flex and Beadalon. They come in different weights, but the weight we'll be using for our projects is .014 or .015, depending on the brand. This number refers to the diameter of the strand in inches. When we're done, you'll know how to put on a clasp with crimp beads and have your first experience using two different kinds of pliers.

Roll up your sleeves and grab your beading stash—or make this a good excuse to go shopping if you don't have all the supplies—and let's go.

Fire and Ice Bracelet

This bracelet has plenty of sparkle and "fire," and it's so easy to make. You won't want to stop at just one! (See the photo at the end of the chapter for my Fire and Ice bracelet.)

Supplies:

> 1 (size .014 or .015) spool flexible wire
>
> 2 sterling silver crimp tubes
>
> 6 (8mm) round clear or AB (aurora borealis) Czech or Austrian crystal beads (I used Swarovski Austrian Crystal.)
>
> 6 (8mm) round Czech or Austrian crystal beads (I used Swarovski Light Siam.)
>
> 24 (3mm) round silver spacer beads
>
> 1 lobster claw clasp
>
> 1 silver split ring or chain tab

Tools:

> Chain nose pliers
>
> Crimping pliers
>
> Flush wire cutters

1. Lay out your beads on your beading board or textured surface, starting with the clasp, then a crimp bead, then 1 (3mm) silver bead, a clear bead, 2 (3mm) silver beads, 1 red bead, 2 silver beads, 1 clear bead, 2 silver beads, 1 red bead, and so on until you reach approximately 7 inches, which is the standard size for a bracelet.

2. Now, cut about 10 inches of flexible wire with your wire cutters.

3. Slide a crimp bead or tube (some people like to use two for extra security) on one end of the flexible wire. Thread the wire through the loop of the clasp and then back through the crimp bead and leave a ½-inch tail.

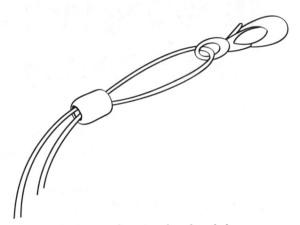

Findings

I have an average-size wrist, and I ended up using 6 of each of the 8mm beads and 24 of the silver beads. If you're not sure about your wrist size, you might want to measure it. You won't want the bracelet too snug, but remember to allow for the two crimp beads and the clasp and ring in your measurements; otherwise, your bracelet might end up being too loose. With everything put together, my bracelet measured a total of 7½ inches, which is a perfect slightly loose fit for my wrist.

Putting on the crimp bead and clasp.

4. Push the crimp bead up snug with the clasp. Squeeze the crimp bead flat with the section of the crimping pliers closest to the handles, flatten it, then move it up to the part of the crimping pliers closest to the tips and fold over the flattened tube.

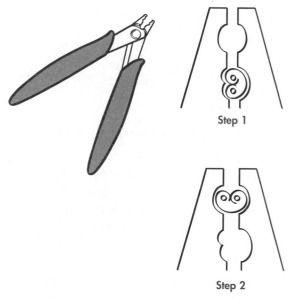

Step 1

Step 2

Flattening a crimp with crimping pliers.

5. Add the first few beads, and tuck the tail into the holes, then trim close to the bead it's coming out of. *Be careful to only cut the tail, not the main wire!* Finish stringing on the rest of your beads.

6. Check your length with a ruler. At the end, thread on a crimp bead, then thread the wire through the second half of the clasp or jump ring and back through the crimp bead.

7. Pull everything taut, leaving just a little gap so there's some "play" in the ring. Squeeze the crimp bead flat with the crimping pliers as you did before, then fold the crimp bead over as before. Cut off the wire tails with wire cutters very close to the bead it's coming out of. Put on the bracelet, and enjoy it!

Now, that wasn't hard, was it?

Ready to stir the pot a little more? The second bracelet you're going to make uses beading thread instead of wire. You'll still be using a clasp, but the method for attaching it will be different.

Blueberry Parfait Bracelet

This is a project where you get to use whatever supplies you have on hand. I simply went through my bead stash and pulled out a variety of beads of all different shapes and textures in the same color family and an assortment of antique finish silver beads, all approximately the same size. We'll be using a random design, so play with what you have until you like the way it looks! (See the photo at the end of the chapter for my Blueberry Parfait bracelet.)

Supplies:

Assortment of purple beads, all similar in size, of varying shapes

Assortment of small silver beads of varying shapes

Beading thread (I used Beadalon Dandyline size .011 for this project.)

2 clamshell bead tips with hook for attaching a clasp

1 clasp (I used a toggle clasp.)

Clear nail polish or G-S Hypo Cement

Beading needle that fits through your beads and also has a eye that takes the thread you've chosen

Tools:

Chain nose pliers

Scissors or thread snips

Findings

If you don't have a beading needle or don't feel like threading one, you can dip the end of the Dandyline in clear nail polish and let it dry to "make" a needle. This needle works fine if you don't handle it too roughly!

1. Assemble your beads, findings, and materials, and lay out a pleasing series of beads on your bead board. Keep in mind some of the design principles we talked about in Chapter 4.

2. Cut approximately 10 inches of bead thread, and make a *double overhand knot* at one end.

A-Bead-C's

A **double overhand knot** is made by simply bringing the tail through a regular overhand knot twice, instead of once.

Dab some clear nail polish or cement on the knot and let it dry.

3. Bring the needle and thread through the clamshell bead tip so the knot at the end of the thread is in the "cup" of the bead tip and the thread is coming through the bottom with the hook pointing away from the needle and thread.

Attaching a clasp using a clamshell.

4. Attach one half of your clasp to the hook of the bead tip, and gently close it with your chain nose pliers so it fits just inside the open clamshell. Then, close the bead tip with your chain nose pliers so it's snugly closed, but not mashed, encasing the knot inside.

5. Thread all your beads onto the string until you have a length that's approximately 7 inches (or whatever you've determined is a good length for your wrist), including the bead tips and both halves of the clasp.

6. Bring the thread through the second bead tip so the needle and thread are going in the same direction as the little hook at the end of the bead tip. Tie a double overhand knot, and pull it up snug inside the bead tip. Put a dab of clear nail polish or cement on the knot and let it dry.

Findings

If the knot isn't big enough to stay securely inside the bead tip, tie a small seed bead into the knot and then add glue and fit into the bead tip.

7. Fit the other half of the clasp on the hook, closing it, and then closing the clamshell snugly over the knot. Voilà! Another bracelet!

For our last bracelet, we're going in for the stretch. You won't need a clasp for this one, but you will use a stretchy stringing material so you can just slip it on and off.

Ambrosia Bracelet

You can't get much easier than this! (See mine at the end of the chapter.)

Supplies:

> 10 inches of elastic cord, such as Stretch Magic
>
> 12 (12×10mm) lightweight oval pink and white glass beads
>
> 12 gold E beads
>
> 1 (2×2) sterling silver crimp bead
>
> Plastic tape

Tools:

> Crimping pliers

1. Put a piece of tape at one end of the elastic cord to act as a "stop" and string your beads, alternating a small gold E bead and a large oval bead. Start with one type of bead and end with the other. You'll want this bracelet to fit fairly snug around your wrist, so string just enough beads to fit comfortably.

2. I've seen several ways to finish off your bracelet if it's made with Stretch Magic or similar plastic stretch cord. Just tying an overhand knot won't work because the knot eventually will slide out and your beads

will end up on the floor. I like the crimp bead method: Just put one end of your finished bracelet through the crimp bead, and put the other end through the crimp bead going in the opposite direction. If you have trouble getting both strands of cord through the crimp, stretch out the cord that's already through the crimp to make it "thinner" and make room for the second strand to go through.

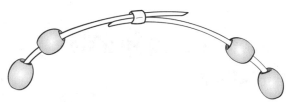

This is how your stretch bracelet will look once you've attached the crimp bead.

Pull the ends up snug (but don't stretch the bracelet), and using a crimping pliers, make a two-step crimp like you learned in the Fire and Ice Bracelet instructions earlier in this chapter. The crimp is nice and neat, holds well, and will most likely hide itself inside the adjacent bead.

Variation: Use the crimp bead as a design element along with an accent bead, and add it to the bracelet. Put the two ends of your bracelet through an accent bead then through a crimp bead—but this time going in the same direction—then crimp the crimp bead and cut the ends evenly.

Knots!

Stretch cords do sometimes lose their "memory" after a while. If you notice your bracelet getting loose, just restring it to avoid any problems. Also be careful with old-fashioned covered elastic cording. It doesn't last as long as some of the more expensive elastic cords available specifically for beading. For added security, knot the cord between beads.

Never-Ending Sparkle Necklace

You can only use this technique on a necklace that will fit easily over your head without needing a clasp to open it. A 26-inch or larger necklace should work nicely. (See my version at the end of the chapter.)

Supplies:

> 13 (10mm) bicone or round crystal beads, in color(s) of your choice
>
> 13 (6mm) bicone or round crystal beads, in color(s) of your choice
>
> 132 clear, silver- or gold-lined E or other 4mm beads
>
> Plastic tape
>
> Nylon or silk beading thread
>
> Glue for securing knots (I like G-S Hypo Cement.)

Tools:

> Scissors or thread cutter

Findings

When choosing which cord or thread to use, be sure it doesn't stretch (or pre-stretch it) and that it will go through your beads twice. You can either use a beading needle or make a needle (see the first Findings sidebar in the Blueberry Parfait Bracelet project), using glue or clear nail polish.

1. Cut a 36-inch length of thread, and make or thread your needle. Put a piece of plastic tape securely at one end to act as a "stop" for your beads.

2. Thread on your beads starting with 1 (10mm) crystal, then 6 silver E beads, then 1 (6mm) crystal, then 6 silver E beads. Repeat until you've reached approximately 26 inches.

3. Move your beads so you have approximately the same length of exposed thread on both ends. Put the needle end of the thread through the first large crystal bead you strung. Pull both ends up snugly, and make an overhand knot on either side of the first large crystal bead.

4. Dot some glue on both knots and let dry. Cut off the excess thread, and wear your necklace!

Findings

Just for extra security, I like to thread the tails through a few more beads on each side and make another set of knots.

This necklace works up quickly, and you can use any beads you like. With a pair of earrings to match and a stretchy bracelet strung in the same repetitive pattern using the technique you learned to make the Ambrosia Bracelet, you have a lovely set for an impressive gift. (You'll learn how to make earrings in Chapter 11.)

To Knot or Not To Knot? Let's Answer That Question!

Imagine you were in a crowded restaurant when your pearl necklace broke—and it *wasn't* knotted! You'd be chasing pearls all over the floor and may not even find them all. If the pearls are knotted individually, the most you can lose is one pearl.

Knotting is a stringing technique where you tie a knot after stringing on each bead or pearl. It is usually used when stringing pearls, very special beads, or fine gemstones. It takes considerably more time and a little practice to get the knots even, but it is well worth the time when what you're stringing is valuable or rare. Knotting between beads prevents beads from rubbing together and wearing, as well.

Findings

I taught myself how to knot from a book and video in a couple of hours. The best instructional beading video I've found is called *Pearl and Bead Stringing with Henrietta*, with instructor Henrietta Virchick. There's a book that goes with it that makes it even clearer. Another good video that uses a slightly different method is *Pearl Knotting Like a Pro*, available from The Bead Shop. I highly recommend using a video, as it really helps to see someone else do it several times. (I've listed these resources and how to get them in Appendix B.)

Before you tackle a new project, you can practice knotting by taking a necklace you already have and restringing it using the knotted method.

Bead Clasp Potpourri

You can do so much more with beads than simply hang them from thread, string, cord, or wire. The skills you've learned in this chapter will get you started and happily stringing beads for years to come. However, I'd like to leave you with a few additional instructions so you can add even more variety to your designs.

Attaching a Cord Coil or Crimp

If you decide to use satin cord or leather cord, you can, of course, simply knot the ends together when you're ready to finish your piece. But you could also add a clasp. If you do, you'll need to know how to attach a cord coil or cord crimp:

1. Cut the end of the cord flush.
2. Push one end of the cord inside the cord coil or crimp at the open end. (The other end has a loop for attaching a clasp.)
3. Using your chain nose pliers, press down and flatten the first ring or two of the coil against the cord. If using a crimp, flatten the whole tube.
4. Pull a little on the cord to be sure it's secure. Now you can attach a clasp to the loop end of the coil. Repeat this procedure on the other end, and add the rest of the clasp. You're done!

Findings

Thin cording or leather might pull out of a cord crimp or coil if it's used in a single thickness. To fix this, just double the cord or leather inside the cord crimp. Trim any excess close to the cord crimp after crimping.

A creativity note: You can attach feathers to your beadwork by using a cord crimp. It basically turns the feather into a bead!

Knotting on a Clasp with Thread

You might just want to attach a clasp to your thread end without a clamshell, or maybe you just don't have one handy. Here's how you do that:

1. Thread the clasp onto one end of your nylon or silk thread, and bringing the end around several times through the clasp, make a double overhand knot. Leave a 3-inch tail.

2. Put a drop of clear nail polish or glue used for securing knots (see Chapter 3) on the first knot and let dry.

3. String a few beads onto the other end of the thread using a needle, and thread the tail at the clasp end through the first few beads. Make another overhand knot, dab with polish or glue, and let dry.

4. After stringing on all your beads, thread the other end of your thread through the second half of your clasp, and tie a double overhand knot, pulling everything taut as you do. Put some clear nail polish or glue on that knot as well and let dry. Thread this tail back through a few beads, and make a second double overhand knot and dot with polish or glue. Trim the tails on both ends close to the nearest bead. Be careful not to cut the main thread!

Attaching a Clasp Using Bullion

When you do individually knotted pieces or any time you use thread to attach a clasp, you can add strength and durability to the thread that goes around the clasp and make it look more elegant and finished by using bullion, also known as French wire.

Knots!

Be sure you have the right bullion for the job. It comes in both gold and silver tone and in three sizes: fine, medium, and large. Get the right size, or it will snag and pull apart. And store your bullion carefully (I keep mine in a little plastic box) because it catches on things and is easily crushed.

As you might remember from Chapter 3, bullion is a very fine coil of wire. It snags and pulls apart very easily, so you'll want to work with it on a smooth surface and be very gentle with it. Here's how you use it to attach a clasp:

1. For our example, we're going to say we have size F or FF thread and we're using medium bullion. Cut off ⅜ to ½ inch bullion, making sure the edges are cut clean. Pass your threaded needle through the last 3 beads you intend to string, leaving a 4-inch tail, then put your needle through the strand of bullion, holding the bullion gently between your fingers and being sure not to catch the thread on the wire.

2. Add one side of your clasp to the thread, and move it so it's over the center of the piece of bullion.

3. Pass the needle and thread back through the end bead, making a loop with the bullion-covered thread, and knot tightly on the other side of the bead. Keep your thread and bullion flat as you make the coil. Don't twist it.

4. Continue stringing and knotting using whatever method you've chosen, and repeat the bullion procedure on the other side of the project.

> ### Findings
> I was able to get the hang of using bullion the first time, thanks to Henrietta's video and book, but it's a good idea to practice making a bullion coil with thread a few times before actually using it on a project. Having your thread well conditioned is a good idea, too.

Clasp attached using bullion or French wire.

Multi-Strand Necklaces or Bracelets

Making multi-strand pieces means basically using any one of the techniques we've used for single strand ones multiple times. (That's a no-brainer, right?) There are a few special findings you might want to use and some tips, but we'll look at those when you make a multi-strand bracelet in Chapter 19.

Which Stringing Material Is Best?

Knowing which stringing materials to use with each project is something you'll learn with experience. Definitely consider using flexible wire with heavy beads or anything that has an abrasive hole or edge because it will wear longer. Definitely knot between valuable beads. I prefer silk thread when knotting pearls, and that's what Henrietta advises as well, but some people prefer nylon. Threads tend to produce a more fluid piece although some of the finer flexible wires are quite amazing. Try them all and decide for yourself.

Look at your beads. Determine their weight and whether they're smooth or sharp at the edges. Look at the different materials available. Also, choose your findings based on how the item will be worn and how heavy the beads will be when they're all strung.

Not sure? Ask! Most of the people in today's bead stores are beaders themselves and have lots of experience with different materials. Share your concerns and questions, and you'll undoubtedly get good advice based on what you tell them you want to do.

Sometimes we have to learn lessons the hard way. My best beading buddy made a beautiful Victorian beaded purse. Not long after she finished it and started using it, she noticed it was coming apart. The thread she had used just wasn't strong enough. The purse took many hours to bead, and we were both heartbroken.

Once I made a lariat necklace with some wonderful sparkly cut seed beads. It came out great, and I even went through the entire necklace twice with thread. Now it's coming apart. I plan to totally rethink the materials I used and will probably string it again with a very light flexible wire or Fireline. Even seeming failures are learning experiences!

Put On Your Beadin' Cap

Let's get a little more practice attaching findings using two of the methods you've learned in this chapter. Measure the length from one side of your beading cap's "beak" to the other. Cut flexible wire or beading thread to that length, plus several inches. Attach a soldered jump ring or split ring to the ends using the methods you learned in the Fire and Ice or Blueberry Parfait Bracelets. String with beads and attach a ring to the other end. Sew each end onto your beading cap. These caps are starting to look smart!

This is how my bead cap looked after I added my "bead spaghetti." What does yours look like?

My assortment of bead spaghetti! From top to bottom: Fire and Ice Bracelet, Blueberry Parfait Bracelet, Ambrosia Bracelet, and Never-Ending Sparkle Necklace.

The Least You Need to Know

◆ Flexible wire is a great way to string heavy or abrasive beads.

◆ You can attach clasps several ways with bead thread.

◆ Knotting between beads when stringing pearls or other special beads is a good idea so you won't lose but one if the strand should break.

◆ Bullion or French wire is helpful for strengthening a clasp where the thread goes through it—plus it looks finished and attractive.

◆ You'll learn which stringing material is best through experience (including failures) and by asking experienced beaders when you're not sure.

In This Chapter

◆ Learning two commonly used peyote stitches

◆ Mastering an alternative method for those difficult first three rows in flat peyote

◆ Working with flat and spherical netting

◆ Using the ladder and brick stitches, square stitch, and the right-angle weave

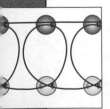
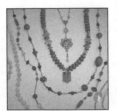

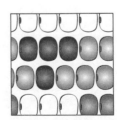

Chapter 7

Dream Weavin': Off-Loom Bead Weaving

When most people think of weaving, they think of fiber and looms. But you can also weave with beads and, as with fiber weaving, you can create a woven object in many ways without using a loom. In beading, these freehand weaving techniques that don't require a loom are usually referred to as "off-loom bead weaving" or "freehand bead weaving."

You can use many stitches in off-loom bead weaving, and in this chapter, we're going to learn the ones you'll see most often. You're sure to find one that suits your fancy!

Needles and Threads Revisited

Off-loom weaving is mostly a needle-and-thread game. You might use a few findings on some projects, but you can make many things using just a needle, a length of thread, and some beads.

You'll mainly be using seed beads for off-loom weaving, although the stitches can be used for any beads. Some of the more sculptural pieces you may have seen in the bead magazines and books are done with many different size beads woven together freestyle.

In this chapter, we'll be making a sampler of patches that you'll sew onto your beading cap at the end. You can expand any one of these sample patches into a bracelet, an amulet bag, or any of a number of things. (We'll be doing some of those projects in Chapter 20.) All your sampler patch instructions will be for size 6° "E" beads. If you're feeling confident, you can move to a smaller size seed bead at any time, or try the technique first in the E beads and then again in the more common size 11° seed beads.

Peyote Stitch: It Can Become Addictive!

The use of the term *peyote stitch* is actually somewhat controversial. It is also called gourd stitch, and some Native Americans believe we should use the latter as the proper term, because peyote beadwork is a specific technique used for a sacred ceremony. Yet "peyote" seems to be the term that's "stuck" in the beading world.

A-Bead-C's

Peyote stitch is the term commonly used to describe the gourd stitch, a highly versatile bead weaving stitch common in Native American beadwork. Peyote is actually a small, wooly, buttonlike cactus with hallucinogenic properties that is used as part of a sacred ceremony performed by a wide variety of Mexican and Native American people. Peyote beadwork is that beadwork specifically used to decorate some of the ritual objects used in the peyote ceremony.

The peyote stitch is difficult for some, but others pick it up easily. Whichever category you fall into, I definitely advise you to start small (our patch for your beadin' cap will work just fine) but with big beads. The little sample we'll be making is wide enough to get the idea, but not so wide that you'll have to struggle to keep it from curling or twisting. Starting with large beads also helps you see where the thread is going and how the beads should lay. Using a contrasting thread will make it even clearer. Make several samples if you need to, and practice until you feel like you've got it.

The first three rows of a peyote project are the hardest. I suggest keeping the first row laying flat on your working surface and weaving in your second row, being very careful as you set down your first three or four rows to not twist your thread. Or you might find holding your work between your thumb and forefinger works better for you. Once you get your first three rows down, the thread will be easy to control.

By using contrasting colors to create your sample, you can see the pattern the beads develop through the weave. By working with two different color beads, you can also guide your pattern and compare it to the pattern pictured to see if you've done the weave correctly.

Flat, Even Count Peyote Patch

There are basically three types of flat peyote: even count, odd count, and circular. Even count is the easiest to master. Let's make your sampler patch with that stitch, and you'll see how it works.

Supplies:

> Thread, size D or F
> Needle, size 10
> Size 6° "E" beads in color #1, a generous amount
> Size 6° "E" beads in color #2, a generous amount
> Thread conditioner

Tools:

> Sharp scissors

1. Cut about 2 feet of thread from your bobbin or spool. Condition the thread, and thread the needle. If you have trouble threading your beading needle, an easy way is to hold the end of the thread firmly between the thumb and forefinger of your nondominant hand so that only a little protrudes and put the needle onto the thread, rather than the other way around. Tie on a "stop bead" of a color other than the two colors you'll be using by going through it twice with your needle. (You will take this bead out when you're done, so it doesn't matter what color it is.) To tie on the stop bead, bring the needle through the bead, leaving a tail of about 6 inches, then bring the thread around your forefinger and through the bead again. Pull snug.

Knots!

Seed beads can often be quite irregular. Before you begin beading your sample patches, sort through your beads and remove any that are misshapen, especially small or especially large. You want beads that are all of the same general shape and size. Your finished work will look much better if you presort your beads.

2. String on 8 beads, starting with 1 of color #1 and then 1 of color #2, alternating colors until you have 8 beads altogether. This first string of beads will become the first 2 rows, and each row will be 4 beads wide.

3. String on 1 bead of color #2, and go through the second from the last bead of the first 8 you strung with the needle. *Do not twist or turn your work!* So for example, if you started with a white bead, then a black, and so on, you would have ended with a black bead and the second from the end would be a black bead. You would

then string a white bead on the needle and go through the second from the last bead, which would be black. You'll be able to see this easily from the following illustration.

4. Put another color #2 bead on your needle, and go through the fourth bead. Do the same for the sixth bead and the eighth bead, and your first three rows should look like a small zipper similar to the following illustration. You should have 4 beads of color #2 on the bottom row, 4 beads of color #1 in the middle, and 4 beads of color #2 on the top row. Your stop bead should be on your left if you've laid your work out flat in front of you.

5. You've just completed the hardest part! Turn your work so you're always working from the bottom up, from right to left. Put on 1 bead of color #1, skip the middle row bead (which should be color #1 also), and go through the "high" bead (color #2). Continue doing this, using color #1, skipping the lower bead and going through the high bead until you've finished the row. Turn and change colors and repeat until you've completed enough rows to make a patch approximately 1-inch square. Your patch should look like the following illustration, with alternating vertical stripes.

6. Now, to tie off your work: On the outside of your patch, weave your needle and thread through the connecting threads between the two beads closest to your needle. Make a loop, go through the loop with your needle, and make an overhand knot. Pull snug and repeat. Weave your needle and thread through several beads in a diagonal row up or down following the thread path, then cut the tail with sharp scissors. *Be careful only to cut the tail!* Pull off your stop bead, and do the same thing with that tail. You're finished!

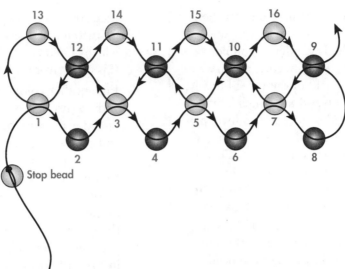

Your four rows of flat, even count peyote should look like this.

Findings

Keep your work flat, and don't let it twist. Keep your tension even and snug, and be especially careful on the first three rows while you lay your foundation.

If you have trouble doing flat count peyote this way, you might want to try the two-needle start. I first encountered this method on Suzanne Cooper's website (www.suzannecooper.com). She gives credit to Barbara Grainger, peyote beader extraordinaire. Barbara says she's seen it published as far back as the 1930s, but she's expanded and adapted it to all three types of peyote.

Let's try the two-needle start. We'll make the same patch as the one we just did, but this time we'll be using one piece of thread with a needle at each end. We'll also be using three different color beads, so it'll be easy to see how this works. When you're finished, you'll have a different color on each row.

Flat, Even Count Peyote Two-Needle Start

Again, you'll be working from the bottom up if you follow these directions. If you want to work from the top down, swap rows 1 and 3 so row 1 is on top.

We'll be using the same supplies as we did making the previous patch, only this time you'll need two needles.

1. Cut and prepare your thread as we did in step 1 of "Flat, Even Count Peyote Patch," and thread two needles, one at each end.

2. Pick up 2 beads, 1 of color #1 on the right needle and 1 of color #2 on the left needle. Lay your work out so both needles are pointed to the left and the two beads are centered one above the other, all the way to the right. The color you chose for row 1 should be on the bottom and the one you chose for row 3 should be on the top. Bring the beads to the center. Lay your work out so both needles are pointed to the left and the two beads are centered one above the other, all the way to the right.

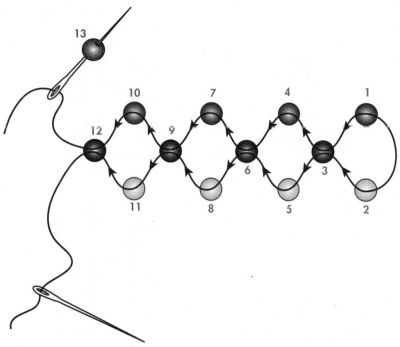

Your first 3 rows of flat, even count peyote using 2 needles to start should look like this.

3. Pick up 1 bead of color #3, and either pass it through both needles at once, or, if you can't get them both through at once, put one needle through and slide the bead down past the eye, then slide the other needle through. Remember, threading both needles through the bead at once makes it easier to twist the thread, so be careful if you do it this way. Bring this bead next to the first 2 beads. This becomes row 2. Be careful not to cross your 2 threads and needles. Keep them separated.

4. Pick up a row 3 (color #3) bead on the top needle and a row 1 (color #1) bead on the bottom needle, and slide them next to the single row 3 bead you just put on. Hold things snugly to keep everything in position. This third up-and-down configuration should look like the first row's 1 and 3 beads did.

5. Repeat steps 3 and 4 until you've got the number of beads you want for the width of your project, ending with a single row 2 bead.

6. Turn your work. Pick up a color #3 bead with your needle, and pass through the last row 3 bead (which should be color #2 and the "high" bead) and continue working with that needle back and forth. Later you'll tie off the bottom thread and weave it into your work, then trim it off.

If you've done everything right, you should have one vertical solid stripe of color #3 and alternating beads of color #1 and color #2.

Findings

For instructions on using the two-needle start with odd count flat peyote and both even and odd count tubular peyote, there's a great article in the August 1999 issue of *Bead&Button* magazine (#32) by Barbara Grainger that explains each with diagrams. Just go to their website at www.beadandbutton.com and print out a copy or contact the magazine about getting one. I've given you all the info for *Bead&Button* magazine in Appendix B.

Tubular Peyote

Tubular peyote is the easiest way to get a peyote cylinder or little amulet bag. All you have to do is bead a cylinder, flatten it, and close the bottom. Add a strap, and you've got an amulet bag. It's also the method you'll use to cover any kind of bottle, needle case, or other vessel with peyote stitch. You can even use this method to cover cord to make a beaded snake!

For this project, we're going to make a large tube bead using odd count tubular peyote. Here's how to do it:

1. Using the same ingredients and equipment you did for Flat Even Count Peyote, cut a thread approximately 4 feet long and double it for strength. Put the doubled thread through the eye of your needle. Add a stop bead at the end, leaving a 6-inch tail. Choose one color to use for your beaded tube bead or a variety of beads—whatever you like.

2. Put 7 beads on your needle and thread. Bring the first and last beads together, and create a ring of beads by going through the first bead in the same direction and tying off (making two overhand knots) behind the first bead.

3. Insert a graduated stick such as a chop stick through the ring, and bead your tube around the pointed end until you can maintain a good hold on your beaded tube. I found I could do this after three rows. Be sure to keep your thread taut and maintain the tension.

4. Put a bead on your needle and thread, skip the next bead in the circle of beads, and go up through what is actually the third bead of your circle. Pick up a bead, skip bead 4 on the circle, and go though bead 5. Pick up a bead, skip bead 6, and go through bead 7.

5. Now pick up a bead and go through the first bead added in the second row you just did. Continue doing this (picking up a bead, skipping a bead, and going through the next bead) until you've completed several rows and have created a beaded tube bead. I made my bead 12 rows high altogether. You might want to make yours longer or shorter.

6. After you've gone through the last bead in the row, tie off by making two overhand knots. Thread your needle through several beads following the diagonal thread path, then snip off the tail.

7. Remove the stop bead, and do the same thing at the beginning end—tie two overhand knots, thread through, and snip off the tail. Throughout this process, be sure you are keeping your threads taut and your work snug.

Sew your tube, together with your two flat, even count patches, on your beadin' cap!

Knots!

Be careful to read directions thoroughly and determine *which* peyote stitch is being called for. Many variations of the stitch exist, and a common mistake is to use an even count peyote when an odd count is what the design calls for. If you want to learn more about the many variations of peyote stitch in all their glory, I highly recommend Barbara Grainger's book, *Peyote at Last*. The Internet also has some very good directions, complete with diagrams, tips, and projects. Suzanne Cooper's site (www.suzannecooper.com) is a good one. Type in "peyote stitch" in a good search engine, and you'll find scads more.

What's in Your Net?

I love doing netting. It goes so fast, looks lacy, and has lots of applications. The year I learned how to do circular netting, I made everyone beautiful beaded ornament covers which hang over glass balls. I'll show you how to do that in Chapter 20, but let's learn the basics now and make a sample to put on your beadin' cap.

We're going to make a flat netted circle to put on the top of your beadin' cap, so we'll need the initial circle to be large enough to fit over the button at the top of the cap.

1. Using the same supplies and tools we've been using for the projects in this chapter, string an *even number* of E beads to make a circle large enough to go over the button on the top of your cap. I used 18 beads to make mine. I suggest using several different colors, switching with each "round" so you get a rainbow effect, but use your own creative judgment here. Bring your thread around and go through all the beads again, creating a circle. Come out of the last bead you threaded on the circle.

2. Thread on 15 beads. I used 7 of one color, 1 of another, then 7 of the first color again. Skip 2 beads and go through the third. Repeat this sequence until you arrive at the beginning single bead. At this point, your work should look like a circle with 6 "petals" projecting out from it if you started with the same number of beads I did. Go up through that single bead and up into the first 8 beads you strung on. In my case, this put me through the one odd-color bead I had in the center of my "petal."

This is how your netting should look with the petals complete ready for the third round.

3. Thread on 11 beads, and go through the center bead of the next "petal" (which would be the eighth bead as before). Continue doing this until you meet the first 11-bead sequence in this round. Join and tie off.

Sew your finished beaded netting piece onto your beadin' cap! I stitched through the circle and at the outside-points to put it on my cap. You can see what I did in the photo at the end of this chapter.

As with peyote, there are many versions of beaded netting, including vertical, horizontal, and spherical. You can use netting to make elaborate fringes and trims. Look in Appendix B for places to learn more about beaded netting stitches.

Right-Angle Weave

This stitch can be done using one needle or two. We'll be learning the one-needle method, using the same materials as our previous patches. You'll note in the illustration that I've numbered each bead consecutively so you can see the exact order the beads are put on, which is somewhat difficult to follow in right-angle weave. I would suggest you use two contrasting colors so you can follow it more easily.

1. Using the same supplies and tools we've been using for the projects in this chapter, cut 2 feet of thread and thread on a needle. Pick up 4 beads, and tie them into a ring using an overhand knot. Repeat the knot so your work will hold fast. Be sure the tension is snug before you tie your knots.

2. Pass the needle through beads #1 and #2. String on three more beads (#5, #6, and #7), and pass the needle back through beads #2, #5, and #6. Repeat this pattern, following the illustration, until you have a circular row of beads approximately 1 inch wide. You should have used 13 beads total on your first row.

3. To do the next row, turn your work and go across in the opposite direction. Start by coming out of bead #11; adding beads #14, #15, and #16; and going back into bead #11 and down through beads #14, #15, and #16.

4. Go through bead #10, add 2 beads (#17 and #18), and go around in a circle coming up through beads #16, #10, and #17. Add 2 more beads, and go around in a circle again, going through the bottom bead from the upper circle (bead #5) and the left side bead from the previous circle in the same row (bead #17), then back through beads #19 and #20.

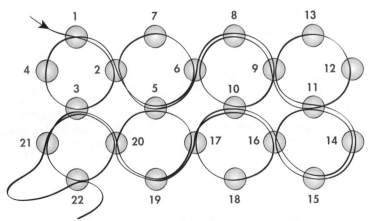

Your first row of right-angle weave and beginning of the second row should look like this.

5. Now go through bead #3, the bottom bead from the first circle you made in the first row, add 2 beads (#21 and #22), and repeat.

6. Continue creating enough rows until you have a patch the size you want. Knot and tie off.

Now sew this patch onto your beadin' cap!

Findings

If you're starting to get confused with all your different sample patches on your beadin' cap and you're not sure which is which, neatly label underneath each patch on your cap with a fabric pen.

This Stitch Is for Squares!

By now you should really be getting the hang of this off-loom weaving thing. Isn't it fun?

I'd like to teach you three more stitches in this chapter, and then you can go exploring wherever you'd like.

The next sample patch we're going to make uses the square stitch. This stitch approximates what you would get if you used a loom and makes it possible to use a counted cross-stitch design chart to create a pattern. This is a very strong stitch and is good for anything that might receive some stress or regular wear.

1. Again, using the same supplies and tools we've been using for the projects in this chapter, cut 3 feet of thread, tie on a stop bead, then string on 8 beads of color #1.

2. To do the second row, add 1 bead of color #2 and bring your needle and thread through the last bead of the first row (bead #8) then back through the bead you've just strung on (bead #9).

3. Add a color #2 bead, and go through the next bead in the first row and back through the bead you've just strung on. Continue with color #2 until you reach the last bead in the first row (bead #1). Pass the needle through the entire first row and the row you've just done to reinforce your work.

4. Work back in the opposite direction the same way with color #1 and back again with color #2 until you have created a patch approximately 1 inch by 1 inch. You'll have alternating rows of colors #1 and #2. Reinforce each row as you complete it. Knot and tie off.

You guessed it: Sew this patch on your beadin' cap!

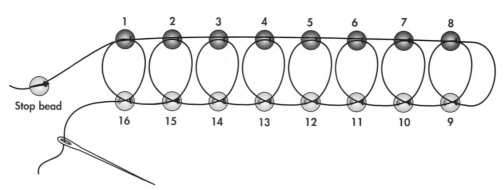

Your first two rows of the square stitch should look like this.

Bricks and Ladders

The brick stitch is also known as Comanche stitch and, as with most off-loom stitches, has several variations. For this sample, we're going to combine the brick stitch with a ladder stitch base to produce a diamond—so you'll get to learn two stitches at once! You'll often see the ladder and brick stitch combination used to create earrings. (I give you a pattern for one with an added fringe in Chapter 20.)

1. Using the same supplies and tools we've been using for the projects in this chapter, cut a 3-foot length of thread and put on your needle. First, we'll make a base row using the ladder stitch with 7 color #1 beads. Use two needles for this, and you'll have thread for both the top and bottom triangles without having to add thread.

   Pick up 1 color #1 bead with 1 needle, and bring it to the center of your thread. Go back through the bead with the other needle in the opposite direction, so with

1 needle you've gone from right to left and with the other from left to right. Keep adding beads and making a threaded circle by crossing the 2 needles until you have 7 beads on your "ladder." This is your foundation row for your 2 brick stitch triangles.

2. We'll make the triangles with color #2. Remove one needle. Working right to left, string 1 #2 color bead and bring the needle under the top thread between the first two beads, then through the bottom hole of the bead you just added. Add another #2 bead, and repeat until you reach the space between the last two beads. You should have 6 beads on this row. You are actually *decreasing* the number of beads with each row and forming a triangle.

3. Turn your work, and add the next row in the same way. When you get to the fifth row from the base row (the one with two beads), add the final bead to form the top of the triangle and go through one of the two beads below it. Then knot and tie off.

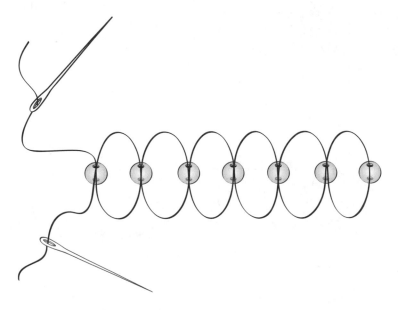

Using two needles to make your foundation row of ladder stitch.

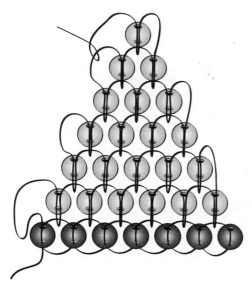

The first brick stitch triangle of your patch should look like this.

4. Add a needle to the other thread, and repeat to create another triangle on the bottom, using color #2 as well. Knot and tie off.

Sew this on your beadin' cap! It's starting to look great, isn't it?

Does your beadin' cap look similar to mine after you've added all the samples from this chapter? Looks good, don't you think?

Put On Your Beadin' Cap

You should now have a ton of sample patches to put on your cap! If you've made one and don't like it, make another. The more you practice, the better you'll be. I've done everything in large beads so you could easily manipulate them and see how they go together. You'll mostly be using these stitches with smaller seed beads, most commonly size 11°. If you want, remake your patches with the smaller seed beads. It'll be a cinch now that you know how!

The Least You Need to Know

◆ The peyote stitch, or gourd stitch, has many variations.

◆ You can do netting in the round, vertically, and horizontally. This stitch gives a lacy, open effect.

◆ Brick stitch and ladder stitch are often combined to create earrings and other beaded objects.

◆ Peyote and netting can both be adapted to cover objects such as glass bottles, vases, pens, and needle cases.

In This Chapter

- Knowing your *warp* from your *weft*
- Working with threads, needles, and beads for loom work
- Putting it all together
- Designing your own pattern

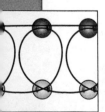
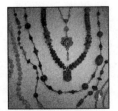

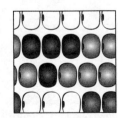

Chapter 8

Your Destiny Looms!: Getting Started Beading on a Loom

If you've ever been in Scouts or gone to summer camp as a kid, you've probably dabbled in loom work, either with beads or with fiber. In fact, this is probably the most familiar kind of beadwork to many of us.

Usually associated with the work of Native American and African tribes or elaborate Victorian chokers and purses, loom bead weaving is a versatile technique that produces strong beaded fabric in a tight grid. It's fast and easy—you can make a simple bracelet in just 2 or 3 hours—and because it forms a square grid (like the square stitch you did in Chapter 7), you can use counted cross-stitch patterns or design your own on graph paper. You can make everything from bracelets and necklaces to belts and purses with a beading loom. Your only limitation is the size of your loom.

What Makes a Loom a Loom?

A typical loom, beading or otherwise, is made of some basic parts. Most important, perhaps, are two sets of threads: the *warp threads* and the *weft threads* (also called the weaving threads). The warp threads run lengthwise along the loom, and you weave the beaded weft threads first under and then over the warp threads, going through all the beads in the row at once.

A-Bead-C's

Warp threads run lengthwise on a loom. **Weft threads** form the woven beaded fabric, under and then over the warp threads.

To hold the warp threads, you need a *frame*. This is usually made out of wood or metal, but looms can be made from almost anything, from a simple piece of bowed flexible wood to a wooden cigar box or a cardboard shoebox.

Next, you need some way to separate the warp threads evenly and at the distance apart that will accommodate the size beads you'll be using. In a primitive loom, you would make a *thread separator* for the specific project you were making, piercing a thin piece of wood or leather with the number of holes you needed for each thread and spaced at the distance required by your beads. Some simple, more versatile "hardware" is a pocket comb (if you can find a metal one, even better), a threaded rod such as a long screw, bolt, or spring. Even modern commercial looms use springs as thread separators.

Knots!

Whatever loom you choose to buy or make, be sure the design allows you to space your warp threads evenly and keep the tension even. If it's too loose, your bead weaving will look "sloppy." If it's too tight, your weaving won't lay flat.

A *spool* is an extra-added convenience. Many looms are not adjustable in any way, and you can only make your work as long as the length of the loom. However, other looms, including some inexpensive hobby looms, have wooden spools at both ends that enable you to adjust the warp thread tension and create pieces that are longer than the length of the loom frame. You cut your threads as long as you need and roll up the excess on one roller, then roll out this thread as you work, rolling up the completed work on the roller on the other end. Each spool is usually held on with a bolt and a wing nut. Screw heads or rivets in each spool hold and separate the warp threads. While you work, be sure the spool stays tight in the slot and doesn't slip out when the warp thread tension is tightened.

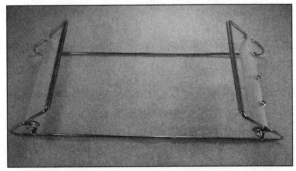

This is a typical inexpensive loom you can find in a hobby or crafts store. Note that it has spools at either end so you can make items longer than the loom itself.

A Weaver's World of Choices

I believe in starting with the best equipment you can afford (or make), without going overboard, to build a strong foundation for success. For a little more money than the cost of a small plastic "toy" loom, you can have something you can bead on for a long time.

I purchased my first loom at a large hobby and craft store for about $25. It's strong and fairly large and has a metal frame and wooden spools or rollers with a spring to separate the warp threads. A nice thing about these "hobby" looms is their portability. They're lightweight and small enough to pack up and take with you on a trip. In addition to the larger deluxe loom I have in my studio, I have my "little loom" just for this reason.

I've written the instructions for Chapter 9's beadin' cap patch assuming you have a similar hobby loom. You could do the patch for your beadin' cap on just about anything, but if you can beg, borrow, or buy a basic well-made loom, I heartily encourage you to do so.

but you might outgrow this loom fairly quickly if you really take to loom work and want to do larger pieces.

Also, check that the spools on the loom will tighten and stay put when you put a little pressure on them. Once you string your loom, there will be tension between the two spools. The design of some cheaper looms I've seen make it difficult to keep the spools in place.

If you decide you like loom work, you might want to invest in a professional loom. I've been working with a Mirrix loom recently, and I must confess, I'm in love. I can use it not only for beadwork but also to make woven fiber pieces. It can be adjusted to sit upright, like an easel, so I can position it in many different ways for my comfort. Mirrix looms come in all sizes and types but are not inexpensive. (See Appendix B for more information.)

Another option is to make your own loom. It's not very hard, and you'll get a lot of loom for very little money and effort. All you really need is some wood, two springs, some screws, and some basic tools to assemble it.

Knots! _____

If your loom is flimsy, you'll have trouble keeping a tight warp tension, which is essential to good results. Do yourself a favor and find (or make) a sturdy loom.

Try to get a loom at least 12 inches long and 5 or 6 inches wide. That's a good size for making a wide variety of items. Some hobby looms are shorter and narrower. They'll still work fine,

Findings _____

If you think you'd like to make your own loom, check out rogue.northwest.com/~ahawley/loom.htm for some of the simplest instructions I've seen. This one is made from artist's canvas stretcher bars, screen-door springs, and some wood screws. The total cost of this fairly large loom is about $10, and the instructions and illustrations are clear and understandable.

Also, Virginia Blakelock gives easy-to-follow instructions on making a loom in her classic bead weaving book *Those Bad, Bad Beads.*

Whatever loom you choose, give it some thought and purchase or make something that will give you good service and grow with you as your interest in beadwork grows.

Threads and Needles Revisited (Again)

Each kind of beadwork requires a re-examination of materials. Let's look at what needles and thread we need for loom work.

For on-loom bead weaving, you need two sets of thread—one for the warp and one for the weft, or weaving, threads, and you can use the same kind of thread for both. I usually use size D Nymo for both my warp threads and my weaving thread, although in articles and books, I've seen a wide variety of preferences. Experiment and find your own favorite combination.

As for needles, size 10 or 12 beading needles are usually the best. A fairly long needle works nicely because you can put on several beads at one time. If you have trouble threading the small eyes of some beading needles, try one of the "big eye" needles.

Knots!

Technically, you can use almost any kind of thread to make your warp threads, and you can use any thread that will fit through your beads for your weaving threads. But in reality, you want a good, sturdy thread that won't break or stretch to ensure your finished product will last for a long time. Check the thread you're thinking of using for strength, durability, and stretch before you start working with it, or you could be in for some unpleasant surprises down the road.

Most modern patterns in books and magazines call for size 11° seed beads. Modern loomed beadwork is often done in Japanese cylinder beads, which give the finished product a completely different look. The grid structure of the loom and the somewhat square and very regular shape of the Japanese cylinder beads give the work an even more geometric feel, if that's what you're going for. However, if you like the authentic look of native or Victorian loomed beadwork, use a more common round seed bead.

You can also work in larger size beads, but you'll need to string the warp threads far enough apart to accommodate them without having a too-big space between threads. Experiment with your loom and various beads to see what effects you can get and which size beads you can use. If you have a particular size bead you want to use and your loom just doesn't seem to work properly with that size, you might have no other alternative but to make your own loom just for working with those beads.

As with any beading, you'll want to sort your beads and remove any irregular or misshapen ones. Lay them out on your beading surface and presort, then sort again as you work, rejecting any beads that don't look fairly uniform.

Setting Up Your Loom

Loom setup might vary somewhat from loom to loom, but the steps are basically similar for any loom. Obviously, you'll want to read and follow the instructions that come with your particular loom. I'm going to give you the fundamental steps based on a loom with adjustable spools at either end, like the one pictured earlier in this chapter. You might have to adapt the following instructions for your loom, but here are the basics:

1. Decide how many beads per row across you need for your design and how long your beaded piece is going to be. That will tell you how many threads you'll put on your loom and what length they need to be. If you do not have spools on your loom, your design cannot exceed the distance between the two ends of your frame—and, in fact, they'll need to be shorter so you're not working right up against the frame on either end.

2. Create your design. You can design your own on graph paper or use one of the many designs available online or in books. You might have even received some nice ones with your loom.

Findings

Several websites offer free loom beading designs. Here are just a few:

users.easystreet.com/sequoia/patterns.html

members.tripod.com/~beadnik/patdex.html

home.flash.net/~mjtafoya/patterns.htm

www.nfobase.com/html/loom_patterns.html

3. Cut the number of threads you'll need for each of your beads across, plus one. You'll always need one more warp threads than the number of beads you want in width because a bead goes in between each warp thread and you need to have a thread on the outsides of each side of your work. Cut each warp thread between 16 and 24 inches longer than the length of your design.

This will give you some extra room if you decide to make your item longer or if you want to add fringe or finish your piece in a variety of ways (I'll give you some ideas in Chapter 9). Remember, the *minimum* length has to be the length of your frame, plus enough thread to attach your warp threads securely at either end of your loom.

4. Lay all the threads together and tie a knot at one end. Trim any excess thread. Without tangling them, separate the loom threads into two halves in the direction going away from the knot. If you have a wide loom, it might have several places along the spool where you can attach groups of warp threads. If you're making a very wide piece, divide your warp threads into several "bundles" and knot them. However, for your first piece, your beadin' cap patch, we're going to keep it fairly narrow.

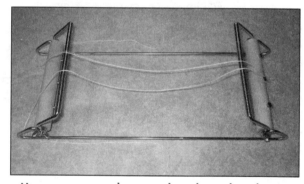

Here you can see the warp threads ready to be put on the loom.

5. With your loom in front of you, going from left to right, hook the knot under the rivet head on the left side and divide the threads in half. Bring the divided threads up over the spool on either side of the rivet head. Wind the threads around the spool

on the left side until the threads on the right side are about 8 inches long. Tighten the spool on the left so it doesn't move. Then pull the threads snug and knot them on the right side.

6. Hook the new knot over the rivet head on the right side of the loom. Pull the thread a little tighter (but not too tight!) by turning the right spool and tightening the wing nuts.

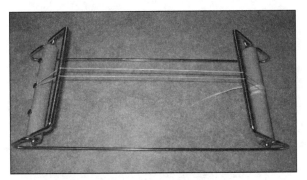

This is how your loom should look after you've made your two end knots and adjusted your tension.

7. Using a toothpick or other similar device, lift one thread at a time and place each in one groove of the thread separator. Keep doing this until you have each thread in side-by-side grooves. Repeat on the other end so the threads run separated and straight across. If you need to, adjust the tension by loosening the wing nuts, turning the spools, and retightening the wing nuts.

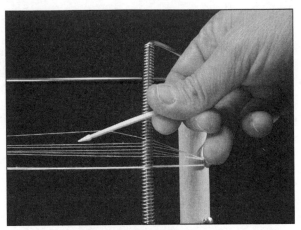

Separating the warp threads.

Reading a Pattern

Now that your loom is threaded and ready to go, what design will you weave? As I've mentioned, you can create your own or use a pregraphed pattern.

Reading a graphed pattern is easy, as you might already know. Each square represents a bead. Depending on the size of your beads compared to the size of the squares in the graph paper, your design might be actual size or larger or smaller. If you want to see what your design will look like when it's actual size, use the graph paper you have to color in your design, then reduce or enlarge it on a photocopier. You might even want to enlarge an actual size design and use the larger version to work from for your eyes' sake.

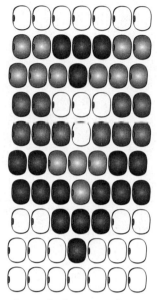

A graphed pattern design.

When reading a charted design, be sure you know which way the design runs on the chart. Which way is lengthwise on the loom (along the warp), and which way is widthwise? If you don't determine this before you start, you could run into trouble later.

Also be aware that if you use just regular graph paper rather than graph paper made especially for beading, your design won't be completely in proportion, because a row of beads is a bit taller than it is wide, as you can see in the previous figure.

An absolutely wonderful website where you can get files for almost every kind of graph paper you might need in beading is shala.addr.com/beads/resources/graphpaper/index.html. A small donation is requested, and if you find these useful, it certainly would be a nice thing to do!

Knots!

It's easy to get interrupted or distracted and lose your place on your graphed design. Use a sticky note or a metal board with magnetic strips to move up each row as you complete it so you can't get lost. You can also get a clear plastic line magnifier, which has magnets on each end to hold it securely in place over the row of your drawing on the metal board. You can order these online from www.beadcats.com, which is a great place, by the way, for all your loom work supplies. Also check out the cross-stitch and quilting areas of your local crafts shop for more helpful tools.

The Least You Need to Know

- Loom weaving is easy, and the results are strong and durable.
- You can choose from many kinds of looms or make your own. Whatever loom you decide to work on, be sure it will hold an even tension.
- You can use Nymo thread for both the warp and the weaving threads.
- The World Wide Web offers lots of free loom work designs; plus many patterns are available in books. You can also create your own patterns using beading graph paper.

In This Chapter

- ◆ Weaving basics
- ◆ Adding new thread
- ◆ Increasing and decreasing rows in your project
- ◆ De-looming and finishing your work
- ◆ Putting your work to use

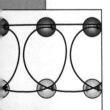

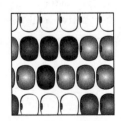

Chapter 9

Becoming a Loom-a-Tic

Your loom is strung (if it's not, go back to Chapter 8), and you're ready to begin weaving. Where do you start?

In this chapter, I'll go over the basics of weaving beads onto a loom, adding new thread, increasing and decreasing rows in your piece, and then I'll walk you through making a patch (well, actually it's a strip) for your beadin' cap. When you're done, you'll learn how to finish your piece and remove it from the loom. And finally, you'll learn all the different things you can do with your loomed beaded piece.

Now You're Weaving!

Thread your needle with 18 to 24 inches of thread that you've conditioned with either beeswax or Thread Heaven. This will help the thread go through the rows of beads more easily and make it less likely to tangle. You will probably find your own preferences for thread. I usually use size D Nymo for both my warp and weft threads. Some people prefer size D Nymo for the warp and size B Nymo for the weft. If you're using Japanese cylinder beads, you might prefer size B Nymo for the warp and A or 0 for the weft. The important thing is to use thread thin enough to pass through your work more than once, as you'll be weaving threads back through your work when you add a thread or when you finish your piece.

Findings

If you decide you want to work with larger beads than size 11° seed beads, make both your warp threads and your weft (weaving) threads heavier. Then warp your loom at the correct distance apart evenly to accommodate the size bead you've chosen.

Leaving at least a 6-inch tail, tie the end onto the first warp thread (lengthwise thread) on the left, about an inch above the thread separator. This is usually the best way to start if you're right-handed, although you can start from the right side if you're a lefty and that feels more comfortable. You can weave this thread in and out of your warp threads a few times to anchor it if you like.

The way you position the loom is up to you. I've seen it a variety of ways. The directions I've given you here assume you are holding the loom perpendicular to you, with the longest part going away from you, and that you will be looking at your pattern in the same way. You'll be starting to add beads at the bottom of your loom, or the end closest to you. Any extra warp thread should be rolled up on the spool at the top, away from you.

Pick up the number of beads you need for your width. If you're following a charted design, look at the order of the colors and put them on from the lower left-hand corner of the chart to the right.

Findings

If you use regular seed beads and you're following a charted design for counted cross-stitch, your design will not be exact because the beads are not perfectly square. You'll notice they're wider than they are high. Japanese cylinder beads are closer to square, though. If you use them, your design will come out closer in proportion to the original. Japanese cylinder beads have a larger hole, which is a plus, but they usually cost more.

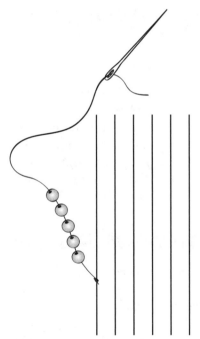

Preparing to weave the first row.

Use your left hand to push the beads down to the end of your weaving thread. Bring the thread, beads, and needle *under* the warp threads and to the right. Using your left index finger, push each individual bead up through the warp, one bead between every two warp threads. Be sure to keep the row straight.

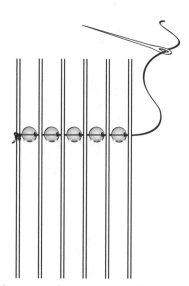

This is how your first row should look before you get ready to bring the thread through the beads and over the warp threads.

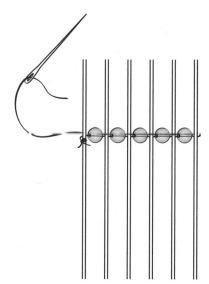

This is how your first completed row should look.

Hold the beads tight between the warp threads and bring your needle through all the beads again, going from right to left *over* the warp threads. Be sure the weaving thread is *over the top* of the warp thread on every bead! You'll want to check this carefully, because if you "miss" a bead, it's very difficult to correct it later.

After you've gone back through the first row of beads, pull your thread snug (but not too snug or your work will curl), then bring the needle and thread back under the warp. Add your next row of beads, and repeat. Keep your rows even and close together.

(For finishing instructions, see "What Do I Do Now?" later in the chapter.)

Knots!

Be careful not to go through the warp threads as you go through the beads. If you catch the warp thread with your needle, undo the row up to before your mistake, push up the beads higher from underneath and try again.

More Thread, Please!

What happens if you run out of thread before you're done? Bead weaving uses a lot of thread, so sometime during your beadwork, you probably will encounter this problem. But don't panic. Here's how to add new thread:

End weaving with the old thread at one side, left or right. Remove the needle, and thread it onto the new length of thread you've cut. You can add the new thread before you hide the old thread and deal with concealing the old thread later. I like to find a juncture between the warp and the weaving threads, knot the new thread twice, then weave until I come out where the old thread was. You can also simply start a new thread on the outermost warp thread on the same side you started from, right next to where you ended the old thread. Be sure to leave a long tail just as you did when you started so you can weave it back into your work. Weave the old thread back through your work. You can add some glue or clear nail polish to your knots for extra strength.

Then, simply add your beads on the new thread and continue weaving as before.

A Little Bigger, a Little Smaller

What if your pattern calls for a shape within your design, where you'll have more or fewer beads in a particular row? For this, you'll need to know how to increase and decrease. All the off-loom weaving stitches you learned in Chapter 7 can be increased and decreased as well. I've referred you to further information about each stitch in Appendix B, and you can learn how to do this once you've mastered the stitch.

Increasing and decreasing on a loom is easy. To increase, you need extra warp threads, so you will have to plan ahead for increasing in your design and add the extra warp threads at the beginning. You can increase only as much as the number of warp threads you have strung. When you're ready to increase:

1. Bring the weaving thread under the warp thread just as if you were going to start a new row. Then bring it up in between the warp thread next to the last bead and the second warp thread from the left and then back down underneath the warp threads you're going to add beads to.

2. String the number of beads you want to add, push them up through the warp threads (you'll be going in the opposite direction than you usually work), then bring your needle around, through the beads, *over* the warp threads from left to right (again, the opposite of what you usually do).

3. Then bring the needle down through the warp thread just before the last bead in your original row, add beads as usual, and begin weaving again in the same manner you did from the start. This is difficult to explain in words, but I hope the drawing will make it clear to you.

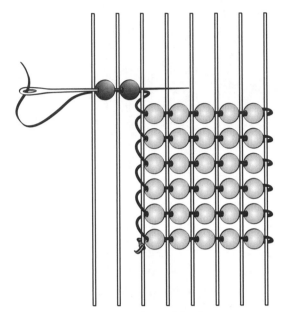

How to increase the width of a row.

Decreasing is even easier:

1. Once you finish your regular row, go under the last warp thread on your loom from left to right (this should be on your far left), bring your needle around, and pass back through the last bead in the row and through the total number of beads you want to decrease the row by.

2. When you reach the other side of the row (right side), bring the weaving thread *under* the warp thread again this time, then loop back around and go over that same thread and through your shorter row of beads.

3. Bring the needle and thread under the warp thread at the left and begin weaving as normal unless you need to decrease more. Then repeat the same procedure.

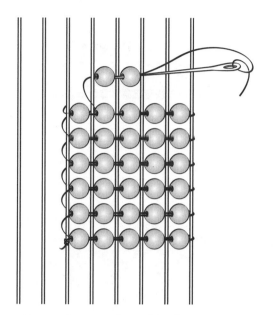

How to decrease the width of a row.

What Do I Do Now?

When you get to the final row of beads and have gone through it from right to left with your needle over the warp threads, be sure everything is tight (but not too tight!) and uniform, then knot off your thread. Weave back through your work, come up in the middle somewhere, and clip off your weaving thread closely, being careful only to cut the weaving thread.

But before you take your work off the loom, you need to decide what you want to do with it, as that will determine how you finish it.

You can finish your piece in a variety of ways. One way is to tape the ends and secure the piece to a backing. Put some tape across the warp threads to hold them before you take your work off the loom. Then clip the warp threads up to the tape and fold the whole thing under the beaded "fabric" you've made—tape and all. Then glue the piece to a backing you've chosen, such as leather, velvet, or felt. Don't use too much glue, but use enough to hold everything firmly. Wipe off any excess glue quickly and thoroughly.

You can also make a selvage edge and apply it to a backing. Weave the weaving thread back through the warp threads alternating under and over for about 1½ inch and make a selvage. Make an identical selvage with the tail you left at the beginning of your work. Then tie the first two warp threads into a tight knot and repeat across for every two warp threads. Seal the knots with glue or polish, then clip the threads. Turn the selvages under the piece, and hide them by gluing or sewing a backing on the piece such as thin leather, velvet, or felt.

If you choose not to put your work onto a backing, you still have the problem of what to do with all those warp threads! You can simply remove your work, put a needle on each thread, and one at a time, weave them back into your work. Knot the warp threads right up against the beads first to ensure they won't unravel.

Findings

By now you might be able to see why it's so important to choose a thin enough thread so you can go through your seed beads several times.

You can also knot the warp threads and braid them, if they're long enough. Then tie a knot at the end of your braiding and tie the piece on a necklace or bracelet with the braided string.

Or you can decrease at each end and come to a point before you take your work off the loom. Using the threads closest to the point, thread on enough beads to make a loop, and add a clasp on one end and a split ring or other closure on the other. Knot and weave your thread into your work. Do the same for the other warp threads you haven't used for the loop.

If you've decided to simply square off your ends and weave in the warp threads (directions a few paragraphs up), you can add a button closure. Sew the button to one end of the strip by knotting in and leaving a tail, making a loop of beads, going through the button (you'll need to use a button with a shank), and bringing your thread back down through your work then knotting off. Then make a beaded loop at the other end, being sure it's snug enough that it won't fall off the button, but not so snug that you can't get it over the button. You might have to play with this a bit to get it just right. Test it several times before you finish off the loop.

You can also use the warp threads to make a fringe. This works nicely if you're sewing your beaded piece onto something else or using it as a self-contained unit, as in a bookmark. If you have enough warp thread, take each one and add beads, then go up through the second to the last bead and all the ones above. Work the remaining thread up into the work, knot at a juncture between the warp and weaving threads, add a drop of glue to the knot, then weave a little more and cut the thread with the needle on it close to your work. Repeat across the piece.

More for Your Beadin' Cap

You've been making sample patches for your beadin' cap for several chapters now, and this chapter is no exception. However, this patch is longer than it is wide—more like a strip. By the time you complete this patch, everyone will know you're a beader!

If your loom won't accommodate the entire strip, you can leave out "My" and still have a fun piece.

This piece uses four colors. I suggest you use a light color for the background and bright, contrasting colors for the letters. You can use different colors for each word, as I have done, or use a rainbow of colors and alternate each of the letters.

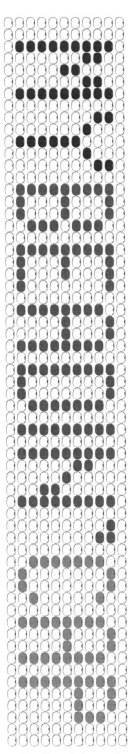

Here's a beading diagram for your beadin' cap strip.

The Least You Need to Know

◆ You can choose charted designs or make your own.

◆ If you use counted cross-stitch designs, choose a more square bead such as Japanese cylinder beads for a more accurate pattern.

◆ You can increase or decrease rows easily, but you can only increase to as many extra warp threads as you have strung.

◆ How you want to use your loom-worked piece will determine how you finish it. Think about this before you remove your work from the loom.

In This Part

Part 3

Getting Wired!

Knowing how to do wirework will give you a whole other world of options for working with beads. Whether you're making simple earrings and dangles for pendants or designing elegant connectors and wire wraps, wirework and beads just sizzle!

In addition to a quick course in "Wire Choosing 101" and learning the basic tools and techniques for working with wire, you'll also learn the steps for both French and Victorian beaded flower-making, using tiny seed beads to create lifelike flowers and leaves for beaded flower arrangements.

In This Chapter

- ◆ Learning wirework—a good idea for every beader

- ◆ Choosing wire by shape, hardness, material, and size

- ◆ Gathering essential wirework tools—and others that are nice to have

- ◆ Wireworking "extras" and finishes

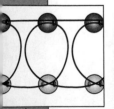   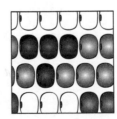  

Chapter **10**

All Wired Up

Wirework is my thing. It was the first beading technique I learned, and it's the one I do the most. Wirework jewelry is created without soldering or casting and is held together only by twisting, bending, and cutting the wire. Stones or beads may be wrapped or strung and incorporated into the finished product to produce some really beautiful pieces.

This kind of jewelry goes back to antiquity. Biblical scholars have dated wirework jewelry to the fifteenth century B.C.E. Wirework was an art known to Egyptian and Phoenician craftsmen and has been found in the pyramids and the tombs of pharaohs.

And it's still as popular as ever. Let's find out why.

Why Wire?—Why Not!

Working with wire has so many pluses: Wire is strong. Wire is versatile. Some wire is dirt-cheap, and even precious-metal wire is pretty reasonable.

Knowing some wirework will make your beading life easier—and *cheaper!* You can make earrings, earring wires, clasps, and simple connectors at a fraction of the cost of buying them. Plus, with a little wirework experience, you can repair a lot of your own jewelry.

There's also the matter of individuality. If you don't know wirework, you're somewhat restricted to the findings you can find in stores or online. If you *do* know wirework, you can make your own clasps, earring wires, eye pins, and a whole host of other items and really make your work unique. Add some metalworking skills and some practice with precious-metals clay, and the things you make will *really* be unique!

Which Wire?

Wire is both simple and complicated. It's easy to find in a hardware store, keeps your electricity working, and comes in a variety of materials. There's electrical wire, floral wire, telephone wire, antenna wire—all kinds of wire! But when we think of wire for making fine jewelry or other kinds of crafts, we need to look a little closer. The main qualities you'll want to look at are shape, hardness, size, material, and finish. Let's examine each before we start to twist and bend.

Shape

I bet you think wire is round, don't you? Yes, it is, but it also comes in half-round, square, and triangle forms. For the beginner, round wire is pretty much the way to go, but it's good to know other shapes are available. If you decide to do more work with wire, you might want to try some of these nonround wires.

Hardness

The hardness of wire directly corresponds to the wire's bendability, or how malleable the wire is—the harder the wire, the less pliable, or bendable, it is.

You can make soft wire harder by drawing it through a plate (known as a *drawplate*) or by hammering it (called *work hardening*). By heating and cooling the wire at specific temperatures (what's called *annealing*), you realign the material's molecules and create a harder, more malleable wire.

> **A-Bead-C's**
>
> **Anneal** is the process of heating glass or metal to a predetermined temperature for a set period of time, then cooling it slowly to make it harder and less brittle. Small pieces can be heated with a torch. A kiln or an annealing oven is needed for larger pieces.

The common categories of hardness are *soft* or *"dead" soft*, *quarter-hard*, *half-hard*, *hard*, *extra hard*, and *spring hard*. The ability to bend and shape wire will also be affected by how thick it is, but we'll get to that in a minute.

These hardness terms also correspond to a numbering system, which refers to how many times the wire has been drawn through a drawplate. Dead soft is #0 because it isn't drawn through a plate at all but is fully annealed. Quarter-hard is #1, half-hard is #2, and hard is #4. Extra hard is #6, and spring hard is #8, meaning it has been drawn through successively smaller holes eight times.

What hardness wire you use will be determined by your application. For example, dead soft wire can be manipulated just by using your hands, but it doesn't take much stress. You would use this wire for more decorative applications that won't get a lot of action.

Findings

Just by working with your wire, you will harden it. This, along with applying a hammer to the wire, is called *work hardening*. You can change it just by bending it and straightening it again. But be careful: Although the wire will become harder, it will also become more brittle and can break.

Half-hard wire is the most commonly used for wire jewelry work. It is fairly malleable, but you'll need tools to bend it into the shapes and forms needed for jewelry. Half-hard will hold its shape well and will take a moderate amount of wear and tear.

If you're going to be putting a lot of stress on a particular part, you might want to think about using full hard wire, although this will be a little more difficult to manipulate. You can also add strength by moving up in gauge, which I'll talk about next.

Size

In the past, wire was made by hammering metal into a form. It was then drawn through a drawplate full of varying-size holes. Those holes today correspond with *gauge* or diameter.

Wire for jewelry ranges in gauge from 4 to 34 gauge. The smaller the wire gauge number, the thicker the wire. You will primarily be using no smaller than 26 gauge and no thicker than 18. I find myself using 22-gauge wire the most, although I also use 20 and 24 gauge for pieces that warrant it. I like 20 gauge for making earring wires and 24 gauge for small dangles that won't be getting any stress. Remember, the higher the number, the smaller the diameter of the wire, so if delicate is what you want, go with the 24-gauge. Just be sure it's strong enough for your application. You also might find you have to use a thinner wire with certain gemstones, especially pearls, unless you want to have to enlarge the hole of every bead with a bead reamer (see Chapter 3).

Findings

Wire may also be sold by millimeter designation, especially in places other than North America. I've provided a chart in Appendix C for wire with corresponding gauge and millimeter measurements.

Cheaper wires in brass, copper, or other base metals are usually sold in spools. Gold, gold-filled, gold-plated, silver, silver-plated, anodized niobium, and aluminum are sold by the foot or ounce (or centimeter or gram, if you're in Canada or across the pond). Know how much you want when you go to the bead store, and they'll cut the wire for you. Some bead stores precut and package wire in common lengths. Now, if you get *seriously* into wirework, you might buy gold or silver wire wholesale by the spool, but its price will still be determined by weight or so much per foot.

Knots!

Be careful about wire you buy in the hardware store. It is great for practice and can be used in some applications, but it's usually not hard enough for jewelry making. Find good-quality jewelry-making wire from your bead store, online, or though mail-order catalogs. (I've listed some sources for the latter two in Appendix B.)

Materials

Wire comes in a variety of materials, including precious metal, alloys, and plated wires.

The two precious metal wires you are most likely to work with are silver and gold.

Gold is the most malleable but also the most expensive. Gold fineness is measured by karats; 24 karat is nearly pure gold. Gold is also alloyed with other metals to make it harder, more durable, and less expensive, but anything refined to less than 10 karat can't be called "gold" in the United States. You might have heard the terms *white gold*, *rose gold*, *yellow gold*, and *blue gold*. These are the result of adding different alloys to alter the color of the gold.

As a beginner, you will probably not want to work in gold wire until you have practiced your skills because it's expensive, soft, and mars easily. When you want a gold look, you might want to try *gold-filled* wire or "rolled gold." This is a bit of a misnomer: The gold is actually on the outside, covering an inner core of base metal. Often that core is brass or silver. Look for 14-karat gold-filled wire or "14/20" when you want a gold look.

A-Bead-C's

Gold-filled or *rolled gold* wire is made of a core of metal such as copper, brass, or sterling silver, with a 14-karat gold coating. Its quality is determined by a number ratio: 14/20 means 1/20 of the weight of the overall wire is 14 karat gold heated and bonded to the outside of a core of another metal.

There's also gold-plated wire, but the plating is much thinner than the outer coating of gold-filled wire, and it is usually 10 karat rather than 14.

Silver is an especially nice wire material and is quite affordable as well. Even sterling silver is within the reach of most beaders. Sterling is actually silver (92.5 percent) combined with copper to increase its hardness. Its only disadvantage is that it tarnishes or oxidizes when exposed to air, so if you want to keep it shiny, you'll have to polish it periodically.

You can also easily find silver-plated wire, which is less expensive and equally easy to work with.

You might also see anodized niobium, titanium, aluminum, and even platinum wire while you're wire shopping, but unless you become a serious wireworker, I doubt you'll work with these materials.

Knots!

You might want to practice with some copper or brass wire before you use gold or silver in your beadwork. The former materials are less expensive than the latter two and are perfectly fine for practice.

And then there's "craft wire." You'll see this on spools in craft stores and even bead stores in a variety of colors and gauges. The problem with these wires is that the packaging often doesn't say what it's made of. Most likely it's a combination of base metals. You also don't know how hard it is. Again, this is perfectly fine for practice and for many applications, but you might want to experiment with it and even wear a sample before you put a lot of time and effort into a piece only to have it turn green on your wrist or give you a nasty allergic reaction.

Knots!

Craft wire can be coated to give it a color or make it look like gold or silver. It looks nice enough, but if you're going to be working with it a great deal in the fabrication of your finished piece, some of that color can be scratched off. The same is true if it's going to receive a lot of wear or stress. Before you use it, test it! Give it a good going over with your tools. Bend it and unbend it. Rub it against something hard and see how easily the finish comes off.

And of course, there's wire you just stumble upon. How about telephone wire or floral wire? If you want to play with it, be my guest! But the same cautions apply if you're going to wear it. Just test everything before you make something important with it!

Findings

For an excellent discussion of wire in general as well as an extensive glossary of wire jewelry terms, check out Preston Reuther's site at wire-sculpture.com/wire.html.

I Remember ...

There's another wire you should know about that's kind of in a class by itself. It's called *memory wire*. If you have ever played with a slinky toy, this is kind of what memory wire looks and acts like. It's shaped like a spring and is usually made of stainless steel, so it doesn't rust.

Memory wire comes in bracelet, necklace, and even ring sizes. Its great advantage is that you don't need to know the size of the person you're making the item for. It stretches and then goes back to its original shape. All you need to do is put a small loop or glue an end cap on one end, string your beads on the wire, then do the same on the other end. If you use a loop as a "stopper," you can add a dangle of beads or a charm or both for added interest.

Tools Revisited (This Time for Wire!)

The two most important categories of tools for wirework are pliers and cutters. I talked about these very briefly in Chapter 3, but now I'm going to make you a pliers and cutters expert!

Pliers

Essentially, a pair of pliers acts as an extension of your hand, giving you precision and strength you couldn't have with just your hand alone. Basically, pliers are constructed pretty much the same—the differences are in the jaws, which vary in shape, size, and application. Sometimes the same pliers will have different names, depending on the industry they're used in or a quirk in a supplier's catalog. I'll be using their most common names and have given you a picture of the major ones so you can identify them on sight.

You want tools that have been drop-forged as opposed to die-cast because forged tools are stronger. Look at the surface of the metal. If it's cast, you'll see little holes. Look, also, to see that the joint where the two sections of the pliers are put together is tight. The best kind of joint is a box joint, although most cheaper pliers are constructed with a lap joint. A box joint actually requires that the two pieces interlock, where a lap joint is just the two pieces criss-crossing each other. Start looking at tools more carefully, and you'll see the difference.

You'll also need to decide if you want a spring-action joint or not. This is basically a piece (or two) of metal on the inside of the handle. Some pliers come without any springs, some come with one spring that rests against the opposite handle, and some come with two springs that push against each other. This spring automatically opens the pliers when you relax your hand. If you're doing a lot of opening and closing of the pliers as you work, this is a helpful feature and is less fatiguing to your hand.

My favorite tools are my German-made ones. I reach for them every time. They have a box joint and two springs, and for me this is the best configuration.

It's also important to consider what the tools are made from. Carbon steel is stronger but needs to be protected from moisture or it will rust. Stainless steel doesn't rust, but isn't as strong. I live in dry Arizona, so moisture isn't as much an issue as it might be in New Orleans or the Northeast, so think about your environment and the conditions where you'll be storing your tools.

As you work with wire, you'll find that one of your main concerns will be marring or scoring the wire. Some marring will occur no matter how careful you are, and the more skilled you become, the less you'll have to handle the wire with your tools and the more pristine it will stay. But your tools are part of the equation.

Be sure the pliers you buy have smooth inner jaw edges. Don't purchase those with serrated edges or "teeth." These are for gripping and will leave a mark on your jewelry. When I get a new tool, I examine the inner edges under a magnifier and file down any rough spots. You can also dip the jaws in a substance made for coating tool grips. I would recommend doing this on an extra set of tools, though, not your best ones. I can't work well with coated tools. I sometimes need the feel of the bare metal tool. So I have one set of really good German tools that I use as is and a coated second cheaper set for when I need to do a lot of touching and gripping with my pliers.

What shape pliers do you need? I guess we have to define the word *need*. You can definitely use just two types of pliers to do almost all your wirework and never need anything else. I certainly did for a long time. But when I found I was doing a lot of a certain type of work, I acquired some different tools specifically for that work. They simply made the job easier. Now I regularly use four or five types of pliers.

The three basic types of pliers are flat-nose, round-nose, and chain-nose. Round-nose and chain-nose are essential for doing wirework, and flat-nose can be handy to have.

Chain-nose pliers—so named because they're used to open and close chain links—have half-round tips—they're round on the outside and have a flat inside edge. They can come with teeth or without, but for what we're doing, smooth is the right choice. You'll need to have two pairs because certain techniques will require one pair for each hand. Chain-nose pliers are sometimes called "needle-nose pliers," but the latter is actually a different animal.

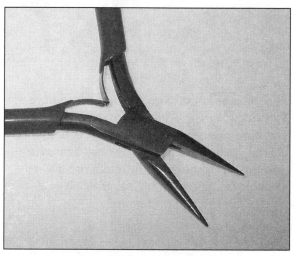

A pair of chain-nose pliers.

Round-nose pliers have round tips with tapered points and are used for making loops. Because they're graduated in size, you can make loops of various sizes. Round-nose pliers are also called rosary pliers, although true rosary pliers have cutters at the base. Forget the ones with cutters. They're awkward to use. Use your flush cutters instead.

Round-nose pliers come in different lengths. I have two—one standard length and one extra long for making various-size jump rings.

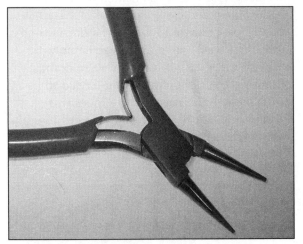

Round-nose pliers.

Two other pliers you might want to have are flat-nose pliers, which have flat, rectangular tips, and bent chain-nose pliers, which look like curved chain-nose pliers. I use my bent chain-nose pliers all the time, although other wire-workers I talk to say they never do. It's a matter of taste and preference.

Cutters

Cutters are a very important tool because you need something to cut your wire cleanly and accurately—you don't want a stray wire sticking out in your beadwork, and you don't want to accidentally cut the wrong wire with dull cutters and ruin your work.

When you shop for cutters, ask for "flush cutters." Try them out before you buy them if you can. Be sure they make a nice clean cut with only a little burr on one end of the side of the wire. A small tapered point is helpful so you can get close, and the cutting edges shouldn't be too thick, as you'll often have to get into tight spaces with your cutters.

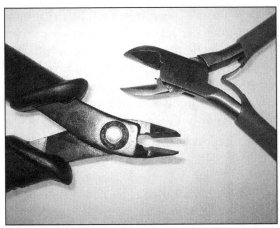

Cutters.

Findings

If you take care of your tools, they can last you a lifetime. You can hang them so they're readily available and less likely to come in contact with moisture or caustic substances—pegboard works nicely. If you want to keep them in a tool kit, be sure they're not thrown in a jumble on top of each other. A toolbox with separate compartments to hold each pair of pliers is best. Rub a thin coat of sewing machine oil on your tools if you're not using them regularly, especially if they're made of carbon steel.

What Else Do I Need?

In addition to pliers and cutters, you might need (or want) some additional tools. If you looked in my toolbox, you'd find some of the following:

Block and hammer   Sometimes you want to hammer wire flat either for looks, to harden the wire, or to keep beads from slipping off. You can get something called a steel bench block (also called a "jeweler's block") and a small ball-peen hammer. (If you often carry your work with you, a small bench block isn't as heavy and is easier to tote around when you need it.) Be sure both the block and the hammer are smooth with no dents or abrasions. You can temper the wire without marring it by putting a piece of leather under and over it, then hammering. This is especially important with coated wires.

Split ring pliers   The more I work with even simple jewelry, the more I don't like jump rings unless they're soldered closed—and then they aren't right for many applications. I prefer split rings. These look a lot like tiny key rings, and just as you probably have had trouble pulling those blasted rings apart to put your keys on, so it is with pulling split rings apart to connect things together in jewelry making. Enter the split ring pliers. When I got mine, I exclaimed out loud "Wow, these are great!" In my opinion, split ring pliers are the difference between obscene language and a pleasant wire-working experience!

Files   You'll need a file or two to smooth rough edges and burrs on wire. You'll want your files to be pretty small and fairly fine. I found some that weren't being used scattered around my husband's toolbox in our garage.

Cap burr   This is a small drill bit used in a Dremel tool to smooth out the ends of wire. It's shaped like a cup and is covered with diamond grit. It's easy to use: just insert the wire into the cup and move it around until it's smooth and burr-free.

Sanding block   A block covered with fine-grit sandpaper is handy to have. Get the soft kind of block that is more like a sponge. They're easier to use with wire.

Jigs, gizmos, and wire twisters   Again, you might never use these, but they're great fun to play with. And if you want wire components that are repeatable and look the same each time, a jig is the way to go.

The best jigs I've found are made of metal. They basically consist of a base with lots of holes and pegs of different sizes that you can place in the holes, then wrap wire around them to get different designs. You can then hammer your components flat or leave them as they are.

There are also various devices for twisting wire, although you can buy wire already twisted. But why not do it yourself for a fraction of the cost? Watch the catalogs and stores for various other gadgets and gizmos for working with wire.

Findings

You can make a jig with a block of wood and some nails. The only disadvantage is that you'll have to make one for each design because they're not adjustable. But hey, wood and nails are cheap!

There are lots of other tools and aids for working with wire, but these are the ones you're most likely to encounter your first time out. As you work, you'll either see the need for other things or you will find that what you have works perfectly well just as it is!

Coats That Suit

Want your wire to look rusty? Aged? Different? You need patina! Patina is a coating or film that forms on metal. It can happen naturally, or you can help it along with various actions or chemicals.

Depending on which chemicals you apply, you can bronze your wire, add a verdigris finish, or make it look antique. You'll need to observe some safety precautions and be sure you get adequate ventilation. After you've worked with wire a while, you might want to explore some of these. A good place to start is The Science Company website at www.coscosci.com/patinas/patinasintro.htm or Tim McCreight's classic handbook *The Complete Metalsmith*. Both have recipes to try.

Even if you decide you don't want to go into wirework in a big way, you'll need to know at least how to make a pair of earrings and a closed-circuit closure for clasps and stuff. So let's move on to the next chapter, and I'll teach you the basic techniques you need to make those items—and more.

The Least You Need to Know

◆ Wirework is useful to any beader, even if all he or she wants to make is some earrings, clasps, and connectors.

◆ Knowing wirework can save you money!

◆ Wire comes in various shapes, metals, sizes, and finishes. Wire also has a scale of hardness.

◆ The two tools you need most to work with wire are a pair of round-nose pliers and a good wire cutter. Good tools are worth the investment.

◆ Memory wire is a fast wire-working technique, but it can ruin delicate jeweler's tools, so have separate heavy-duty tools for working with memory wire.

In This Chapter

◆ Making a simple wrapped wire loop

◆ Dangles made from head pins and loops for just about everything!

◆ Forming your own French ear wires and clasps

◆ Using wire to make connectors and attach clasps

◆ Creating a memory wire bracelet

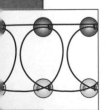 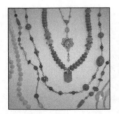   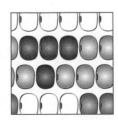 

Chapter 11

Connect-a-Bead:
Basic Wirework Techniques

Bends and loops, with some twists thrown in—no, I'm not talking about a roller-coaster ride, but it sure can bring some thrills. This is wirework.

Although wirework is very simple and requires very few tools to do the basics, it can produce very complex and spectacular results. There are primarily two applications for wirework—connecting and enclosing. Eventually, every beader will need to connect something, so that's what I'm going to concentrate on in this chapter.

I'll be using two wirework terms throughout this chapter: *closed circuit* and *open circuit*. A simple jump ring is an open circuit. If you yank on it hard enough, it will pull apart. In closed-circuit wirework, you make a loop and then wrap the wire under the loop a number of times to "close" the circuit. This type of circuit is stronger, and the wrapping itself actually becomes an element in your design. The open-circuit technique is fast and economical, but once you see the advantage of closed-circuit wirework, you won't want to use anything else!

Findings _____

Note: Everything you make in this chapter calls for half-hard round wire.

Wrap That Loop!

Let's start by learning how to make a basic wrapped loop. This is strong, and the wraps become part of the design. You can wrap once or many times, that's up to you. But you will need to plan to have enough wire to make the number of wraps you desire.

First, cut a length of wire. Make it at least 6 inches. If it's a little rounded from being wound on the spool, stroke it outward with your fingers to straighten it. You can grip it on one end with your chain-nose pliers and pull against that. A pair of wire-straightening pliers with nylon jaws is a handy luxury tool to have, but it's not necessary.

To start, I'm going to suggest you use 20-gauge copper or brass wire. These are not expensive, so you can afford to waste a little. You'll find wirework isn't hard, but it does require some practice to get the hang of it, so having some wire to play with is a good idea. You'll be making loops, cutting them off, and making more, so have a wastebasket handy.

Now, before you actually make your first loop, let me show you how to hold your pliers correctly. This will make all the difference when you actually make your loops.

Knots! _____

If you don't normally wear glasses, I strongly suggest you wear safety glasses when working with wire. The ends can go flying as you clip them, and you don't want a sharp piece of wire to go into your eye. The same goes for people nearby, and watch out for pets. Once you're done, do a clean sweep. There's nothing worse than walking out into the kitchen in the middle of the night in your bare feet and stepping on a piece of wire.

First, don't grip them too tightly. You want to have a firm enough hold that you have good control but not such a tight grip that you're rough on the wire and your hand gets fatigued easily. Look at the following photo for the correct position for holding your pliers. You might even take some scrap wire and try bending it in different directions just to see how your grip is working for you.

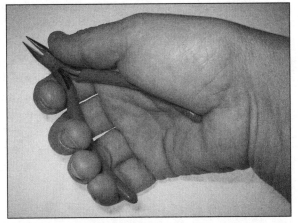

This is the correct way to hold your pliers for wirework.

1. Now that you've gotten the feel of your tools, grab your chain-nose pliers and grip the wire about 3 inches or a little more from the end.

2. Pushing away from you, press the short end of the wire over the top of the pliers into a 90-degree angle. Make the bend crisp. This first bend is very important because it becomes the foundation of your loop.

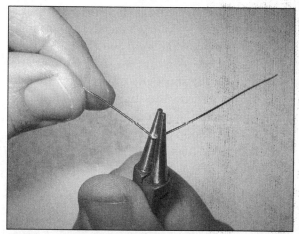

Placement of your round-nose pliers in preparation for making a loop.

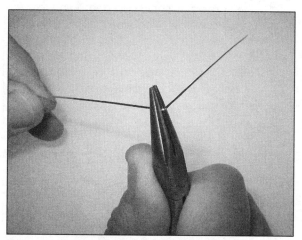

The first bend, a 90-degree angle.

3. Put down your chain-nose pliers and grab your round-nose pliers. Snug the jaws of your round-nose pliers in the 90-degree-angle bend of your wire. The wire should be held between the jaws. Bring the wire up the graduated shape of the pliers' jaws until everything fits snugly. The short end of the wire should still be facing away from you.

4. Place the index finger of your nondominant hand (you're holding the wire with the pliers in your dominant hand) *under* the short end of the wire, and push up. With your index finger and thumb, push the wire up and around the top jaw of the round-nose pliers and back down again, but stop just before you would form a complete loop.

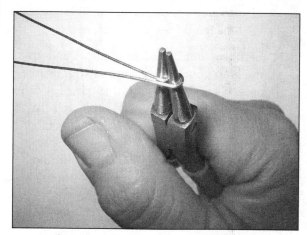

Configuration of wire after completing step 4.

5. Now, remove your round-nose pliers and slide them up and around so the bottom jaw is now in the loop and the top of the loop is between the two jaws. Continue moving the short end of the wire around until you cross the straight, longer piece of wire and have formed a complete loop. Give the loop a very slight turn to the right to center it over the straight piece of wire.

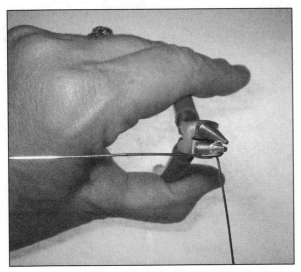

The formed and centered loop.

6. Remove your round-nose pliers, and grab the loop between the jaws of your chain-nose pliers firmly but not too hard. With a second pair of chain-nose pliers (I like to use my bent chain-nose pliers), grab the short end of the wire and, in a circular motion, wrap it 180 degrees around and under the loop. Then reposition your

hand and do another 180 degree turn and repeat this until you have wrapped close to the loop two or three times. You'll want these wraps to be as close to each other and as tight as possible. This will take a little practice, but you'll get it!

Findings

Some people recommend holding the loop with a pair of chain-nose pliers in your nondominant hand and doing the wrapping with your dominant hand. If that's what works best for you, then by all means, do it! I find this very awkward and prefer working the other way around. There is no one right way. Do it whatever way works best for you to get perfect loops.

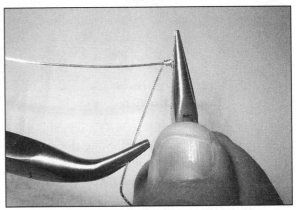

A completed wrapped wire loop before finish cutting.

7. With a flush cutter, very closely clip off any excess wire on the short piece that you just made the wraps with. You'll still have a little bit of wire protruding no matter how close you cut. Taking your chain-nose pliers, just lightly snug that protruding tip down close to the wrap you just made.

There! You did it! Your finished loop should look like the following figure.

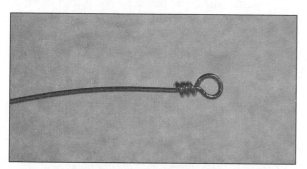

A wrapped wire loop after cutting the excess wire and tucking in the end.

These instructions are what I've developed over years of experimenting, and it's what works for me. Beginning wirework classes that I've taken and several videos and books on the subject offer different ways of doing it. Some people like to do the wraps with their fingers. I find I get a closer, tighter wrap using bent chain-nose pliers. Some people like to keep the round-nose pliers in the loop and grip it that way, then do the wrapping. I find that this mars the wire more than holding the whole loop flat with my chain-nose pliers. This might not be the case for you.

So *practice* and *experiment* and find what's best for you! Keep making loops and cutting them off until you've used up all your first cut of wire. Then do it again. Keep practicing until it becomes smooth and effortless. You'll be ready to tackle almost anything once you master this first wireworking skill.

If you'd like to see how this works visually, check out a video from those I've given in Appendix B. You could also grab a wireworking friend and ask if she could demonstrate for you. Or go to your local bead shop and take a class or ask if someone could do a quick demonstration for you. A "look see" is sometimes worth a thousand words *and* pictures!

Knots!

Don't slump! It's easy to do when you're beading, but especially when you're doing wirework because you're bearing down with your pliers and your shoulders just naturally seem to want to sink forward. Sit up straight and lean back in your chair. Your back, neck, and shoulders will thank you for it!

Baubles, Bangles, and Dangles

Now that you know how to make a wrapped wire loop like a pro, you're going to use that know-how to make your first wire dangle. So what is a dangle? It's a beaded unit with a loop on one end and some sort of stopper or finishing on the other. The dangle can be used for a multitude of things. The most obvious is to suspend it from an earring wire or post and voilà! You have an earring. But dangles can also be used to hang from necklaces, to embellish key chains, and to serve as zipper pulls. You can dangle a dangle from just about anything!

To make your first dangle, I'm going to have you use a head pin, but I'll also show you two ways of making your own termination at the end to act as a stopper for your beads.

If you remember from Chapter 3, a head pin looks like a sewing pin, except it doesn't have a sharp end. Head pins come in different lengths and diameters just as wire does. Get some that are fairly long and thick to start, but be sure they'll fit through the holes of whatever beads you want to use for your first dangle.

1. Put your beads on the head pin, leaving about 1 inch to make your loop and wraps. Now, hold the tips of your chain-nose pliers up against the last bead at the top of the head pin, and make a loop like you have practiced. Remember? Make a right angle by pushing the wire over the top of the pliers away from you with your fingers.

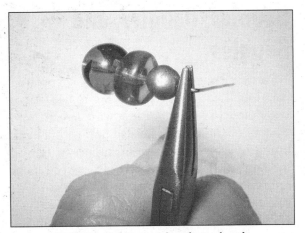

The first bend in your head pin dangle.

2. Switch to your round-nose pliers, and make the first part of the loop over the top of the pliers just as you did before.

Reposition the round-nose pliers and complete the loop. Then grab the loop with your chain-nose pliers and grab your bent chain-nose pliers (or just a second pair of straight chain-nose pliers) and do the 180-degree turns to make your wraps.

Knots!

When you're making earrings, be sure to make the same number of wraps on both dangles. Otherwise, they won't hang evenly, and you'll have dippy dangles.

3. Make enough wraps to fill the space between your loop and the last bead. Tuck in the sharp end of your wire (trim if needed), and you've got a dangle.

This is how your finished head pin dangle should look.

You can attach your dangle to anything you want using a jump ring or a split ring (preferred), or you could have made a direct connection and slipped on the dangle before you completed the loop and wrap. I'll show you how to do each.

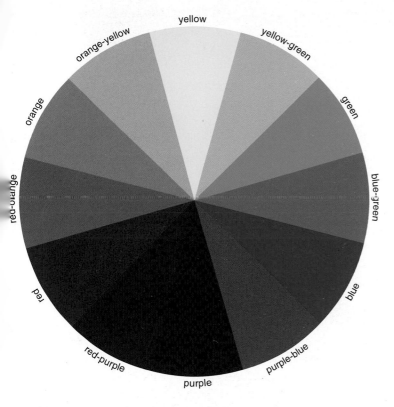

yellow

orange-yellow

yellow-green

orange

green

red-orange

blue-green

red

blue

red-purple

purple-blue

purple

The color wheel is a great way to learn about color relationships and families. The color opposite the color you'd like to work with is its complementary color, and they're just made for each other. The colors to the sides are analogous and will look well together.

Here are two different versions of the beadin' cap, full of projects made throughout the chapters of this book. As you learn different techniques and make samples, your own beadin' cap will evolve in a unique way.

(Photo by Georgene Lockwood)

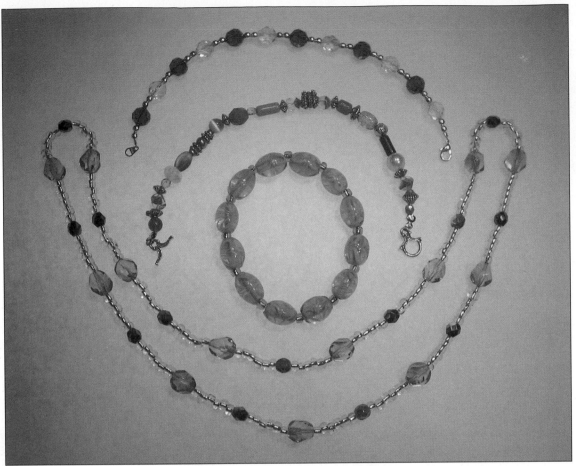

(Photo by Georgene Lockwood)

You'll find directions for making these Fire and Ice, Blueberry Parfait, and Ambrosia Bracelets, plus the Never-Ending Sparkle Necklace, in Chapter 6.

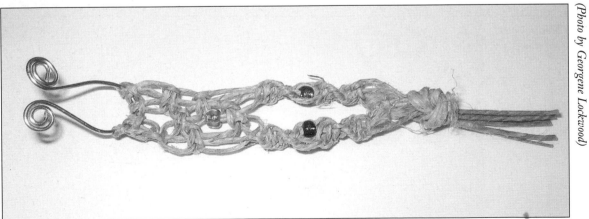

(Photo by Georgene Lockwood)

You can attach this macramé sampler from Chapter 15 to your beadin' cap using the loops at the ends of the wire finding.

(Photo by Georgene Lockwood)

Here you can see the color harmony of analogous colors in these random pattern Multi-Strand Bracelets, the first project in Chapter 19.

(Photo by Georgene Lockwood)

Pictured here are just a few of the many possible versions of the Simple Looped Earring project in Chapter 19.

(Photo by Georgene Lockwood)

Who would have thought you could make beaded jewelry for your car? Here's one version of the beaded Car Sun-Catcher project in Chapter 19.

Using beads to decorate your home is as easy as looking up! This Fan Pull is from Chapter 19. You can use the same idea for window shade pulls, too.

(Photo by Georgene Lockwood)

The Daisy-Chain Continuous Loop Necklace from Chapter 20 makes a delicate statement in pastels. You can use bolder colors if you like, and choosing different size seed beads changes the texture and weight. Just add or subtract daisy-chain sequences to get the length you want.

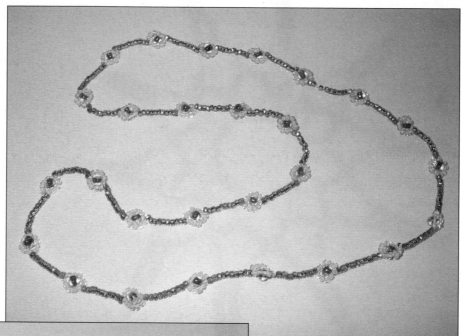

These elegant earrings from Chapter 20 are a combination of ladder stitch (for the foundation row) and brick stitch. Varying the length and sequence of the fringe will change the look, as will different colors and finishes of seed beads.

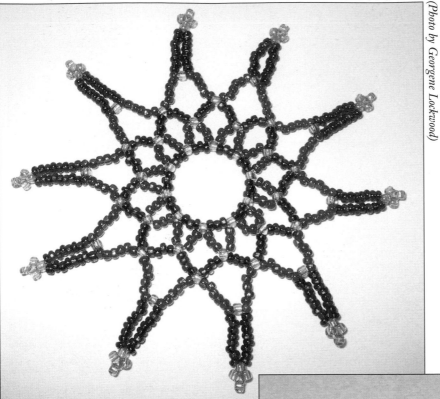

Beaded ornament covers make gifts friends will treasure for years. Find instructions for this netted version in Chapter 20. (See more examples created by Bobbi Wicks later in the color insert.)

You can use wirework dangles in singles or multiples to create many exciting styles of earrings that will add pizzazz to any outfit. These Chandelier Earrings from Chapter 21 use a purchased 3-to-1 finding, but you can make your own using wire.

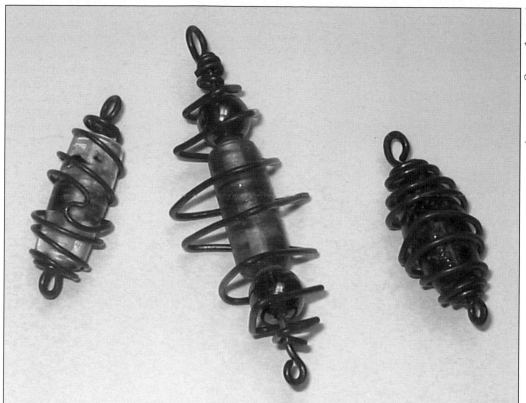

Use wirework to capture beads or marbles in a "cage" and add an interesting design element to your beaded pieces. Here is an assortment of caged beads illustrating the project instructions in Chapter 21.

The simple wrapped loop dangle can be used for any number of beaded objects. Here a dangle has been added to a purchased brass bookmark finding to illustrate the project in Chapter 21.

Add beads to fine wire, and twist into forms from nature. Simple beaded flowers or snowflakes, like this one made using the instructions in Chapter 21, make lovely decorations, gifts, or "bonuses" on gift wrapping.

Enhance everyday objects made from fabric with beads to make them something special. Here is a sachet made from fine netting with a simple beaded motif and a pincushion made from velvet that serves as a mini-sampler for some bead embroidery stitches. Find instructions for both these projects in Chapter 22.

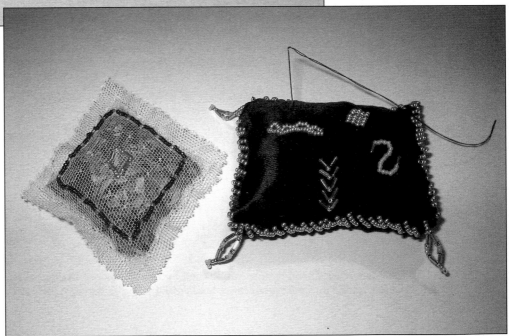

Surrounding a flat stone or cabochon with bead embroidery creates a stunning brooch. Turn to Chapter 22 for the pattern and instructions to make this one, or design your own.

Macramé and beads just go together. You can learn to make this simple bracelet (or expand it into a choker if you like) from just a few easy knots. Turn to Chapter 22 to learn how.

Bead artist Rowena Tank uses a variety of her handmade glass lampwork beads along with seed beads to create a one-of-a-kind necklace called "Love's Merlot." The focal beads are made from recycled merlot wine bottles, and the necklace is finished with tubular peyote and other off-loom weaving stitches. (To see additional examples of Rowena Tank's unique creations and for sales information, go to www.rowenaart.net/. You can also view her work at www.artsprescott.com/Tank_Rowena/.)

This piece by Rowena Tank called "Prescott Fishing Expedition" includes more of her lampwork beads and is worked in Ndebele, brick, and peyote stitches. Rowena also hand made the copper clasp.

This necklace by Rowena Tank of purple seed beads with faceted silver bugle accents is made using off-loom weaving, and incorporates multiple loops. It can be worn symmetrically or asymmetrically.

Bead artist Wendy Blair often uses freshwater pearls in her designs. These two variations are strung on, and each uses a lobster claw clasp with an adjustable chain. The necklace and earrings on the right are made of freshwater and keishi pearls. The necklace on the left is made from "copper coin" pearls. Both are strung on flexible wire. (To contact Wendy Blair about her beadwork, e-mail her at fishdish@cableone.net.)

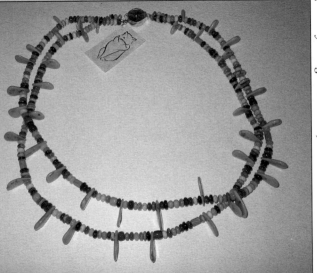

Turquoise, coral, citron, sugilite, chrysoprase, spurite, lapis, pink shell, and gaspeite make up this colorful, playful necklace strung on flexible wire by Wendy Blair. Note how the choice of clasp enhances the overall look of the piece.

Carnelian leaves in many shades of the same color family make for a dramatic piece by Wendy Blair. Again, the choice of clasp adds to the graceful lines of the design. This piece is also strung on flexible wire.

This cherry quartz choker and earrings made with Turkish and Balinese sterling silver beads were created by Lana Ante for Arts Prescott Gallery in Prescott, Arizona. The choker is strung on fishing line. (View more of Lana Ante's fine beaded jewelry at www.artsprescott.com/ Ante_Lana.)

These green Tibetan turquoise and handmade Turkish sterling silver beads are strung on fishing line. Lana Ante created these for Arts Prescott Gallery in Prescott, Arizona.

Lana Ante created this amethyst and handmade sterling Balinese beaded bracelet and earrings set for Arts Prescott Gallery in Prescott, Arizona. The bracelet is strung on fishing line.

Rosemary Topol created this French beaded flower arrangement of gardenias with a beaded hummingbird from a pattern by Dalene Kelly. (View more of Rosemary Topol's exquisite beaded flowers at www.geocities.com/roetopol.)

These magnolias ar[...] calla lilies were cre[...] ated with the French beading technique [...] Rosemary Topol. Th[...] calla lily pattern is [...] Virginia Nathanson

Rosemary Topol created and arranged these French beaded cotton blossoms.

Bobbi Wicks created these amulet bags in tubular peyote stitch from designs adapted from Suzanne Cooper. (Bobbi Wicks can be reached to discuss her beadwork at bwicks@commspeed.net.)

These three bracelets created by Bobbi Wicks use a variety of techniques. The top one is done on a loom and is from a pattern adapted from Eagle Spirit (www. eaglespirit.co.uk). The middle and bottom ones are strung using flexible wire and crimps.

Bobbi Wicks worked these beaded ornaments in netting adapted from a variety of sources.

A glass aromatherapy vessel called an amphora is the focal point in this Victorian-inspired necklace and earrings, which include vintage brass filigree beads and drops and Swarovski crystals, crafted by Georgene Lockwood using flexible wire and crimp beads. (Georgene welcomes inquiries about her work, her jewelry company Victorian Vices, or this book. You can reach her at glockwood@bigfoot.com and view more of her work at www.victorianvices.com.)

Georgene Lockwood created these amazonite, freshwater pearls, and sterling silver necklace and earrings using closed-circuit wirework.

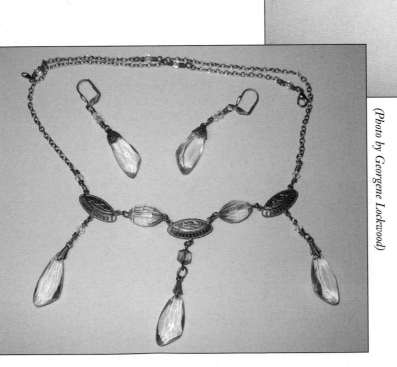

This aquamarine glass set is inspired by Art Deco. The brass findings are actual designs from the period, and the glass drops and faceted oval beads are vintage. Georgene Lockwood created these pieces using closed-circuit wirework.

Opening and Closing a Jump Ring

To open a jump ring, never just pull it apart with your pliers. You'll weaken what is already a "weak link." Instead, take two chain-nose pliers and twist with your wrists in opposite directions, bending and opening it sideways. Slip on your dangle and whatever else you want (zipper tab, key ring, earring wire or chain, for instance), and close it the same way. Be sure the ends meet and that the ring is closed completely.

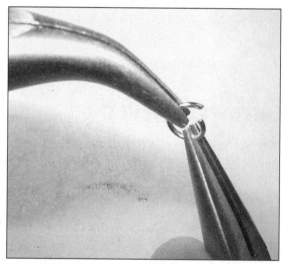

This is how to hold your pliers to open a jump ring correctly.

Findings

If you decide to use a jump ring as a connector, please use a heavy gauge and work harden it by covering it with leather and hitting it with a hammer on a block a few times so it's less likely to pull apart. You don't want to flatten it; you just want to harden it.

Attaching a Split Ring

A split ring, as you might remember from Chapter 3, is like a miniature key ring. Just like its big sister, it's difficult to open but it's strong! I prefer split rings to jump rings any day. Here's where I find a specialized tool is truly the best way to go. Before I got myself a pair of split-ring pliers, I rarely used split rings. Now that I have the pliers, I use them all the time.

To open, simply push the bent end of the pliers inside the split ring, and it magically opens. Then slip in whatever you're connecting and let go. Snap! It's closed, and it's not going to open unless you play tug-of-war with a gorilla!

If you can open a split ring with your fingers, you're a better woman (or man) than I am. I just can't do it and remain a composed, well-mannered person without the pliers.

Making Your Own Head Pins

I told you I'd show you how to make two kinds of head pins. One is more decorative than the other, and I use both. I actually rarely buy pre-made head pins, but they do have their place on occasion. When to buy versus make them is a design decision you'll learn to make with experience and based on your project.

The first method of making a head pin is the simplest. After cutting an appropriate length of wire, take your round-nose pliers and, using the very tip, the smallest part of the pliers, make a sharp turn at one end of your wire as tightly as you can. Then close the little loop with your chain-nose pliers. That's right—just mash it shut. This will create a little nub that keeps the beads from falling off, plus you've added a small decorative element at the end. You can even hammer this little nub flat if you want to for another look.

A homemade head pin.

The second method is to make a small coil at the end by making that small little turn I just showed you with your round-nose pliers. This time, though, don't mash it closed. With your round-nose pliers still in the loop, twist your wrist and start making a little turn. This is the beginning of your coil.

Then, holding the wire and nub flat between the jaws of your chain-nose pliers, start to turn with the wrist that's holding the pliers and pull the wire up and over with the other hand, making the wire follow the shape of the circle. Like magic, the wire will begin to coil itself around that first little turn you made. Keep coiling until you make it the size you'd like, then add your beads. You can keep the coil off to one side, or use your pliers to center it under the wire that holds your beads.

A homemade coiled head pin.

Once you've got this technique down, you can make different shapes around your coil like a star, a heart, or a triangle.

Variations on the coiled head pin.

Earrings on Your Own

You can buy French wires for making earrings, which are quite inexpensive. However, if you run out, you might want to try making your own. You can make them unique and personal—plus they're really easy.

Findings

Kate Drew-Wilkinson sells a jig for making earring wires, and I use it all the time. It helps keep them uniform and speeds up the process. Check Appendix B for the scoop on Kate's jig.

Before you begin, it helps to have an ear wire (or at least a picture of one) in front of you for reference.

1. To make your first ear wire, cut about 3 inches of 20-gauge wire. This is the best gauge for ear wires.

2. Start by making a tight loop on the end of your wire with your round-nose pliers. This is the part your dangle will hang from.

3. Next, place a pen or something similar in diameter against the side of the wire opposite from the direction of the loop about ½ inch from the loop. Hold the wire tightly, and press it against the pen, coming up over and around, making an arch. It should look a little like a candy cane with a loop at one end.

4. Then, come down and flair out just a bit with the last ¼ inch or so of where you want the ear wire to end. Cut off the excess wire. You've made your first ear wire!

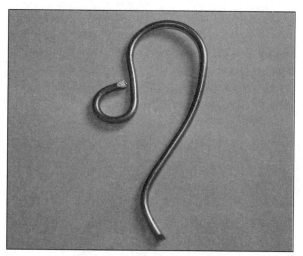

A do-it-yourself French ear wire.

Again, this is something that takes a little practice, especially to make them uniform, but it's easy once you get the hang of it. Be sure you file off the end of your wire so there are no little burrs to scratch the ear hole when you insert the ear wire.

Add a small bead after you make the first little loop but before you start the upper turn for a nice addition. You can also hammer the top part of the ear wire flat for some added interest. Just be sure you don't make it sharp up where the wire goes through the ear. This could slice a tiny cut in the ear and cause problems.

Now, create identical dangles, open your little loop by twisting it slightly to one side with your chain-nose pliers, add a dangle to each ear wire, close the loop the same way, and you've got your first pair of earrings!

Making Important Connections

You've learned how to make a wrapped loop at one end of a head pin to create a dangle. But you can also use wire to make separate beaded units with loops at both ends and connect them to make bracelets, necklaces, or whatever else you want.

Basically, you're creating your wrapped loop first, putting on your beads, then making another wrapped loop at the other end. When you connect the next unit, you'll need to slip on one of the looped ends of the first unit, then close the loop of the second unit to securely connect them.

A wrapped loop connector unit.

You can also put lengths of chain in between units for a more delicate look. This particular design is very popular, very lightweight, and always looks classic.

Make the first unit by making a wrapped loop on one end, adding your beads, then beginning the loop for the other end and adding your chain while the circuit is still open.

Then, when you make your second unit, add the other end of the chain before closing the first loop. Add your second length of chain on the other end, and so on, repeating until you're ready to add your clasp.

Wrapped loop connector units with chain in between.

You can use a closed-circuit unit to add your clasp as well. I usually connect my final clasp unit with a wrapped loop, add a small silver or gold bead, then make my second loop and add the clasp before I close the circuit, then wrap. This makes a very strong clasp connection. You then add the other end of your clasp or a split ring as the termination on the other end. I use the same kind of clasp unit—a loop, a small bead, and a loop with the other end of the clasp connected to the end.

A clasp attached using closed-circuit wirework loops.

Keeping It All Together

Another finding you can make easily with wire is a clasp. So I'm going to show you how to make two simple but beautiful clasps.

Making an S Clasp

The first is the S clasp, and it's exactly what it sounds like—an S shape. To use it as a clasp, you'll need split rings at the ends of your necklace or bracelet. These then hook on to the open-ended hooks formed by each side of the S clasp.

You'll want 18-gauge wire for your clasps so they're strong enough to take the weight and tugging of your beads and findings.

1. Cut off about 2½ or 3 inches of 18-gauge wire.

2. Grasp the wire with your round-nose pliers about 1 inch from one end. Push the wire all the way up until it's almost up against the hinge of the pliers. You want it at the fattest part of your round-nose pliers.

3. Bend the wire around the top of the pliers, and bring it all the way around until it intersects with the straight part of the wire. As you do this, keep pulling on the end of the wire you're bending. You want a curve and a straight end, not a loop.

4. Remove the round-nose pliers and move them up the wire about ½ inch from where the first curve you made intersects. Bend the wire in the same manner going in the opposite direction so you have a figure eight. At this point it should look like this.

The first part of making an "S" clasp.

5. Clip off the ends of each of the wires about ¼ inch past where they intersect, then turn up each of these ends into a little loop with your round-nose pliers. One loop should be larger than the other. The finished piece should look like the following figure.

This is how your finished "S" clasp should look.

6. You can leave the curves round or flatten them with your block and hammer. You now have a finished clasp!

Making a Hook-and-Eye Clasp

I learned to make this hook-and-eye clasp from Mark Lareau's book *All Wired Up*. In it, he also explains how to make a double wire clasp that's incredibly strong, even when it's made with thinner, more delicate wire. If you want to learn more about wirework, this is one book I definitely suggest you put on your bookshelf.

1. Cut a 3-inch piece of 18-gauge wire that you've straightened.

2. Using a chopstick, pen, or dowel as a form, pull your wire around, holding the end out straight—form an arch, not a loop—until you cross over your wire on the other side. Your formation should look like a teardrop.

3. Using your chain-nose pliers, grab the short end of the wire and bend it back right where it intersects the long part of the wire to about a 45-degree angle. Clip the wire a little past this bend.

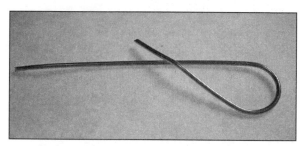

A partially finished hook-and-eye clasp.

4. Clip the long end of the wire about ½ inch past the end of the hook you just made, and bend that end backward to form a loop. You can hammer the whole thing flat, just hammer the big curve, or leave it as is.

The finished clasp.

You can use a large split ring for the other side of the clasp or make an eye. For an eye, make a figure eight similar to what you did when you made the S clasp, making it somewhat smaller and rounder, and butt up the ends against the center.

The finished "eye" part of the hook-and-eye clasp.

You could also attach a clasp by making a wrapped loop with a small bead as I showed you earlier in the "Making Important Connections" section. Experiment. Look at handmade jewelry and see how the clasps are made. Are they prefabricated clasps, or did the designer make his or her own?

Memory Not Lost

I talked a little about memory wire in Chapter 10. Now let's use some and make a bracelet. You can buy memory wire in long coils or pre-cut for bracelets, rings, or necklaces. Cut or buy a bracelet length, and you'll be ready to start. This one's about as easy as it gets. Just remember to use heavy-duty tools (not your good pliers and cutters) for this.

1. Using a heavy-duty pair of pliers, make a loop at one end of your coil.

2. Put on your beads.

3. Finish off with a loop at the other end.

What could be easier? I like to add some dangles to both end loops—usually a couple of small beads and a charm. You decide what you'd like to do.

Some examples of beaded memory bracelets.

Now that you've had some fun playing with wire, you can make earrings for every occasion and clasps for all your beadwork, and you might even want to try working with a jig. (I've listed several brands and where to find them in Appendix B.)

Put On Your Beadin' Cap

You can use any one of the elements you've created in this chapter to add to your beadin' cap. How about sewing on some dangles? Or you could thread a few dangles on a large safety pin and pin that on your cap. If you don't like what you've made so far for your cap, make something just right. You're in control!

The Least You Need to Know

- You don't have to be "into" wirework in a big way, but knowing how to make a few basic things will save you money and make your work unique.

- The best gauge wire for earring wires is 20 gauge; 18 and 20 are usually best for clasps. You'll want to use half-hard round wire for most beaded wirework.

- It's important to file the burrs off the end of your ear wires so you don't scratch the ear and cause an injury or infection.

- Don't use your good tools to work with memory wire. Heavy-duty tools are better.

In This Chapter

- ◆ A little history on the origin and use of beaded flowers

- ◆ Growing a beaded garden: the materials and tools you'll need

- ◆ Making a basic beaded leaf or petal using the French and Victorian methods

- ◆ Assembling beaded flowers and arrangements

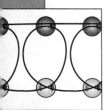 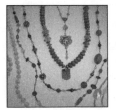   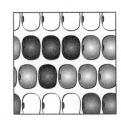 

Chapter 12

In a Beaded Garden

Beading flowers had nearly become a lost art, until it saw a revival in the 1960s and 1970s. It then seemed to disappear as a favored craft once more until the past few years, when a hardy group of beaders who were willing to put in the time and practice it takes to become accomplished at this technique took up the task.

Now many out-of-print books on the subject are being reprinted, and new ones are appearing with new patterns and approaches for modern beaders. The Internet now boasts a legion of beaded flower websites and e-groups, and more and more beaders are checking out this time-honored craft. Although elaborate flowers and arrangements take some skill to execute, even beginners can learn to make some simple wire-and-bead creations in just a few hours.

From Peasants to Parlors: How Beaded Flowers Grew

Although the exact origin of the art of beading flowers is not known, some bead historians believe it might go back as far as the Roman Empire.

According to Virginia Nathanson, author of the classic 1960s how-to book *Making Bead Flowers and Bouquets* (see Appendix B for more information):

> The art of bead-flower making originated many centuries ago with the peasants of France and northern Italy who tended the vineyards in wine country. Because these people were idle during the winter months, enterprising glass manufacturers gave them homework—the making of glass beads that were to embroider the magnificent ball gowns and jackets worn by the members of the French court. Imperfect beads were rejected, but rather than discard the beads, the thrifty peasants made them into beaded flowers which altar and choir boys carried in church processionals for Easter and Christmas services.

Late nineteenth-century Victorian decorators, according to Nathanson, discovered these flowers and fashioned them into embellishments for wall sconces and lamps.

It is also known that beaded flower wreaths were made in Venice during the sixteenth century for church celebrations, to decorate the church altar, and eventually to commemorate the dead at graves and tombs. This practice was also widespread in the nineteenth century.

Today, these botanical masterpieces attend happier occasions—they decorate homes, are fashioned into one-of-a-kind brooches and hair ornaments, and accompany the bride on her special day in bridal bouquets and headpieces.

Tools for Twisted Gardens

You don't need a lot of tools to get started making beaded flowers. Essentially, making beaded flowers requires three things:

- ◆ A method for getting the beads on the wire
- ◆ Cutting the wire
- ◆ Twisting the wire

If you've done stringing with flexible wire or wirework, you already have the tools you need for cutting. Good wire cutters are essential. You most likely will want your chain-nose pliers for some of your beaded flower work as well.

But there are a few other tools you might want to think about if you get bitten by the beaded flower bug.

Bead spinner This is a special gizmo for getting loose beads onto your wire for beading—without you picking them up one at a time.

Make a slight hook on the end of your wire, pour loose beads into the bead spinner, rotate it with one hand, and hold your wire into the "bowl" of the spinner with the other. The beads will literally fly onto the wire.

Once you get the hang of it, you'll see how fast and easy it is. However, if you're not sure beaded flower making is for you, you can thread beads onto the wire directly from hanks (pretty quick and easy) or pick up individual beads on your wire (slow and tedious). Either method is just fine, at least until you can see if this is a form of beading that really grabs you.

Bead spinners aren't inexpensive, except for a plastic version that I don't recommend. The better wooden types run around $40 to $60, but if you get into flower beading in any serious way, you'll want one.

A wooden bead spinner loaded and ready to "fly."

Hemostat   A hemostat kind of looks like a pair of scissors, but it locks in place. It's actually used in the medical profession to compress bleeding blood vessels.

For nice tight twists in your stems and branches, this tool is invaluable. Again, you can live without it, especially to start, but I picked up one at a bead show for only $2 and started using it right away.

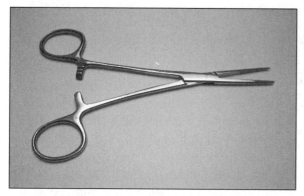

A hemostat is not a necessity, but it can come in handy when you're making beaded flowers.

Nylon-jawed pliers   These are just plain nice to have for straightening wire. Because your wire can get kinks in it, having these wire-straightening pliers is really handy. If the nylon jaws wear out, you can get replacements. I've seen these pliers in various places for less than $15.

The Stuff of Flowers

As you can see, tools required for making beaded flowers are minimal. But as with any kind of beading, you can never have too many beads!

You'll most often use seed beads in beaded flower making. And because flowers and foliage come in all different colors, you'll want a sizable stash of seed beads in a variety of colors and finishes to start growing your beaded garden.

Size 11° seed beads usually work best, although size 10° seed beads are somewhat easier to work with to start. Some more experienced beaded flower "gardeners" work in smaller sizes to make really delicate blooms. If you use smaller beads, you must be sure they'll fit on your wire. I've also seen some lovely flowers made in larger Swarovski crystal beads.

You can purchase seed beads either loose or on hanks. If you don't have a bead spinner, you'll want to buy hanks so you can transfer the beads directly from the hanks to your wire. Different finishes for seed beads give different effects, so experiment or follow your pattern's directions to get the right look.

You'll find you will work mostly with 28-gauge wire, although if you're using very flexible craft wire, you might want to use something a little heavier, like 24 gauge. You'll use 30 or 32 gauge for lacing and assembly, so you'll need to have some of that on hand as well. You can work in silver- or gold-colored wire or buy one of the many colored craft wires available to match your beads. Although these craft wires have some liabilities when used in other applications, because beaded flowers don't normally get a lot of wear and tear, they are fine for this use. The fact that they come in so many colors is an added bonus, because you can match them to your bead colors and they almost seem to "disappear."

You can also use floral paddle wire found at floral supply, craft, or bridal supply shops. Just be sure whatever wire you use won't rust over time. You don't want to put all that effort into making a beautiful floral arrangement and have it marred by rusty or discolored wire.

You can purchase precut heavy wire floral stems, or you can cut your own, using 16-gauge wire for larger flowers and 18 gauge for smaller ones. For a really heavy flower, you can use ⅛-inch rod stock from the hardware store or even a piece of wire coat hanger.

You'll also need floral tape—the typical paper floral tape you'd use for wrapping any kind of floral stems found in any craft or floral supply store. This tape is coated in wax and adheres to itself when you wrap it and rub it. It has a tendency to stretch, so you'll want to give it a little tug as you work to prestretch and prevent it from bunching up as you wrap.

Leaves of Glass

You can make the same petals or leaves in beads by many different ways. The method I'm going to show you is the most common I've found in my research. But if you see another method that makes more sense to you or seems easier, try it! As long as you get the results you want, who cares how you get there?

To start, it helps to know that there are two traditional methods of making beaded flowers—French and Victorian. The most popular is the French method. Most French method instructions teach you to put all your beads on your wire first, keeping the wire attached to the spool. This keeps the beads from falling off on one end, and you can string enough beads to make your finished project before you start. (We'll make a petal using this method a little later in this chapter.)

The easiest way, in my opinion, to get the feel of working with seed beads and wire to make flowers is to start with very simple open continuous loop flowers. This technique is very quick to pick up, and you can use it to make some lovely little blossoms to decorate a barrette or a Christmas ornament.

Continuous Loop Technique

Mastering simple loops means you can make lots of small flowers, centers, small leaves, and stamens. Let's practice and make a single flower.

1. Cut a 12-inch length of wire. If you're using size 11° seed beads, I recommend 24-gauge wire. Bend the wire in a U shape—but don't crease it into a V shape—and thread on 7 or 8 beads so they fall to the bottom of the U.

2. Cross the wires snugly just above the beads on each leg of the U, and make a full twist. You should now have a beaded loop in the center of your wire.

3. Add the same number of beads and make another loop next to the one you just made, keeping the loops close to each other and always twisting in the same direction. Repeat until you have the number of loops you want, then join and twist the two end wires together to make a closed circle of loops.

4. Bend the two wires down to make a stem, continue twisting them together, and you're done.

The steps to making a continuous loop flower.

You can add a larger bead in the center if you want, by putting a wire through the bead and twisting the center wires together with your loop wires. You can also make several different sizes of continuous loop circles and layer them for a different look.

Findings

You're going to spill beads. That's a fact, so accept it. If it's just a few, you can pick them up by moistening your fingertip, pressing down on the beads, then sifting them back into your container. If a lot of beads spill, resort to the handheld vacuum method. You want the kind of vacuum that doesn't have a bag but has a little removable filter cup instead. Clean out the vacuum thoroughly, suck up the beads, and dump!

You can use single loops made the same way as the first loop of a continuous loop flower many ways. They can be the tips of stamens or even little buds or blossoms. You can also make a double loop by completing the single loop and then threading beads onto one of the two

wires and bringing it back over the top of the single loop. This can also be a bud, a flower center, or the tip of a stamen at the end of a longer beaded wire.

Center Bar Method

To make the basic leaf or petal for a wide variety of flowers, you'll need to know the center bar method. There are basically two shapes to learn: the completely rounded shape and the rounded bottom with pointed top. I'll give you general directions for both. When you actually make a flower, you'll most likely be following a pattern, so you'll need to adapt these to the specific directions for your pattern.

Findings

Remember to always secure your wire once you open it. If there's a notch or metal hook on the spool for you to wrap it around, use it. You'll be glad you did. The first time I tried making a beaded flower, I ended up with a mess of wire that sprung from the spool like a runaway watch spring. I quickly learned to secure it right away so it couldn't get away from me.

1. Use size 11° seed beads and 24-gauge wire for this practice piece. Try a little sample first and see how easy it is to wrap one piece of wire around another and then twist the two wires together. Use whatever feels best to practice or, if you have several different wires, make samples in each and compare your results.

The first step is to get the beads onto the wire. If you don't have a bead spinner, you'll want to use hanks of beads. Pull one strand of beads from the hank (don't let them spill!), and thread the wire through the beads a couple of inches at a time. Then pull the string away from the beads on the wire, being sure to hold onto the hank so the remaining beads don't slip off. Let the beads you've strung on the wire fall down toward the spool.

Another tip: Put some plastic tape over the knot in your hank of beads. As you pull out individual strands, the knot becomes looser and eventually all the strands will come loose so you have loose beads rather than beads on a string. If you don't need all the beads on a strand, you can also stop the beads from coming off with a piece of plastic tape wrapped around the individual strand in front of the first bead.

Findings

Most directions for beaded flowers ask you to transfer a certain number of strands from a hank of seed beads to your wire. If you're working with loose beads, it helps to know what this means in terms of numbers of beads or length. For example, a hank of size 11° Czech seed beads is usually made of 12 loops or strands of beads, each approximately 20 inches long. A size 11° seed bead is approximately 2.1mm in size.

If you must work with loose beads, put them into a shallow dish and string one at a time from there, using your index finger to catch them as you go and tipping your wrist up to force them down the end of the wire toward the spool.

Seed beads on wire that's still connected to the spool.

2. When you have enough beads, you'll need to make a loop between your center row (the *center bar* or *basic row*—you'll see both of these terms used in different sets of instructions) and the rest of the beads you'll be using to make your wraps around the center row. These beads will be between the loop and the spool. It helps to keep the spool to your right. For your practice leaf, make a center bar of 7 beads.

3. To make your basic loop, you'll need about 6 inches of wire between the center bar and the rest of your beads. Make a kink in the very end of the wire to keep the center row of beads from falling off. Bring the bar wire around the first couple fingers of your left hand and across itself and make a loop, then twist it tightly in one direction a couple times.

   Once you've created your basic loop, you'll be holding it at the bottom, and your center row with the wire end will be pointing upright.

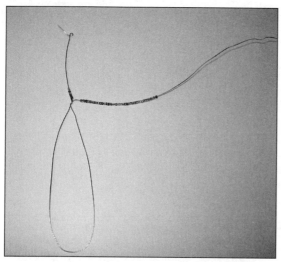

This is how the wire assembly should look for making a leaf or petal using the center bar method.

![Knots icon] **Knots!**

There is a right side and a wrong side, which you'll see when you begin to wrap your rows. Keep the right side facing you and the wrong side underneath, facing away from you.

You'll finish your petal or flower at the bottom of your work. This way you'll always have an odd number of rows, which is usually what is called for in your pattern. If your pattern calls for an even number of rows, you'll finish at the top, where your single wire is.

4. Now, bring enough beads up from your "stash" of beads near the spool to make a nice tight gentle arc alongside your center bar. With the wire at a right angle to the wire with the center bar, bring it around the back of the center wire, across the front, then around the back again, and come down the other side, making another arc on the other side of the center bar. Wrap completely around once, and bring up the next arc of beads.

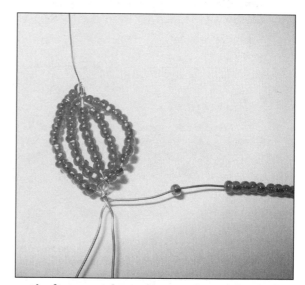

The first two right-angle rows of a petal or leaf using the center bar method.

Don't worry about counting how many beads you have on these next rows. Just be sure they fill in nicely and are close to the center bar.

5. Keep going up, around, and down in the same manner until your petal or leaf is the desired size. Do your best to keep the top wire and your basic loop wire straight so your petal is smooth, tight, and round. End at the bottom, and wrap the wire tightly at least three times. Use an alligator clip or make a circle in the wire that's still on the spool above the remaining strung beads so they don't fall off, then cut the wire. Cut the basic loop you made, too, so now you have three strands of wire hanging down as a "stem."

6. Cut the top wire so only about ¼ inch remains. With a pair of pliers, bend this end down against the beads at the back of the petal or leaf.

After you've cut the top wire, bend it neatly behind the petal or leaf to hide it.

Findings

Cut all your wire on a slant to make a good point to make it easier to string your beads.

This technique will give you a leaf or petal that is rounded both at the top and at the bottom. If you want one with a pointed top, you'll need to increase the angle of your wire strands. Instead of going straight across as you wrap, angle your wire at a 45-degree angle and then wrap. Dalene Kelly suggests adding single beads between the rows of arced beads to get a more elongated look. Do this by cutting off the loop you made in the top of your basic loop assembly and adding a single bead between a couple of rows near the top as you go.

Adding extra beads between rows to make a more pointed leaf or petal.

When you're using the center bar method and making a very large or long petal or leaf, you might need to do some bracing. Using very thin wire (30 or 32 gauge), simply create a crosspiece of wire by wrapping it around each lengthwise row in between the beads. Cut the ends, leaving about ¼ inch, and fold under to the back of the leaf or petal, as you did with the top wire.

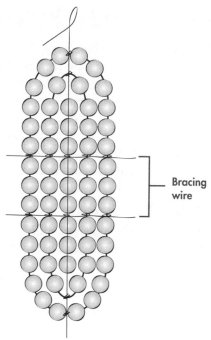

Bracing wire

You might need to add bracing to especially large or long leaves or petals.

Findings

As you complete parts, keep them safe by putting them in separate baggies or small boxes so they don't get tangled with bead hanks or other flowers. I like to put all the petals in one baggie, stamens in another, and leaves in another. This makes it easy to see how many I have and keeps them from getting bent or tangled.

Beading Flowers with the Victorian Method

The Victorian method for making a leaf or petal gives a completely different look. This technique is also called the Dutch method and is similar to the ladder stitch you learned in Chapter 7.

1. Cut a 12-inch length of wire and thread on 3 beads. If you're using size 11° seed beads, 24-gauge wire works well. Bring the beads to the center of the wire, and thread one end of the wire through the last 2 beads you put on. You'll end up with a triangle formation.

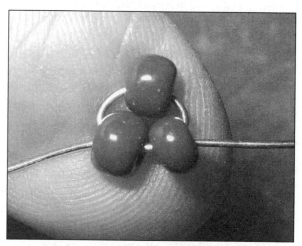

This is how your first 3 beads should look.

2. Add 3 beads to one wire and again make a loop through these 3 beads.

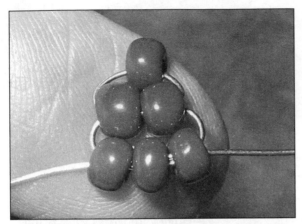

This is how your flower should look with 6 beads.

3. Repeat, adding 4 beads, then make a row of 3 beads, a row of 2 beads, then a single bead row.

4. Twist the 2 wires at the bottom. There you have it!

This is the basic technique. If you'd like to learn more about the Victorian technique of beaded flowers, join the VictorianBeadedFlowers e-group at Yahoo! Groups (groups.yahoo.com), and they'll help you along.

Findings _____

Learning to make beaded flowers is a visual thing. It really helps to be able to see this three-dimensional art being done step by step as you try to duplicate the techniques. If you don't have a beaded flower instructor in your area, there is a video to help you along. It's called *How to Make Your Own Beautiful French Beaded Flowers* by Rosemary Topol. (I've given you the information for ordering it, plus a host of other beaded flower resources, in Appendix B.)

Some Assembly Required

Once you've made your petals and leaves, you'll need to assemble the flower. First, lightly tape the heavier wire or rod you're going to use for the stem with floral tape. Then, starting with the smallest inside petals, hold one so the rounded base of the petal is even with the top of the stem wire. Wrap the thinner wire of the petal around the heavier stem wire with floral tape. Do this with each petal of the same size around the stem.

When all the petals are secure, move on to the next "round" of petals larger in size. Keep this next round up snug against the first one so there's no space between them. Tape these to the wire stem. If you will be adding *sepals* or a *calyx*, they come next.

A-Bead-C's _____

If you look at some flowers, you'll notice some have a green "cup" or separate small green leaves that sit at the base of the flower. The whole thing is called a **calyx**; the individual green leaves are called **sepals**. Think of the honeysuckle, for example. If you pull on the flower, it comes out of the calyx. Some flowers also have centers or stamen. You'll need to study the flower to see all of its parts and then replicate them in beads. Pattern books do this for you. You never thought college botany would come in handy, did you? If you never took botany, just study some good garden catalogs or books.

Bedazzling Arrangements

Now that you've assembled all these components, turn the flower upside down, cut the wires even, and tape the entire stem. If you're adding leaves, you'll make them in a separate assembly and tape them to the stem as well.

Some leaves are close up to the flower; some are lower down on the stem. Some are directly across from each other; some are staggered down the stem. Look up how your flower appears in nature if you're not sure. A good pattern will tell you how to place the leaves along the stem or at least offer an accurate picture.

When you have all your flowers made, complete with leaves, you're ready to choose a container and secure them inside. Remember, these flowers are top-heavy, so you're going to need to weight the container. You can use stones, nonhardening clay, or even plaster of paris if you want a permanent arrangement. Cover the clay or plaster with sheet moss or a layer of stones or stone chips.

Findings

You can find containers in thrift stores and at yard sales—and don't forget to check your own cabinets and storage! The container is very much a part of your finished arrangement, so choose something that complements the flowers you've made. Check out floral arranging books to get some ideas.

Practice Makes Posies

At first, you might feel very awkward doing this kind of beading. Even though I do a lot of wirework, when I started flower making, I felt like I was all thumbs. Practice—you will get better!

You'll see lots of things to embellish with your "practice" pieces. Make bunches of leaves and wire them together in a garland to decorate a candlestick or a light sconce. Or make a sprig of small simple flowers as embellishments for a specially wrapped gift. A couple of continuous loop flowers wrapped around a barrette or bobby pin make a nice gift for a special friend or even yourself. Before long you'll be graduating to roses and orchids!

If a complete arrangement daunts you, don't do it. Just play with making small sprigs of flowers or leaves until you're ready to tackle something larger. Even a single rose with leaves looks lovely in a vase. Add a couple of sprigs of baby's breath, and you've got an easy arrangement.

Put On Your Beadin' Cap

It's time to give your beadin' cap flower power. Make a continuous loop flower—or several—and twist the stem wires together well. Form a loop with the stem wires, and sew your flower or sprig onto your beadin' cap. If you're feeling ambitious, add some leaves made using the center bar method. Make as many as you have room for then sew them on!

To become a really good beaded flower maker, you'll become a botanist by default. Start looking at seed and plant catalogs in a whole new way. Ask yourself, if you wanted to make a certain flower, how would you make each of its parts in beads? Put on your beadin' cap, and you'll start to think creatively about flowers and leaves.

The Least You Need to Know

- Make beaded flowers with bead-strung wire twisted in various ways to make petals, leaves, and other flower parts.

- If you're going to do a lot of beaded flowers, you'll want to invest in a bead spinner and a hemostat.

- Buy seed beads on hanks and transfer them directly to your wire, which you keep attached to the spool for the construction of many types of petals and leaves. A bead spinner makes quicker work of stringing beads.

- Choose your flower-arrangement containers carefully, and be mindful that beaded flowers are heavy and will need to be counterbalanced.

In This Part

Beads on Fabric and Fiber

The clothes of kings and queens, brides, and high-fashion designers have often employed the use of beads to make them glitter and gleam. In the first two chapters of Part 4, you'll learn the secrets of beaded embellishment on fabric. Then, I'll show you how to tie your beads up in knots—macramé knots, that is.

In This Chapter

◆ Using beaded embroidery

◆ Finding tools and materials you'll need

◆ Trying your hand at basic bead embroidery stitches

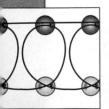

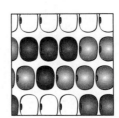

Beads in Stitches

Throughout history, nearly every culture has had some form of bead embroidery for decorating its clothing, religious artifacts, and homes. Even primitive man liked to ornament his clothes: When the remains of a Cro-Magnon man thought to date to 30000 B.C.E. were discovered, his fur clothing was embellished with ivory beads. Other early beads included small holed stones and shells attached with animal sinew.

As more elaborate embroidery stitches developed, beads were a natural to include or add on. And once smaller glass beads and finer needles were commonly available, beads could be incorporated in all other kinds of embroidery and needlework, including knitting, crochet, cross-stitch, and needlepoint.

Victorian crazy quilts became an imaginative canvas for a potpourri of embroidery and beaded embellishment, as did lavish ball gowns and just about any everyday object that could hold a bead. (Humans, it seems, have never met a surface they couldn't embellish with beads.)

The French are known for their exquisite surface beading, and they developed many of the standard techniques, hence the term "French bead embroidery." Some of the most celebrated designers of evening clothes and ball gowns used French beading on their designs.

Today, you can even apply fancy threads and beads using a sewing machine. If you've ever done any type of embroidery, cross-stitch, or needlepoint, just wait until you learn how to add beads!

Embellishment Tools and Materials

You don't need many tools and materials for bead embroidery—and if you do any kind of embroidery, be it crewel, regular embroidery, cross-stitch or counted cross-stitch, you've already got a head start! However, you do need to keep in mind a few special considerations when embroidering with beads.

Thread Talk

When doing regular embroidery, you're most likely to use embroidery floss. This can be used in bead embroidery as well and can even become part of the design, especially when you use transparent beads. You can use as many strands of floss as you need to get through and secure your beads so they don't wobble. I usually use somewhere between 2 and 4 strands.

 Knots! _____

Thread that's too thin for your beads might make your beadwork look sloppy. Try to match the thread to the diameter of your hole or double up on thread to fill the hole more and help stabilize your stitchery.

Nymo thread is especially good for some kinds of bead embroidery. (You might remember Nymo from Chapter 5 or Part 3.) Nymo is great for embroidery because it's strong and durable. Generally Nymo size D will do the job, but use what's best for the size beads you're working with. You can also use Silamide, Conso, or even good polyester sewing thread. Don't forget to check whatever thread you use for stretching. If it does stretch, give it a good tug as you work to prestretch it.

Unless you're using beads as an embellishment on something that's going to be washed or dry-cleaned (see the following sidebar), the sky's the limit. Whatever surface you can use for embroidery, you can add beads to. The size of your bead hole is your only restriction! You can use all those wonderful metallic and textured threads to embroider with beads. Take a look at threads like Sulky and Madeira. And have fun at the sewing and yarn shops! While surfing the Internet, I stumbled across a great article on The Taunton Press website (publishers of *Threads* and many other fine magazines) at www.taunton.com/ threads/pages/t00125.asp (click on the highlighted "Thread types and brands" text in the article). It's a thorough discussion of all kinds of threads for machine embroidery, but it's just as useful for fabric embellishers of every ilk.

Knots! _____

Imagine how horrified you'd be if you sent a garment you'd embroidered with beads to be dry-cleaned and it came back naked. That could happen if you choose the wrong thread.

Carol Perrenoud suggests in her *Bead Embroidery* video that you make two identical samples of the beads you intend to use and ask your dry cleaner to run one swatch through the cleaning process a few times. Compare the two swatches for thread durability so you won't have any surprises later. (You should test your beads for colorfastness as well; see the following "A Need for Beads: 'I'm Going Shopping!'" section.)

A general rule of thumb is to match the color of the thread to the fabric rather than the beads, but, as always, there are plenty of exceptions. If you have transparent beads, you might want to use a contrasting or complementary thread as part of the design.

No Nonsense About Needles

You'll want to have a variety of needles on hand for bead embroidery because the needle you use will depend on what kind of material you're embroidering. It could be something as fine as netting or satin, Aida cloth, canvas, linen, or homespun, or something as thick as leather, felt, or velvet. If you have a variety of needles, it'll be easier to match the needle to the job.

Some good needles to have on hand (and I do recommend *good* needles like John James) are milliner's, tapestry, chenille, quilting, beading, and embroidery needles. Have a selection of sizes and lengths. Definitely have some size 12 beading needles in your supply and some "sharps" (quilters might know these as "betweens"). For leather, you might want to try glover's needles and maybe a curved beading needle or two. Experiment and see what you like working with best.

You'll want to have a thimble nearby. You can use a traditional metal thimble used for sewing, but some of us prefer a leather or rubber thimble, more commonly used in quilting. Experiment and decide which type you prefer.

No Lack of Surfaces

From jeans to gauzy scarves, paper canvas to velvet and silk—the things you can embellish with bead embroidery are endless. Embroider lace, bead a leather pouch, or make yourself a textured pin just covered with beaded stitches.

Some materials to play with are as follows:

◆ **Aida cloth**   This is the most popular cross-stitch fabric. It is specially woven so that there is an even pattern of squares across the surface of the fabric. This makes it easy to place stitches evenly apart. Aida cloth is measured by the number of squares counted per inch, is generally available in 100 percent cotton, and comes in a variety of sizes and colors. Use 14-count Aida cloth for size 11° seed beads.

◆ **Paper canvas and card stock**   You'll need a sharp needle for piercing paper or card stock. A blunt needle works better with perforated paper, such as paper canvas.

◆ **Garment leather and suede**   Look for scraps at your local leather shop or, if you're lucky and just happen to know a leather worker (I'm lucky—I live with one!), ask if you can have his or her scraps. You can also find small pieces of leather and suede sometimes at hobby or fabric stores.

◆ **Fabric**   Ultrasuede, Facile, and similar fabrics have good body and work well. Avoid knits and stretch fabrics. If you do want to use knits, embroider beads in separate units and consider the fabric's "give." Linens and cottons are great for embroidery. You'll want 28-count linen for cross-stitch beading. (You can find this in the counted cross-stitch department of your crafts store.) Felt is also great for bead embroidery (plus you'll need some for your needle weaving in Chapter 14).

Knots! _____

Always prewash your fabrics before beading on them. You don't want any surprise shrinking after you've embellished.

Simple broadcloth can be used for embroidery of all kinds, too. Many decorator fabrics have great designs you can bead over and generally have good body for embellishment. Whether you'll be laundering the fabric or not is an important consideration. Consider moiré for a romantic Victorian look.

Findings _____

Line garments that you embellish with beadwork to minimize the friction on the threads from the underside. When you're buying your fabric, remember to pick up some lining material as well.

◆ **Netting and lace**   Beading on net is an art unto itself. Some of the most beautiful examples come from the Victorian, Edwardian, and Art Deco eras. Wendy Simpson-Connor's little guide to bead embroidery, *The Beading on Fabric Book*, shows you how to duplicate some of these from the days when her grandmother beaded costumes for the *Ziegfeld Follies*. You can add beads and sequins to all kinds of lace and make it even more "frothy."

A Need for Beads: "I'm Going Shopping!"

Perhaps more than any other form of beading, bead embroidery and embellishment open up a whole new world of materials—and, therefore, shopping!

You can incorporate almost any kind of bead into a bead embroidery stitch or embellishment. Think of combining lace, buttons, fibers, and fabric and then encrusting them with beads.

Learn all you can about seed beads because they're a big part of bead embroidery. Become familiar with the differences between Japanese cylinder beads and regular Czech and Japanese seed beads. Mostly you'll be using size 11° seed beads, but look at how slightly larger or smaller beads combine to add texture and design possibilities. Notice the different cuts, colors, and finishes. (For a refresher on the types of beads, see Chapter 1.)

Beads that have color all the way through the glass are the best choices for embroidery on fabric that will be washed or dry-cleaned. Beads with surface finishes or that are painted will most likely wear or change color in the cleaning process. If you're not sure, test some samples.

Knots! _____

Laundering and dry-cleaning can wreak havoc on beads. So you're not surprised with faded or muted-color beads when you pick up your dry-cleaning, test your beads for colorfastness.

If you will be dry-cleaning the embellished garment, leave some beads you plan to use overnight in some acetone (most nail polish removers are largely acetone—check the label) and also a 50:50 solution of bleach and water in a separate container.

If you won't be dry-cleaning your beaded item but will be washing it, test your beads by leaving some in a cup or bowl of warm water and the detergent you'll use on it. See if they leave any color in the water or lose their sheen.

Also consider sequins and buttons when you design your bead embroidery projects. You can use a seed bead to anchor the sequin. Just come up through the sequin's hole, add a seed bead, and come back down through the hole of the sequin again.

Findings

It was through my love of things Victorian and my interest in crazy quilting that I found beading. I've been collecting snippets of antique lace, old buttons, antique beads, ribbon, and trims for years to make that one ultimate crazy quilt. If you'd like to explore the many facets of surface embellishment, including embroidery, ribbon embroidery, and bead embroidery, look into Judith Baker Montano's books and videos. *Judith Baker Montano's Embellishments* is a good video to start with, as is her video on crazy quilting. Her *Elegant Stitches, The Crazy Quilt Handbook,* and *Crazy Quilt Odyssey: Adventures in Victorian Needlework* books are all informative and inspiring. (I've given you information on all these in Appendix B.)

Odds and Ends

Many types of embroidery are done on a hoop, and you can use a hoop with bead embroidery as well. Just be sure your hoop has an adjustable screw on the outer hoop. Beaded fabric can become quite thick, and as you move your work, you'll need to have room to accommodate the beads. Also, when you do use a hoop, be very careful not to pull your work too tightly.

Some bead embroiderers favor embroidery frames over hoops. Some frames attach to a stand so you can work hands free and adjust the tension easier, but these can be expensive.

If your piece is too small for a hoop or a frame, you can cut an opening in a larger piece of fabric and baste your working piece in the hole, then put it on the hoop or frame.

Findings

One of my favorite sources for all things crafty, especially having to do with period crafts and needlework, is Lacis. Check out their embroidery frames and beading supplies at www.lacis.com.

Some people prefer not to use a hoop or a frame. Instead, they like to back their material with iron-on Pellon or similar material (follow the manufacturer's instructions when applying your backing) or simply baste it onto a stiff backing.

The same magnetic board I mentioned earlier for holding your off-loom or loom work patterns comes in handy when you're doing charted and counted bead embroidery. Actually, bring out this gadget anytime you have a list of things to follow and want to keep your place while you work.

You'll also want to have some tailor's pencils, chalk, or water-erasable marking pens handy so you can draw your designs before you bead.

Need ideas for patterns and designs? Plenty of kits and pattern books are on the market, plus you can use iron-on transfers just like you can for regular embroidery. Dover Publications, a great design source for any kind of craft, has wonderful sourcebooks for craftspeople. Like Celtic or Egyptian? They've got it! Medieval? Victorian? Yep. And their books are amazingly low-priced for what you get. You can even purchase designs on CD-ROM and print them out on whatever kind of paper you can feed through your printer. Check them out at www.doverpublications.com.

Another source for patterns is what's printed on or woven into the fabric itself. Just embroider beads on top of the fabric pattern, and match the colors or copy the fabric's pattern onto plain fabric. Simple!

Findings

What if you don't want to use a pattern or can't find one that's just right? You can, of course, draw your own design freehand or trace any design you'd like to create in beads on fabric.

Counted cross-stitch patterns work for bead stitching as well (I'll talk about that a little later in this chapter). If you find a counted cross-stitch pattern you like, why not consider doing it in beads or even partially in beads?

A Stitch Sampler

You can learn hundreds of embroidery stitches and variations, and you can incorporate beads into just about any one of them. (And if you can't find one you like, you can probably invent some yourself!) It's certainly a good idea to practice your stitches before trying to apply them to a garment. There's a reason why folks in days past made samplers.

You might want to create your own sampler to practice your stitches and for later reference. Put some sturdy fabric in a hoop or frame, and try your hand at this small lexicon of simple embroidery stitches—first without beads and then with.

Findings

A fascinating collection of stitches is Dorothy Bond's *Crazy Quilt Stitches*. Also look at Ruth Wilson's *Beautiful Beading: A Beginner's Guide*. On my wish list of books to have someday (is it Christmas yet?) is *Haute Couture Embroidery* by Palmer White, which details the clothing and costume of Lesage and some of the most beautiful fashion embroidery in history. (See Appendix B for more information on these books.) There's even an online "stitch dictionary" that includes bead embroidery stitches. See prettyimpressivestuff.com/stitches/.

Backstitch

Just as the backstitch is a hand-sewing staple, so it is with beading to embellish a surface, and it's the stitch you'll probably use the most. It's great for outlining or filling in. You can use it with single beads or pick up several beads at a time and go back through them. You might want to go back through long rows of backstitched beads a second time to give them some extra stability, especially if the thread you're using leaves some room in the beads and they tend to "wobble" back and forth.

Be sure to push your beads back up against the thread where it's coming out of your fabric and position your needle right in front of the last bead, holding your needle perpendicular to the fabric. Push the needle straight down, not on a slant. If you position your needle too far out from your beads, you'll get a gap between your stitches. If you position it too far in, you'll get an arch or hump in your work.

When going around curves, use fewer beads at one time and go back through each group of beads more frequently to help hold the line of the curve.

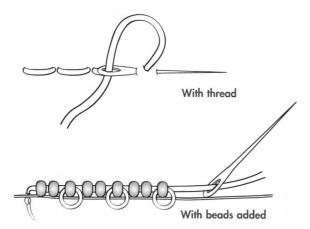

With thread

With beads added

The versatile backstitch, with and without beads.

Stem Stitch

This is an outline stitch or, as the name implies, one for making flower stems.

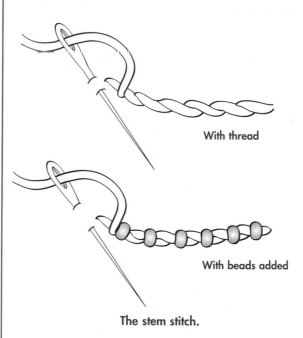

With thread

With beads added

The stem stitch.

Chain Stitch

The trick with this stitch when using beads is to have enough beads to fill the chain and center them.

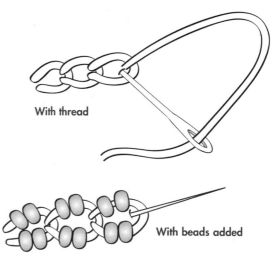

With thread

With beads added

The chain stitch.

Buttonhole or Blanket Stitch

This is another staple stitch in the hand-sewing world. Just add beads to give it a whole new dimension.

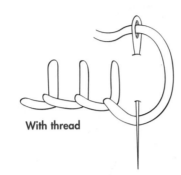

With thread

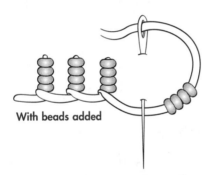

With beads added

The buttonhole or blanket stitch.

Feather Stitch

A favorite on crazy quilts, this stitch adds a lot of texture.

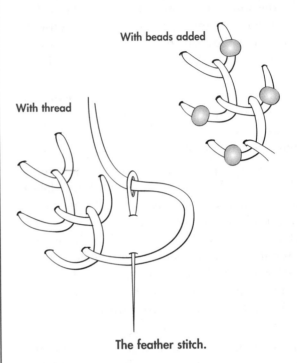

With beads added

With thread

The feather stitch.

Couching

Couching is a great way to fill in large expanses with stitches. Just thread on a long row of beads, and hold them in place with cross-wise stitches known as *couching stitches*. This is generally done using the two-needle method. Pull your thread strung with beads taut, slip your needle into the fabric, and wrap the excess thread around the needle. Then come along with your second needle and thread and do the couching. Or you can do smaller sections and couch as you go. Again, remember to keep your needle perpendicular to your fabric and keep your beads snug against the beading thread where it exits the fabric.

When going through curves, you'll want to couch between beads more frequently to make it easier to hold to the curved line.

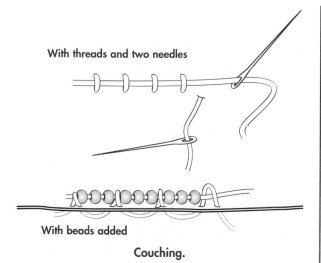

With threads and two needles

With beads added

Couching.

Lazy Stitch

This is a classic Native American bead embroidery stitch. It has other names and is used close together to fill large areas or can be spread apart for a wide variety of designs. (Note I'm only showing you the beaded stitch.)

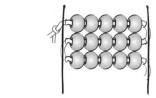

The lazy stitch, with beads added.

Knots!

Watch those sharp-ended beads! When attaching bugle beads or metal beads that have sharp ends, you might want to add one or more round seed beads on the ends to resist thread wear or fraying and eventual loss of beads. Smaller size seed beads come in very handy for this.

Scatter Stitch

This is a random stitch done with beads to give some fill or texture to a large area. It can be done with single beads or multiples in what is also called a *running stitch*.

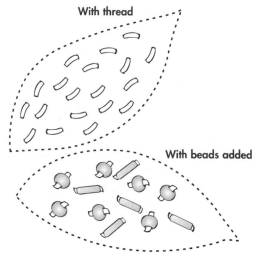

With thread

With beads added

The scatter stitch.

You can do cross-stitch with beads, too. Instead of making a complete X as you do with embroidery floss, do half a stitch. Be sure your stitches are all going in the same direction, from the lower left corner to the upper right or vice-versa.

Beads can be used as part of a cross-stitch design along with floss, the whole design can be worked in beads, or you can first work the design in cross-stitch and add beads to highlight parts of the design. You can do the same with needlepoint and tapestries.

With thread

With beads added

Cross-stitch on canvas.

Another form of beading that looks like embroidery but actually doesn't use any thread is called "pin beading." This is a very Victorian craft and is done with small, stainless-steel pins and glass seed beads poked into a cushion. Suzanne McNeill Design Originals' book called *Pin Beading* is worth checking out. The results are quite delicate and especially lovely when combined with silk ribbon embroidery and lace. If you think this is something you'd like to explore, see Appendix B for information on how to order this book.

If you are a machine embroiderer, there are gadgets you can attach to your machine so you can add beads as you sew. Check out the special feet now available for the newer sewing machines.

Put On Your Beadin' Cap

Find a spot on your cap and, using a light pencil or fading marker (check the quilting section of your craft or fabric store), sketch in some curved lines or a pattern you can follow using some of the stitches you've learned in this chapter. Then embroider it with the beads of your choice. If your cap is too thick to embroider through or if you find it easier working with a hoop, you can make your design on embroidery material, cut out a patch, then stitch the edges under and sew or glue the patch onto your cap.

The Least You Need to Know

◆ Many of the tools and materials used for regular embroidery can be used with bead embroidery.

◆ Seed beads are the most common beads used in bead embroidery. Size 11° seed beads are good for many embroidery applications.

◆ Almost any surface, fabric, or material can be embellished with beads.

◆ Cross-stitch patterns can be adapted for beads.

◆ Beads can be combined with cross-stitch, needlepoint, and tapestry to add depth, texture, and highlights.

In This Chapter

◆ Framing or "setting" flat-back stones or jewels among beads

◆ Choosing the best backing fabric for cabochons and other beaded embellishments

◆ A dictionary of some common edgings that will enhance both fabric and woven beadwork

◆ An introduction to several types of fringes, when to use them and how

◆ The basics of making beaded rosettes

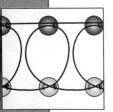

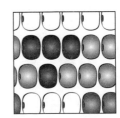

Chapter 14

Embellishments: Cabochons, Edging, Fringes, and Rosettes

Bead embroidery is only part of the embellishment picture. Beads can be used to enhance just about anything. Let's learn some more ways to add dash and sparkle to everyday objects.

A Thrilling "Cab" Ride

Go to any bead store or rock shop, and you'll find trays full of *cabochons*. A cabochon, or "cab" for short, is any flat-backed stone with a domed surface. But that's not the whole story. What beaders commonly call cabs can be made out of semi-precious stones, porcelain, polymer clay, Raku pottery, resin, glass, even metal. I've used antique buttons as cabs, either by cutting off the shank, burying the shank in backing material, or, if the button has holes, beading through and over the holes to conceal them.

You can find some very beautiful antique and vintage cabochons for sale if you look for them, and some lovely reproductions are on the market, too. You can even buy cabochons that look like faces for making beaded dolls or goddesses or just interesting jewelry. So maybe cabs don't have to be smooth after all.

You can make your own cabochons, too. Just as you learned how to make polymer clay beads in Chapter 2, you can make polymer clay cabs. A company called Elite Better Beads actually makes a cabochon frame just for outlining your polymer clay cabs. These are sold at some of the chain craft stores, so look for them if you're interested in making your own polymer clay cabochons.

> ### A-Bead-C's
> A **cabochon** is a domed gem that's smoothed and polished but not faceted.

A wide variety of cabochons are available for your beaded embellishment ideas.

In the jewelry trade, stone cabochons are traditionally set in a metal *bezel* and hung from a chain. However, because we're beaders, we think *beads* rather than simple metal and stone pendants. Why not frame a cabochon or even create a sculpted bezel in beads?

> ### A-Bead-C's
> A **bezel** is that part of a ring, bracelet, etc. to which gems are attached. It is a grooved ring or rim holding a gem, watch crystal, etc. in its setting.

You can frame, set, or capture a cabochon in several ways. I'll show you three methods in this chapter. One builds on what we learned in Chapter 13 on bead embroidery. The others employ the off-loom weaving stitches you learned in Chapter 7.

Watch Your Back!

Generally, you will use some sort of fabric or leather as a backing for your cabochon. Here's an overview of some materials you can use as a foundation for beading around cabochons:

Pellon is an interfacing used in sewing and comes in different weights as well as iron-on and non-iron-on versions. For beading, you'll usually want the heavier weight. You can find pellon in most fabric stores.

> ### Knots!
> Some of these materials are quite expensive, so don't buy lots of one. You might find you prefer something else and then you've wasted your money. Check with some beady friends and see if they have a scrap or two you can fiddle with. Or do you have a sewer, general crafter, or hat maker in your midst? Bet they have some scraps for you to try. You might even find some leftovers in thrift stores or at yard sales or try writing the company and asking for a small sample. That way you can learn your preferences without emptying your wallet!

EaZy Felt is a prestiffened felt that comes in a wide variety of colors. Find it in crafts stores.

E'tal is a newcomer on the market. I was able to acquire some samples, but I haven't had a chance to work with it yet. E'tal is actual metal fibers that have been fused to a backing. We're talking real metal. It cuts cleanly without fraying, can be painted and printed on with a copy machine or ink jet printer, glues easily with E6000 glue, is easy to embellish using standard sewing, embroidery, or beading needles, and can be hot or cold embossed. I can tell you it's really pretty, as well. Go to www.beadyboop.com/e'tal.htm for more information and to order.

Lacy's Stiff Stuff is a specially designed beading foundation material that eliminates the need for embroidery hoops or frames. It's porous, so glues used to affix cabochons soak in and adhere especially well, and the needle glides through easily. A self-adhesive pattern sheet allows you to draw or trace a pattern and then apply it. Check out Lacy's Stiff Stuff online at www.lacysstiffstuff.com.

Timtex is a sew-through stabilizer that was originally created for use in making hat brims, especially baseball caps. You can find it at www.timtexstore.com and at some sewing, quilting, or crafts stores.

Buckram is another foundation and stabilizer favored by some beaders. Buckram comes in different weights, so be sure you can pass a beading or small-eye needle, along with your beads, through what you select. I've seen this in fabric stores as well as online.

A-Bead-C's

Buckram is a cloth made from cotton or linen, usually the former, and closely woven, occasionally with a double warp. It is used most often in book-binding and hat-making and is filled or coated and pressed between rollers to give it a smooth finish, which blocks well and is reasonably durable.

You can also use different materials to finish the back after you use a stabilizer. Chamois cloth, thin leather, Ultrasuede, or Facile all make nice finished backings. Find these at fabric, craft, and leather supply stores.

Setting Cabs: Getting Started

The general procedure for all the cabochon-setting methods I'm going to teach you is the same (although the third method can be done with or without a backing):

First, glue your cabochon onto your stabilizing material. Many beaders prefer a glue called E-6000. You can find this in bead stores and some craft stores. Other adhesives will work well, too. Just be sure it's made for adhering stone or glass to fabric. Follow the directions on the adhesive tube or package, and if you can, let the glue dry overnight. Now proceed to one of the following methods.

Findings

If you don't want to glue down your cabochon because you might want to take it apart and use it in a different way later, the third method gives you that alternative.

Method 1: Embroidery

This is perhaps the simplest method, yet it can produce some of the most gorgeous results. Basically, you're going to glue down the cabochon, then outline it with embroidery. You can use backstitch or couching to create your design. (See Chapter 13 for a refresher on stitches, if you need to.) You might want to draw out what you're going to do first.

I like to use backstitch, laying down three beads and going back through all three beads each time. This gives me an especially strong foundation and adds stiffness to the work. If I want to add edging or embellishment later, I have a good, strong base under my work. Experiment and see what works best for you.

To see how to make a project using this step-by-step method, see the beaded barrette in Chapter 22.

A cabochon framed in bead embroidery. (Instructions for this beaded barrette are in Chapter 22.)

Method 2: Peyote Stitch Bezel

This method works especially well with a cabochon that has fairly high sides.

1. Embroider a backstitch ring or a couched ring around your cabochon. Again, I prefer to do a backstitch, three beads at a time, and go back through the three beads each time. Play with your ring of beads so you end up with an even number of beads.

2. Come up through one bead, and do circular even-count peyote stitch (see Chapter 7 for instructions) around the circle.

3. Do as many rows as you need to reach the top of the cabochon, then, using smaller beads, do your next row. You can even do additional rows with yet smaller beads. In the following figure, I used size 11° beads for my first rows, size 12° for the first row that comes up over the cameo cabochon, then size 14° for the last row.

This lovely cameo has been set in an elegant peyote stitch bezel.

Findings

I must give credit to the Beadnik's page at www.geocities.com/SoHo/Gallery/1216/cabs.html and the links at home.flash.net/~mjtafoya/mycabs/cablinks.htm for teaching me how to do this technique. Those sites are great places to visit, so check them out for tutorials on various netted cab methods and lots of other goodies.

Method 3: Netted Bezel

Netting is a quick and easy way to capture just about anything, and you can enclose and encrust a cabochon in several ways with netting. (Review Chapter 7 if you need a refresher on netting.) I've even seen wonderful pendants made with vintage marbles captured in netting.

You don't need to back your cabochon with this method because you'll entrap it in a net of beads. If you want to, you can glue a piece of leather or other finishing material to the back of the cab to cushion it and give it a more finished look, but that's your choice.

1. Choose your cabochon, and pick out the complementing size 11° seed beads. Beadnik suggests using 2 contrasting colors, and I found this helped me see the netted pattern (much as it did when I showed it to you in Chapter 7). Using your needle (size 10 will do fine) and conditioned thread (I used Nymo D), string on beads in multiples of 6 so you can make a circle around and slightly bigger than the cab. String on 2 of color #1 bead, then 1 of color #2, and end with 1 bead of color #2.

2. Join the circle by going through the ring of beads one time and making a knot where the two ends meet. Leave a long tail for finishing later.

3. For the second row, come up through the first #2 bead, add 2 color #1 beads, 1 color #2 bead, and 2 color #2 beads. Skip one #2 bead on the first row, and go through the next one. Repeat this 5-bead sequence around the row.

4. For the third row, come up through the center bead (a #2 bead) in a second row 5-bead sequence, and repeat row 2. Depending on the thickness of your cabochon, you might want to do another row of the same 5-bead pattern, making 4 rows in all, including your initial ring of beads. Your bezel will begin to curl.

5. For the fourth (or fifth row, depending on what you decided to do in step 4), come up through the center #2 bead in the last row you just did. Add 3 beads of either color #1 or color #2 (your choice), and go through the next center #2 bead. Continue around the entire circle. Carefully pull thread to tighten row. Knot and work thread into beads. Cut off thread.

6. Insert cab carefully in netting, being sure it is balanced all around.

7. Attach thread along first row circle. Weave through a few beads, and come up through a #2 bead. Repeat rows 3 and 4 (and possibly 5, depending on what you decided to do in step 4) on the back side of your cab.

8. If you need to, you might want to do an additional row on the back side, reducing the number of beads in between to 2 beads or 1 bead to tighten the bezel even further. You'll have to adapt these instructions to the shape and size of your cabochon.

Your cab should now be firmly netted inside this beaded "cage."

Cabochon "captured" in beaded netting.

You can work a netted bezel around a cabochon that has been glued down on a backing and surrounded with a backstitch ring, just as you did with the peyote stitch bezel. Just come up through any bead in your backstitched row, make a 3-bead peak, come through the fourth bead from your needle, and then repeat this pattern all the way around. Work your net in rounds to fit the shape of your cabochon. To tighten the bezel, decrease to 2 beads between "peak" beads and tighten, then weave back and knot off.

Findings _____

If you want to learn more about surrounding objects in netting, check out a great book called *The Magic of Beaded Spherical Nets: Techniques and Projects* by Merry Makela. In it are a lot of flat net patterns perfect for encircling cabochons or a large center bead. (I've given you more information on this book in Appendix B).

Beaded cabochons are a quick way to make a beautiful focal centerpiece for a necklace, bracelet, or earrings, depending on the size of the cabochon you decide to use. Experiment and have fun.

On the Edge!

Another embellishment that adds depth and beauty to your work is edging. Just as in sewing or crocheting or knitting, edging can make all the difference between a ho-hum piece and a standout.

You actually learned one form of edging in the previous section on making a netted cabochon. Netted peaks can be done in single or multiple rows to create an edge around any piece. You can also add just enough beads to make more of a scallop.

In the following sections, I give you a short "dictionary" of some edgings you might like to use. Try this on beaded cabochons, scarves, handkerchiefs, pillows, cuffs, sachets, pin cushions, pendants, pouches, earrings, or wherever a little touch of "something beaded" would make it smashing!

Knots!

If you're applying a beaded edging to fabric, be sure the edge is rolled or has a small hem. You could also serge it and then turn it under. Just be sure it's not a raw edge, as your beading could pull out.

Picot Edging

Carol Perrenoud shows how to do this dainty, yet effective edging in her video, *Bead Embroidery* (see Appendix B). I used it on the beaded cameo earlier in this chapter. It also works well to join together two pieces of fabric or thin leather. You can vary this edging by introducing bugle beads into the mix.

The versatile picot beaded edge.

Scalloped Edging

Scallops can be done in a very similar manner. Just space your loops further apart and add more beads. You can create a different look by using a larger bead in the center of the scallop.

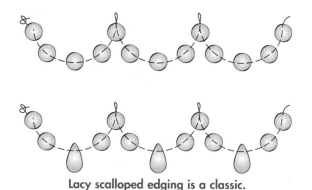

Lacy scalloped edging is a classic.

Netted Edging

Scalloped edging is only the beginning. You can also add rows of netting to your single scallop to make a more elaborate and fancy scalloped edge.

Enter netting once again, only this time it's over the edge!

Combine netted edgings with fringe, and you have a whole other world of fancy edge trimmings.

Fringe Benefits

Getting acquainted with fringe means many wonderful added design possibilities. You can add fringe to cloth fabric, the beaded fabric you've woven in one of the off-loom stitches we learned in Chapter 7, or the loomed fabric you made in Chapter 9. A store-bought scarf, shawl, jacket, or lampshade makes a great item for adding beaded fringe. It can be added to almost any sew-on trim and then sewn separately onto the material by hand or machine.

Findings

Beadwork magazine's book *Beaded Cords, Chains, Straps and Fringe* is a great source for a very clearly explained and exciting collection of fringes, some combined with netted edgings, plus cords, chains, and straps.

In this section, I'll give you some basic fringe styles and instructions, but the sky's the limit. Sketch out designs of your own, or get some help from one of the bead design software packages such as *Beadscape*, which is for Macintosh computers. When you find beaded items in the home or clothing accessory departments of your favorite store, take a look at how they're put together.

Single Fringe

This is the easiest form of fringe to do, yet it looks elegant. If you vary the lengths of the "dangles," you can create a design with the fringe itself. You can add your single fringe strands one at a time directly to the fabric or anchor your fringe to a string of beads you sewed on first (use backstitch to do this).

Use various types of beads on the end of the single fringe to make elaborate "dangles" for a Victorian or romantic feel. You can also terminate the end with a daisy.

Create a branched fringe by first making one side of a single fringe and then branching off with beads on the way back to the top.

Barbara Grainger designed a lovely earring pattern that makes a great fringe—find it at www.ladybead.com. Check the Ladybead newsletter archives for the Basic Weeping Willow Vine in the January 2002 newsletter. If you separated the strands as single fringe rather than using the three branches, this would make a fabulous fringe for a botanical print or embroidered fabric piece. This same basic pattern by Barbara is in *Beaded Cords, Chains, Straps and Fringe*. And for lots of gorgeous and more advanced fringes like this, check for her book *Dimensional Flowers, Leaves and Vines*. You could create a jungle!

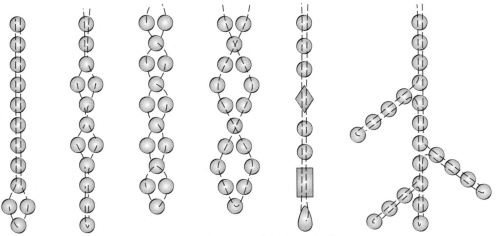

Some single fringe designs and the branched variation.

Looped Fringe

This is similar to the single fringe, but instead of going back through your single strand, you simply make a loop of beads and go back through the top. You can keep the loops independent of each other or pass each loop through the one before, as you see in the following illustration. Turn a basic fringe into a twisted fringe by using an accent bead at the end and twisting before going back up the other side and through the fabric.

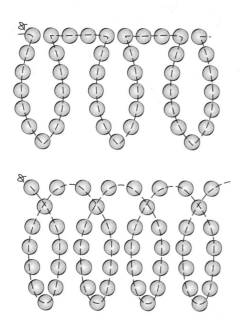

Looped fringe is easy and adds a lovely finish.

Netted Fringe

Flat netting makes a sumptuous edging and fringe. With a glass drop hanging from the netting at spaced intervals, you have a completely "wow!" trim. Think of this on an evening shawl or along the bottom of a special bag or purse.

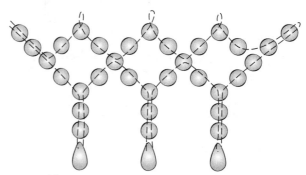

Netted fringe can add the pizzazz you're looking for.

Life Is Just a Bouquet of ... Rosettes

Well, it could be if you wanted to bead them! Rosettes are a form of beaded circular designs very common in Native American beadwork. In fact, specific designs and colors are very special to individual Native peoples.

You can make a rosette directly on your fabric or leather item, or make it on Aida cloth first and then attach it. This is an especially good idea when beading on leather because, unlike fabric, leather doesn't "heal" once a hole has been pierced through it. If you make a mistake, your hole is forever.

These beaded rosettes are basically a form of embroidery, but you can embellish them on with needle weaving and make them even more three-dimensional.

Start with a cross of beads, working from the center outward. Then fill in the design using the backstitch you learned in Chapter 13.

I hope this chapter has given you lots of extras to enhance the beading you've done so far. Pretty soon you'll be adding beaded embellishments to everything you can think of. An inexpensive scarf or pillow becomes a thing of beauty when you bead embellish it!

Put On Your Beadin' Cap

How can you use some of the techniques you've learned in this chapter on your beadin' cap? You could bead-bezel a cabochon, add a pin back, and pin it on your cap. (You can remove it later to wear on a favorite sweater or blouse.) You could add some edging and fringe to that cabochon pin, too! Or do the same with a rosette. You could also edge the brim with one of the more compact edging stitches you learned. Use your imagination!

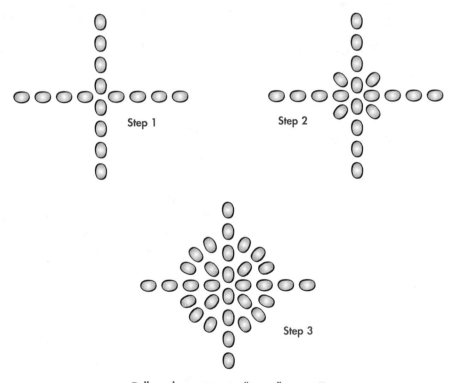

Follow these steps to "grow" a rosette.

The Least You Need to Know

◆ Add beaded embellishments to woven fabric, leather, or beaded "fabric" you've woven on or off a loom.

◆ You have many choices of backing fabrics. Some are easier to work with than others, and some are more expensive than others. Experiment to find what best fits your application and your budget.

◆ Edgings and fringes add yet another dimension to your designs and finished pieces.

◆ You can make rosettes using the simple bead embroidery techniques you learned in Chapter 13.

In This Chapter

- ◆ Decorative knotting origins—from making rugs to today's revival

- ◆ Materials and tools you'll need for macramé and beaded jewelry and accessories

- ◆ Four basic knots you can use for a variety of projects

- ◆ A simple bead and macramé sampler

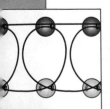

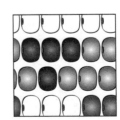

Chapter 15

Beads in Knots

The ability to tie knots has been a staple survival skill for thousands of years. If you're going to climb a mountain, carry water, rig a sail, or ride a horse, you'd better know how to tie a knot or two. But somewhere along the line, knots became more than just a utilitarian skill. They became an art. The people credited with developing the art of macramé, a system of decorative knots, are the Turkish rug weavers of the thirteenth century. What do you do with all those warp ends when you're done weaving a rug? Why not knot them in pretty patterns and create a fringe? Well, that's what they thought, and pretty patterns they were.

As the Arab world was conquered, this system of decorative knotting found its way to Spain and throughout Europe. Sailors, who already knew a thing or two about making knots, took the craft to sea and made hammocks and other decorative items in their spare time.

The height of macramé's popularity was in the nineteenth century, when it even found its way into middle- and upper-class Victorian parlors and on trims for dresses, linens, and many household items.

Macramé's popularity experienced a revival in the 1960s and 1970s, especially among the young. I still have the macramé-and-bead guitar strap I made in my "hippie" days! Macramé was easy to do; the materials were cheap and "natural"; and you didn't need any special, expensive tools to do it. Plus, it was completely portable. I used to tie my work first to a chair leg, and then, when the piece got longer, I tied it to my big toe, barefoot as I often was.

Macramé is again seeing a renewed popularity that's partially tied in with the current beading renaissance. The two techniques are made for each other. Neckpieces, belts, handbags, plant hangers, wall decorations, and jewelry are just a few applications for beads and macramé. Teenagers exchange friendship bracelets made with embroidery floss or very fine hemp, and 20-somethings have rediscovered tie-dye shirts and macramé jewelry.

But macramé has taken on a new face in the hands of serious beaders. The marriage of beaded cords, threads, and other fibers with the wide variety of beads now available is producing some unique and adventurous work. With knotted explorations in new fibers and beads, it's *knot* just your granny's craft anymore!

Findings

If you're serious about macramé, check out the International Guild of Knot Tyers website at www.igkt.net/ and find out how to join more than 1,000 other members worldwide. Among the membership list are academics, surgeons, sailors, sports men and women, Scouts, farmers, miners, magicians, ranchers, rodeo ropers, and anyone else—expert or beginner—interested in knotting. Who knew?

A Little String Goes a Long Way

The tools and materials for making decorative knotted items are actually quite few in number. If you want to keep it really simple, all you need are your fingers and some twine. Add a few beads, and you're all set! If you want to get more serious and have some greater variety, though, you'll want to know more about different fibers and their properties and perhaps invest in a few additional tools to make your experience a little easier and more fun.

Fiber for Knotting

Cords and strings for macramé are everywhere. You might even already have some lurking in drawers and boxes at home. Here's a short list of a few you might like to experiment with:

Jute This is the cheapest material for macramé you can find. Jute is basically packing twine and comes in various "plys," or numbers of twisted strands. Three- and four-ply are usually preferred for making finer macramé pieces and are ⅛ and ¼ inch in diameter, respectively. Be careful about mixing jute with water. It will come apart pretty quickly if subjected to moisture.

Hemp Hemp cord is categorized by strength or "pound test," as fishing line is. Most common are 20#, which is around 1 millimeter in diameter; 48#, which is about 2 millimeter; and 170#, which is about 4 millimeter. You can get it dyed, natural, or bleached as well as polished and unpolished. The most common form is natural.

The "new" macramé cords Since the "old days," lots of cords have appeared for macramé. Check out Crafty Cord, Amy Braid, Braided Elegance, and Bonnie Braid cords and see what you think! I've given you a source in Appendix B, plus you'll find many options in crafts and hobby stores.

Stringth This nylon beading cord comes in different sizes and colors and is another "new" material that's come into the hands of macramé and bead enthusiasts.

Mastex This nylon upholstery thread is 3-ply bonded nylon. It comes in colors, and #18 gauge is most popular for macramé.

Conso Another upholstery store find, Conso is also a 3-ply bonded nylon cord that comes in lots of colors. The most popular size for macramé is #18 gauge.

Perle or "pearl" cotton   If you've ever crocheted, you're familiar with this one. Perle makes a nice macramé material, especially for jewelry.

Embroidery floss   You can use as many strands of multiple-strand embroidery floss as you want. This is what the "kids" are using for friendship bracelets.

Soutache   This is a more unusual material, but I've seen some very attractive pieces done with soutache and silk cord. It is more familiar as a trim or embroidery fiber.

A-Bead-C's _____

Soutache is a flat, narrow braid in a herringbone pattern and is used for trimming and embroidery.

Waxed linen thread   You'll find this at leather supply stores in white, natural, black, and brown, but it is also available in colors. Search the Internet for "Irish Waxed Linen Thread."

Rattail   Remember when I talked about the various satin cords available (see Chapter 5 if you don't)? This one is the best for macramé and gives your projects a sumptuous look. It's slippery, so it might be a little difficult for the very early beginner, but practice a bit and you'll be up for it soon enough. It comes in lots of colors.

Leather cord   Check our your local Tandy or Leather Factory store for all sorts of possible macramé materials, including waxed linen thread and leather cord. P'leather, a simulated leather, also comes in cord. Both come in colors and different widths.

Silk thread   You can use silk thread in the larger sizes like FF and FFF for fine macramé work.

You can use lots of different "found" materials for macramé that weren't intended for it such as parachute cord, other twines, venetian blind cord, or anything else you discover. As long as it's flexible, has body, doesn't stretch, holds a knot well, and feels good against the skin (if it's going to be worn as jewelry), you can call it a macramé cord.

Put On Your Beadin' Cap _____

To raise your macramé creativity quotient, start looking at fibers wherever you go. Hardware stores, marine supply places, fabric and sewing departments, beading and crafts stores, leather supply outlets, and anywhere else that you find string, cord, or fibers are possible sources for unusual macramé materials. Ask yourself *How would this work for knotting?* and use the five is-it-good-for-macramé guidelines: flexibility, body, stretch (something you *don't* want), knotworthiness, and texture against the skin (if it's going to be worn). Then knot, er, knock yourself out!

Beads (Of Course!)

Consider the size of the bead hole when you're picking beads to use with macramé. Heavier cords require very large-hole beads. Natural items you can drill to enlarge the hole also make great macramé "beads." Remember, you'll often need to put two cords through one bead, so the hole must be able to accommodate at least two cords.

Some beads, often wooden, are sold specifically for macramé. They have extra-large holes for use with heavier cords. Take some sample cords with you when you go bead shopping, and try putting them through the holes to be sure they fit.

Odds and Ends

With a bigger macramé piece, it sometimes helps to have a surface to tack down your work as you go. A macramé knotting board is handy to hold wider pieces and is easy to make, using a clipboard and some corrugated cardboard or foam core. Clip the cardboard or foam core to your clipboard, and add a piece of graph paper to help you keep things on the straight and narrow. You can also use a small cork or bulletin board or a polyfoam macramé work board you can find in hobby stores.

You'll want some T pins to use with your board. These are heavy-duty pins with a T-shape head often used in upholstery. You can find them in most sewing and craft stores.

A crochet hook also might come in handy for pulling cords through the beads.

Depending on what you decide to make, consider gathering findings like key rings, belt buckles, clasps, watch face assemblies, or simple O-rings made of plastic, wood, or metal.

Knots Are Basic!

You probably already know some of the knots you'll use in macramé, such as the overhand and square knots. But don't worry, we'll review them anyway!

The half knot is just half of a square knot, and the lark's head is most likely something you've used before but just didn't know its name.

Ready to learn about knots? Then, let's begin!

Lark's Head Knot

Use this knot to set up your work for knotting. You'll need a mounting cord or some type of open finding to practice your knots on.

1. Start by tying a cord onto a chair leg or other solid surface. Then, cut another cord about 30 inches long.

2. Take the 30-inch cord you've cut, and fold it in half so you have a loop at one end. Push the loop behind the mounting device with the loop pointing downward. With your thumb and index finger, reach up through the loop and bring the loose ends down through the loop. Then tighten the loop down into a knot by pulling on the two free ends. You want the free ends to be the same length, and the knot should be very snug.

To practice your knots, you'll need four *working cords*. Cut 2 (30-inch) cords, attach both using the lark's head knot, and you'll have 4 working cords.

> **A-Bead-C's**
>
> In macramé, the **mounting cord** remains fixed and is used to hold additional cords for making knots. The **working cords** attach to the mounting cord and are used to create knots.

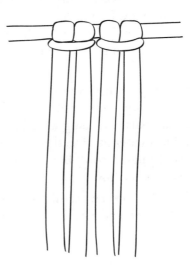

Setting up your working cords using the lark's head knot.

Overhand Knot

This is the simplest knot around. It's the one you make when you want to stop something from unraveling or knot a thread to begin sewing. Basically, you make a loop and bring one end up behind and through the loop in a figure eight.

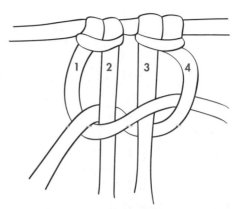

How to do a half knot.

How to do the overhand knot.

Half Knot or Half Square Knot

A half knot is one half of a square knot. Look at your four working cords, and in your mind number them 1 through 4 from left to right. Cords #2 and #3 will remain stationary, and you'll use cords #1 and #4 to make both this knot and the square knot.

1. Bring cord #1 across cords #2 and #3 but under cord #4.
2. Bring cord #4 under cords #2 and #3 and under and through the loop made by cord #1, bringing it toward the front.

3. Pull tight and snug up against your starting lark's head knots by pulling cords #1 and #4 out to the sides and keeping the tension between them even. As you tighten, periodically pull down on cords #2 and #3 to keep them straight. You can even pin them down if that helps.

If you continue making half knots, you'll notice your work will begin to twist in a spiral pattern. By just working this pattern with four working cords and adding beads at regular intervals, you can make an easy and attractive bracelet, anklet, or necklace.

Square Knot

To make a square knot, follow the procedure for making a half knot all the way to the end. Then do the same thing in reverse, using cord #4 as your starting point. Bring cord #4 under cords #2 and #3 and over cord #1. Bring cord #1 down under cord #4 and over cords #2 and #3, then up through the loop made by cord #4. Pull tight and slide the knot up against the first half you already made.

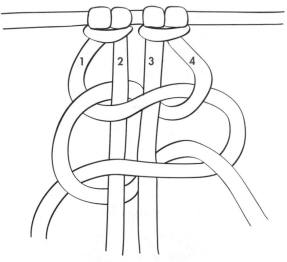

Making a square knot.

There you have it! A square knot. This is a strong knot and can be used with alternating groups of working cords to give you a flat pattern that fills space quickly. And as with the half knot, you can make another easy bracelet, anklet, or necklace using four working cords, tying square knots in succession, and adding beads at intervals—this time in a pattern that will lay flat rather than turn in a spiral.

> **Findings**
>
> For some very easy projects using the simple knots you just learned, plus a couple more, you'll enjoy *Hemp It Up With Beads* by Janie Ray for Suzanne McNeill Originals. I've given you complete information on this and other fun books for you to play with in Appendix B.

Getting Tied Up in Knots

You can now put together the knots you've just learned to create a small sampler.

You'll need a mounting cord or some other finding or material you can attach your working cords to. The mounting cord is the foundation for your knots and can be a piece of wire, a piece of natural wood or a dowel, a key ring, a clasp, a belt buckle, or even a curtain rod if you're making a window hanging or room divider.

For your sampler patch, which you can sew onto your beadin' cap, we're going to use a piece of heavy gauge wire (18 gauge would work well) that you've fashioned into loops at either end. You'll use the loops to attach your sampler patch to your cap. Or if you'd rather, you can substitute a key ring finding and make your own macramé-and-bead key ring.

Choose a fiber to work with. Hemp is a good choice, but if something else catches your fancy, give it a try. I'll be making my sampler out of 20-pound test hemp, but if you'd like to try perle cotton or some other fiber, be my guest. Just know that the diameter of the fiber will affect the size of your patch. Also remember that some materials are more slippery than others and are more difficult to handle.

1. Cut 4 working cords, each 30 inches long. You'll fold these in half, so you'll end up with 8 (15-inch-long) working cords after you've attached them to your mounting cord, wire, or other finding. These are the cords you'll be using to make your knots.

> **Knots!**
>
> Always cut more cord than you think you'll need. In fact, the general rule of thumb is to cut cord 8 to 10 times longer than the finished piece you desire. You'll use up a lot of cord doing knots, and it's basically impossible to add new cord.

2. Attach your working cords to your mounting device with a lark's head knot. (If you've forgotten how, review the process outlined earlier in this chapter.) If you're using a cord or wire, you might want to attach it to your knotting board with pins. I found that by bending my wire slightly it fit nicely under the spring clip on my macramé knotting board. If you're using a key chain finding, you can apply your working cords to the ring and then tie the ring to a chair rung or leg to pull against as you work.

3. Snug all 4 doubled and knotted cords up against each other in the center of your mounting device. Now you're ready to begin knotting.

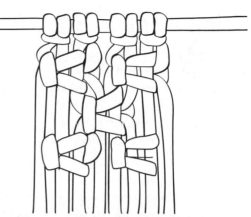

This is what your sampler should look like with the first 5 square knots worked.

Knots!

You can get tangled up with long cords if you're not careful. Once you've attached your working cords, make a little bundle of each cord by rolling it up and adding a rubber band or twist tie to keep it out of the way.

4. Divide your working cords into two groups of 4 cords. Make a square knot with the 4 working cords on the left, then do the same with the 4 working cords on the right. Be sure to keep your cords straight, and don't allow them to twist. Use pins to help you if you need to.

5. Next, make a new group of 4 with the working cords in the center. You should have 2 free working cords on either side of the center group. Make a square knot with the center group of 4 working cords.

6. Now separate your working cords into two groups of 4 again, and make a square knot with each of these groups. Keep your knots tight and close to each other.

7. Find a bead with a hole big enough to fit 2 working cords through (you'll probably want to use a pony bead with 20-pound test hemp), and slide it onto the 2 center cords. Slide it up snug against the square knots you made in step 6.

8. Make another square knot with the 4 center working cords, just below the bead.

9. Now, take the 4 working cords on the left side and make 6 half knots. Make your first half knot just below the square knot you made in the center. You'll end up with some space between knots. Slide another bead onto the 2 center cords of this 4-cord group, and work another 6 half knots. Finish off with a square knot.

10. Repeat this 6 half knot, bead, 6 half knot, square knot sequence on the right side.

11. To finish, tie a tight overhand knot with all the cords. Pull everything tight and trim.

Your finished macramé and bead sampler.

You're *Knot* Finished Yet!

You can finish your macramé piece in many ways, depending on what you're making. On our sampler piece, we could have chosen simply to knot each cord individually and create a different-looking fringe. We could add beads and knot them onto each cord or alternating cords.

If you were making a bracelet, you could make a knot-and-loop closure by beginning your work by knotting all your working cords in an overhand knot rather than using a mounting cord and ending them with one or more overhand knots that will slip through the beginning loop. This works best when using two folded pieces of cord for a narrow band of macramé.

Put On Your Beadin' Cap

Attach your macramé and bead sampler to your beadin' cap, or if you decided to make a key chain decoration, just add your keys!

If you want to learn more about macramé, *Hemp Masters: Ancient Hippie Secrets for Knotting Hip Hemp Jewelry* by Max Lunger will teach you all you would ever want to know about knots. And Wendy Simpson Conner's book *The "Knotty" Macrame & Beading Book* in her *Techniques for Beadlovers* series puts the emphasis squarely on beads with innovative ways of combining fiber and beads using knots.

The Least You Need to Know

◆ Macramé is a system of decorative knots that has many applications and is a natural companion to beading.

◆ Cords of all kinds can be used in macramé as long as they're flexible, have body, don't stretch, and hold a knot well. If the item made is going to be worn as jewelry, it also needs to feel good against the skin.

◆ Very few tools are needed for macramé. In fact, some twine, your fingers, and a few beads are enough to get started.

◆ With only 4 basic knots, you can make a large variety of items to wear as accessories or to decorate your home.

In This Part

Bead Potpourri

Now that you're a bead-a-holic, you need to know the rules for beading responsibly and safely. Part 5 will cover a few safe beading practices, tips on keeping it all together, hints on the best ways to care for and store your loose beads and finished beadwork, and some ideas for decorating with your beaded works.

In This Chapter

◆ Taking care of your eyes while beading and preventing eyestrain

◆ RSI—recognizing symptoms and keeping it from cramping your beading style

◆ Using adhesives and other chemicals safely

◆ Organizing your beading tools and materials so you can spend more time beading and less time dealing with bead clutter

◆ Traveling with your beadwork (You *can* take it with you!)

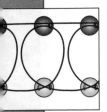    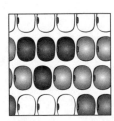 

Chapter 16

Work Safe, Work Organized

By now you've had a chance to experience the wonderful worlds of beading. There are so many different ways to enjoy this craft, and you may be "hooked" already. If this is the case, I'm truly happy for you. I know beading has given me many hours of joy.

But I need to warn you about a few things: Beading and other crafts can be hazardous to your health! Now, don't panic. A little common sense, mindfulness, and some simple precautions should take care of the few dangers. This chapter is just to serve as a reminder to take care of yourselves and the people (and critters!) around you. I'll also give you some tips on how to keep all that beading stuff from taking over your house.

The Eyes Have It

You've heard that your eyes are "the window to the soul," but they're also the window to your beadwork! Eyestrain isn't just the province of computer professionals; it's something anyone who does fine work for long periods of time needs to be mindful of.

But what are the symptoms of eyestrain? Ask yourself these questions to help determine if you may be straining your eyes:

◆ Do you have headaches during or after you do beadwork or any other vision-intensive activity?

◆ Are your eyes irritated, itchy, or dry, or any combination of these three things?

◆ Do you have periods of blurred vision and have trouble refocusing when you look up from your work at something in the distance?

◆ Do you often get lost when you look back and forth from your work and a beading pattern or set of instructions?

◆ Do you sometimes "see double" after working for an extended period?

◆ Do you notice any changes in your perception of color?

◆ Have you had to change your prescription for eyeglasses more frequently?

◆ Do you often finish beading with pain in your neck, back, or shoulders?

◆ Do you experience pain in your arms, wrists, or shoulders after extended beading sessions?

◆ Do you lose track of time and bead for more than an hour at a time without taking your eyes off your work or getting up to stretch?

If you answered "yes" to one or more of these questions, you may be abusing your eyes and should re-think your working conditions and habits.

Many of the things we can do to prevent eyestrain are just common sense, yet we fail to do them. It's easy to get absorbed in what we're doing and say to ourselves *Just one more bead* or *Just one more row* and forget the time and the toll our neglect is taking on our eyes.

However, if we don't take care of ourselves, we might not be able to do the things we love most. On top of beading, many of us are also heavy computer users, scanning the web for patterns, ideas, and materials or participating in beading e-mail groups. So now we're creating a "double whammy" of close work with small objects and, when we're not doing that, we're staring at the unrelenting video display terminal to pursue our hobby.

Well, dear beaders, there's hope! You can prevent eyestrain and some of beading's other occupational hazards with just a little forethought, preparation, and self-awareness:

◆ **Keep your eyes healthy.** When was the last time you had an eye exam? Are your glasses up to date? Do you keep them clean? Are they scratched? If you haven't had an eye exam lately—go get one! If your glasses are scratched, replace them. If they're dirty, well, you know the drill.

◆ **Keep your eyes lubricated.** Another cause of eyestrain in the arid climate I live in is dryness. We have very low humidity and have to be extra conscious of staying hydrated—and keeping our eyes lubricated. Indoor heating is also a culprit for eye dryness.

Blinking is the eye's natural lubricant. If we are staring at a computer screen or our beadwork, though, we might unconsciously reduce the number of times we blink.

That's why looking up frequently and taking breaks is so important. For every 1 hour of intense visual work, allot 15 minutes of rest for your eyes. Your body would probably appreciate a stretch as well!

Drink lots of water. Keep a bottle of natural tears at your work area and use them often. There's even a mist you can just spray into your eyes if you find that easier.

◆ **Give your eyes time to rest.** If your regular job involves heavy computer use or you engage in other activities that may promote eyestrain, you might want to reserve your beading time for weekends, when your eyes are more rested.

◆ **Get a close-up look.** Sometimes our regular eyeglasses are not enough. Magnifiers are available in many shapes and forms. Just using glasses with a higher magnification than normal can help. If you use a 2 power reading glass, step up to a 2.5 or 3 for beading.

Magnifiers are available in various styles that you might find work better. A head-mount magnifier is very helpful, and models are available with lights built in. One excellent brand that's quite affordable is Optivisor. These are large enough to fit over your regular glasses and are adjustable for comfort. Some have several choices for magnification that you can flip down.

◆ **Get a brighter close-up look.** Another option is a magnifying lamp. These come as clip-ons or can also be put on a stand. Couple this with a full-spectrum bulb or one of the new GE Reveal lightbulbs, and you've got an excellent vision aid.

◆ **See the light.** Be sure you have good lighting! Natural light is wonderful, but we can't always work in daylight or near a window. New lighting options can make a big difference, not only in preventing eyestrain but also in seeing bead colors more true to life.

One such option is the Ott-Lite. This is a special fixture that uses something called VisionSaver technology. I've used one of these lights and found it a real pleasure to work under.

◆ **Give yourself a break.** Even the best lighting and magnification are no substitute for frequent breaks and not overusing your delicate eyes. Just do it!

◆ **Wear safety glasses.** In addition to protecting your vision, you also need to protect your eyes from foreign objects. You'll soon learn that it's not hard to break a glass bead, flip a Delica into the air, or snip off a piece of wire only to have it go flying who knows where. Be sure to protect your eyes at all times with glasses or safety glasses.

Findings

An Ott-Lite is a special lighting option to help reduce glare and eyestrain for reading and doing any close work. To learn more about these special fixtures and bulbs, go to www.ott-lite.com.

General Electric has also just recently come out with a new lightbulb called Reveal. This gives a whiter, more true light; comes in various strengths; and is very affordable. To get the skinny on these new bulbs direct from the horse's mouth, point your browser to www.gelighting.com/na/reveal/media_faqs.html.

So please, beaders "old" and "new"—protect those eyes so you can bead for many years to come.

Fight Back Against RSI!

Another hazard of any repetitive activity is something called RSI or Repetitive Strain Injury. This is believed to be the precursor to the more serious carpal tunnel syndrome and can eventually require surgery. RSI is another condition more commonly associated with computer use, but craftspeople are also known to have symptoms and need treatment. And, again, because many craftspeople are also computer users, the possibility is compounded.

RSI actually begins in the neck and is a result of repeating certain physical movements over and over again in a rigid position. Contributing factors are poor posture, an inadequate working arrangement, age, diet, sedentary lifestyle, and fatigue.

I have suffered from the early stages of RSI, so I know it's no laughing matter. For me, the symptoms were constant aching in my elbow and lower arm; having my arm "go to sleep" fairly frequently; and losing strength in my hand, wrist, and arm. At times, my arm ached so much I had trouble sleeping. Luckily, I did my research, totally rearranged my workstation, adding several ergonomic pieces of equipment to help, and started a regimen of exercises, massage, and frequent breaks. I'm happy to say all my symptoms have disappeared.

Findings

Anatomically speaking, the causes of RSI are complex, and I won't go into them here, but many resources are available if you suspect you might have it or would just like to get informed. An excellent book—this is the one I used most to turn my own RSI around—to check out is *It's Not Carpal Tunnel Syndrome! RSI Theory and Therapy for Computer Professionals* by Suparna Damany and Jack Bellis. Some excellent free information is also available at eeshop.unl.edu/rsi.html. This is aimed at computer workers but is equally applicable to anyone doing work that could cause RSI. Take care of yourself!

Be sure you hold your tools properly. Some tools are available with ergonomic handles. Are you using the right tool for the job? I found switching to a bent-nose pliers for some operations in wirework, for example, was much easier on my wrist.

Look carefully at your chair and work surface as well. Are you using a comfortable chair? Does it encourage proper posture? Is your work surface at the right height? Is it cramped and full of debris or spacious and uncluttered? Beaders are beautiful people, and I want you to stay that way! I also believe a beautiful beader is a healthy beader. Give yourself a break—often!

Love Your Lungs

Another minor safety issue in beading is the use of adhesives and finishes that might do damage to the lungs or cause an allergic reaction. Very few of the adhesives used in beading give off toxic fumes, but some of the antique finishes for wire have some cautions.

The best rules of thumb are, again, common sense, but they do bear repeating. Follow these guidelines when using adhesives, dips, finishes, or sealers:

◆ Be sure you have adequate ventilation when using any kind of paint, glue, wash, or finish. If you can, work near an open window or work outside.

◆ Read the label! Whatever product you're using, don't just wing it. Read the label and *follow directions!* And remember, most adhesives are only good for 1 to 2 years. Throw them away if they've passed their "good" date.

◆ Also watch for reactions to adhesives and other chemicals such as rashes or hives. If you start to see an allergic reaction, discontinue their use and find a substitute.

◆ In some rare cases, if you tend to be very sensitive to a variety of chemicals, you might need to wear a mask. If it helps, do it. Most substances used in beading are nontoxic or quite mild, but there are always exceptions. It's up to you to take precautions and action if something seems to be causing problems for you or someone in your household.

Findings _____

If you're not sure about a substance, check the MSDS (Materials Safety Data Sheet). This is available from the seller or you might be able to find a copy online. Cornell University maintains an extensive MSDS search site at msds.pdc.cornell.edu/msdssrch.asp.

Pets Are People, Too! And Don't Forget the Kids!

Let's not forget the "little ones." It's easy to ignore our four-legged friends when we're happily beading away. But cats and dogs do the darnedest things. Our three felines have been known to bat things around the room and then chew on them when they got bored. I have to lock up my beading loom, or one of my cats will chomp on the warp threads. A small bead can choke an animal, and those unidentified flying objects from a beading session can also find their way into a pet's eyes or ears—or paws. Be careful!

Knots! _____

Watch those broken beads and pieces of sharp wire. They can hurt bare feet and paws. Don't wait to pick up the pieces if you see where they land, and sweep and vacuum regularly!

If you have small children in the house, you'll need to be especially mindful. Beads are a dangerous choking hazard. If you are the parent of a toddler or if you baby-sit often (Grandma!), you might have to confine your beading to one space that you can make off-limits to the rest of the household. Be observant, and be cautious.

And with regard to children and pets, something I mentioned earlier bears repeating. Some beads made from natural materials can be toxic. Look out especially for red beads made from plants. If you handle them, don't put your hands in your mouth unless you wash them first.

Remember that beads are also slippery when stepped on. Keep a tidy workplace and pick up after yourself!

The Organized Beader

You've been learning all these new beading skills, and now you've got a pile of *stuff!* How'd that happen? They might be small, but beads can take over your life—and your house. With the various tools, findings, threads, patterns, books, magazines, wire, and needles accumulating, suddenly you're swamped.

The basic principles of organization reign here, as always. Some of you might know I've written a book on that very subject: *The Complete Idiot's Guide to Organizing Your Life.* Here are some tips from that book to keep your beading life running smoothly:

- ◆ **What's essential and what's clutter?** This is a key to getting and staying organized in any realm. Do you really need to save every beading ad or magazine? Unless you write about beading like I do, you probably only need to keep the articles and patterns you're really going to use. Most beaders don't do every form of beading. What's your specialty? Perhaps you do wirework but not bead weaving or vice-versa. Why save *everything* to do with beading when you've actually settled on one or two areas of interest? If you don't use it, it's clutter!

- ◆ **Group like things together.** Keep all your wire together, all your stringing materials together, all your tools together, etc. Find containers best suited to each or a general container that stacks well and works effectively for all or most supplies. I like plastic shoeboxes. They stack, they're clear so I can see what's inside, and they accommodate most things to do with beading. For storing beads, I like divided boxes, like the kind you find in hardware stores for nuts and bolts. They also stack and come in clear plastic.

- ◆ **Consolidate and compress.** When you group like things together, before you know it, you find you have duplicates. Keep the best of what you have, and pass on the rest.

Knots! _____

Be sure your containers lock and if they're turned upside down, beads don't skip from one compartment to the next! There's nothing worse than having to sort a pile of beads after they've spilled out of an insecure container.

◆ **Alphabetize and label.** Putting things in alphabetical order might seem obsessive, but you'd be surprised how much time it saves. Patterns, information files, books—whatever lends itself to alphabetizing is worth the effort. And label, label, label! How many times do you have to go through that box because you forgot what's in it? Label it!

◆ **Go for quality, not quantity.** A few good tools are better than a lot of not-so-good ones. Invest in the best you can afford, and get rid of inferior things. Don't buy a better one and keep the old. That's how clutter starts!

◆ **Think multi-purpose, not single purpose.** People are in the business of selling things, and bead stores, craft stores, catalogs, and websites are no exception. But you don't need a special gadget for every little thing. Sometimes a special tool can make all the difference (I stand by my split-ring pliers and wire-straightening pliers any day!), but we can also talk ourselves into gimmicks and gadgets we don't really need. Look for tools and materials that have a variety of uses and reduce clutter.

◆ **Be realistic about your space and your time.** Before you bring it into the house, think, *Am I really going to use this? Do I have a place for it? Can I afford it?* If beading is your new favorite thing, what unfinished projects have you left behind? Part with them to make way for your beading adventures. Don't use beading as an excuse to add to your clutter! If you don't use it, lose it! Give it away to someone who loves your old craft.

◆ **Put it away.** Set up your work area so it's easy to put away your beads and other supplies, and have a spot to put your work in progress away from little paws and prying hands. If you work on your dining room table, you might be surprised to find what you thought was a green pea is—*gulp!*—a green bead!

In addition to organizing your supplies, you'll need to organize your ideas. Think about what you're doing now and develop a system. I have two: I have a file box with folders for each beading technique where I file articles and ideas. Then I have a set of binders with projects I really want to do organized by type—necklaces, bracelets, earrings, etc. These are contained in plastic sheet protectors, so when I take out the project, everything I need is together in its little plastic "envelope." My system might not work for you, so develop your own. Information is only as good as your ability to retrieve it!

Another helpful tool to help you organize and keep track of your ideas is one of several bead design software programs. I'm a Mac user, so I have *Beadscape*. It makes it easy to get my ideas for loom work or off-loom weaving designs down in a usable form, and I can store hundreds of designs on a disk or CD-ROM. If you're a PC user, you have your choice of the *Bead Pattern Designer* and *Autobead* combo, *BeadCreator*, *Bead Cellar*, *BeadWizard*, and *Bead Painter*. The technical editor for this book tested *Bead Pattern Designer* and *Autobead* and found it challenging but workable. In Appendix B I've given you information on where to buy these programs and in some cases download demos so you can try them out. *Bead Painter* is free for downloading.

Have Beads, Will Travel

If you really become a serious beader, you'll want to take your projects with you. That's not an easy thing, because spilled beads in a car can be even worse than spilled beads on a kitchen floor. Or how about trying to track down an errant bead in an airplane?

You'll have to be realistic about when and where you can bead, but I've taken small bead embroidery projects with me to a doctor's office totally contained in an empty Altoid's box—and I don't think I lost a single bead. Where there's a bead, there's a way.

There are cases specially created for transporting beads and tools for travel. One unit from Fire Mountain Gems has six plastic boxes with secure closures and various compartment configurations that all fit in a zippered case with a handle and shoulder strap. (I've given you their information in Appendix B.) I have this particular case and have taken it on car trips and even on an airplane, carefully packed in my luggage with padding around it. I wasn't able to bead in transit, especially with the new airline restrictions on sharp metal objects, but I had a virtual beading studio when I got to my destination. Additional boxes can be substituted, depending on what supplies you need at a particular time. Save reading your bead magazines or designing for the airplane!

Off- and on-loom bead weaving enthusiasts swear by this method for transporting those tiny sorted seed beads and Japanese cylinder beads: They use porcelain watercolor trays that have sections and look something like a flower. In each compartment is a supply of the different color beads they need for their project. When they want to pick up and go, they cover the watercolor tray with plastic wrap, lay the trays between the two foam layers of a pistol case (you read that right—a *gun* case!), and seal it shut. The beads can't escape no matter how you hold the case, and the individual trays can even be stacked for added capacity. Beaders have been known to share their sources for the cheapest pistol cases around. Who'd have thought? Like I said—have beads, will travel! Just be sure if you're taking your beads on an airplane, you're prepared to explain to authorities what's inside the gun case and open it for them. Are they ever in for a surprise!

The Least You Need to Know

- ◆ Eyestrain can be prevented by using proper magnification and good light, keeping your eyes lubricated, and taking frequent breaks.

- ◆ Repetitive Strain Injury (RSI) can be caused by activities other than computer use. Paying attention to posture and other working conditions, plus exercise and varying activity, can prevent RSI.

- ◆ Good ventilation is essential to working with adhesives and other chemicals.

- ◆ Be mindful of animals and children when working with beads, and pick up and put away your bead projects where they can't reach.

- ◆ Basic principles of organization apply to beading and other crafts. Keeping down clutter and organizing what you have will make beading a more rewarding experience.

In This Chapter

- ◆ Cleaning and caring for loose beads

- ◆ Keeping gemstones sparkling

- ◆ Caring for the metals in your beadwork and special measures required when they're combined with delicate stones

- ◆ Cleaning and storing finished beadwork

- ◆ Preserving beadwork on fabric

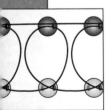

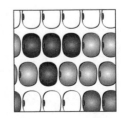

Chapter 17

The Care and Feeding of Beads

If you've been following our adventures in beadwork throughout this book, by now you have a stash of beads and some beautiful finished beadwork. *How*, you might be asking, *do I take care of these things and ensure they last for years to come?*

Generally speaking, beads are hardy souls, especially in their loose form or temporarily strung and stored away for later use. Once they've been strung on some sort of stringing medium or connected with wire or woven, they become a bit more problematic, but nothing we can't handle. By the end of this chapter, you'll know how to properly care for your beads.

Beware of the Destroyers!

Certain forces (I call them "the destroyers") in the environment—some natural, some manmade—can damage beads and beadwork:

◆ **Dust** makes beads and beadwork look dirty, dingy, and dull. It also contains tiny particles that can abrade the surface of some materials when friction is added.

◆ **Light** can fade colors and make things brittle. Just leave something on your car dashboard for a day in the sun, and you'll see what UV rays can do.

◆ **Moisture** can cause some materials to deteriorate—especially natural materials like wood. Some stringing media can break down and give out when exposed to water or even just sweat or humidity, and metals can rust.

Findings

Although most beads and stringing materials don't get along well with moisture, some semi-precious stones, like opals, actually like a good soaking now and then!

◆ **Chemicals** from suntan lotions, skin lotions, hair sprays, and perfumes are extremely damaging to some natural materials, both those used for beads and those used to create finished beadwork.

◆ **Friction** from storage of loose beads and finished beadwork can shorten their lives or alter their appearance. Throwing them in a heap in a drawer, wearing them to bed or while swimming, wearing several pieces of different hardnesses together, and designing pieces so beads rub against each other can lead to chips, cracks, broken beads, kinks, or scratches.

◆ Even **gravity** can take its toll on beadwork if it's hung for long periods of time. It can stretch and eventually weaken and break.

When you choose beads, create a storage system for loose beads, and take care of finished beadwork, you'll need to know a little about your materials and how best to take care of them.

Storing and Caring for Your Beads So They Last

First, let's talk about your raw materials. Before you attempt a beading project that will take many hours to complete, thoroughly test your beads. Galvanized, color-lined, pearlescent (sometimes called Ceylon), and other coated beads can lose their finishes over time. This is better to know now than later.

Findings

A knowledgeable bead store employee should know whether a finish is permanent or not. Most AB (aurora borealis) or Iris finishes are permanent. I have used both of these beads for years and have had no noticeable fading or loss of finish.

Once you've made your bead choices, your storage choices can also affect what kind of shape your beads will be in when you're ready to use them.

If your beads are in containers and remain on a shelf most of the time, they're not going to get a lot of jostling around and probably won't suffer from a lot of friction. But if you travel, your beads could get some pretty rough treatment. Beads with special finishes or delicate lampworked glass beads can really suffer, so think about how you have things stored before you take off for Timbuktu. You might want to have separate containers for special beads or have them wrapped in cotton or another soft material for traveling. Simulated pearls and any other bead that has a coating or "skin" needs to be stored and handled with care.

Wood and some other natural materials suffer from extremes of temperature and humidity, so consider this when storing them for periods of time or transporting them to different climates.

You can clean most beads with just a soft cloth. Most can be subjected to some warm water and, if necessary, a mild clear soap (colored soaps can sometimes transfer the color to the more porous materials). A toothbrush gives you a little more cleaning power, and some beads will benefit from the addition of a little toothpaste, too. Still others can be put into an ultrasonic jewelry cleaner, but be considerate of their fragility and porosity. Stay away from ammonia or alcohol cleaners if you decide to use one. The above are general cleaning methods, appropriate for most glass beads and hard stones.

Knots!

If you decide to use an ultrasonic cleaner, take the beads off temporary stringing media first, and try one sample before putting them all in. Stringing material can swell and become very difficult to remove from the bead holes and an ultrasonic cleaner can craze, crack, or chip some beads. Better be safe than sorry!

Stone Savvy

Although something made of stone seems invincible, some stones are actually quite fragile and need special care. One of the most fascinating side trips you will take as you journey down the beading path is that of learning about gems and minerals, metals, and other materials used in making beads and jewelry.

Not So Tough

Gemstones are categorized by hardness measured by the *Mohs hardness scale.*

A-Bead-C's

The **Mohs hardness scale** is a comparison scale of how a mineral reacts when scratched with a pointed testing object. This scale of scratch hardness, ranging from 1 (softest) to 10 (hardest) was introduced by Viennese mineralogist Friedrich Mohs (1773–1839). The softest on the scale, talc, can be scratched with a fingernail. The hardest is the diamond.

Stones with a Mohs scale hardness of less than 8 are most subject to scratching, but stones higher on the scale can still chip or crack. According to *Gemstones of the World* by Walter Schumann, anything below a 7 can be damaged by dust, as it may contain small particles of quartz—itself a Mohs hardness of 7. You must carefully handle and store these stones.

The following table lists some of the most common stones you may find made into beads and their hardnesses.

Mohs Hardness Scale	
10	Diamond
9	Ruby, Sapphire
8.5	Alexandrite, Cubic zirconia
8	Topaz
7.5 to 8	Aquamarine, Beryl, Emerald
7 to 7.5	Iolite, Tourmaline
7	Citrine, Amethyst, Quartz, Rock crystal
6.5 to 7	Garnet, Agate, Chalcedony, Chrysoprase, Jadeite, Jasper, Peridot, Tanzanite, Tiger's-eye

continues

continued

Mohs Hardness Scale	
6 to 6.5	Amazonite, Aventurine, Labradorite, Moonstone
5.5 to 6.5	Hematite, Opal, Sodalite
5.5	Moldavite
5 to 6	Lapis Lazuli, Turquoise
5	Apatite, Glass
4	Fluorite
3.5 to 4	Malachite
3 to 4	Coral, Howlite
2.5 to 5.5	Serpentine
2.5 to 4.5	Pearl
2.5 to 3	Gold, Silver
2 to 2.5	Amber, Cinnabar

Knots!

Amber and Cinnabar are only 2 to 2.5 on the hardness scale. Handle with care!

Suds for Your Stones

When cleaning gemstones, think both about the stone itself and the stringing medium the stones are on. Many gemstones are very porous and easily stained. Do not use an ultrasonic cleaner, commercial cleaner (although you can use commercial pearl cleaner), or silver cleaning solution. Just use warm water or a very mild soap. If you have a mixture of stones, you'll have to treat them according to the weakest or most delicate component on the piece.

Start with the most gentle cleaning solution and work up. Generally, just some dusting or a damp cloth will suffice. If that's not enough, move up to some warm water. Still not clean? Add a very mild clear soap (not detergent) and water. Dry with a clean, lint-free cloth, and you're good to go.

The next step up might be a weak solution of ammonia and water. This should be safe for stones with Mohs hardness of 7 or higher. A little scrubbing with a soft toothbrush should also be all right. If you have a loose sample of the beads, try cleaning that first before you work on the finished piece. Whenever you can experiment on a sample first, by all means do it!

Porous stones like opals, turquoise, malachite, pearls, or coral discolor easily and are quite fragile. Take them off when you're doing vigorous exercise or work and avoid subjecting them to suntan oils, sweat, perfumes, or lotions.

Ultrasonic cleaners are effective for some things but can be very stressful to others. Opals, pearls, coral, amber, turquoise, lapis, malachite, and tanzanite are just a few stones that are not good candidates for ultrasonic cleaners. If you're not sure, don't do it! These stones are also sensitive to heat, so don't leave them sitting in the sun or in a hot car.

Knots!

Avoid using an ammonia-based jewelry cleaner when you're not sure it's safe for the stone. Many jewelry cleaning solutions for ultrasonic cleaners contain ammonia or alcohol, so you'll want to check that out before using it on your jewelry.

Some people swear by using denture cleaner tablets like Efferdent or Polident. I have used them on clear glass, and they worked like a charm. I'm not sure how this would work on certain coatings, but you could certainly do a sample and find out. Just put your beads in a glass bowl or jar, cover with water, and add a tablet or two. Wait until the tablet stops fizzing, dump the water (a colander works well here to catch the beads and allow the water to flow through), then rinse with clear water. Lay them out on a clean towel to dry.

Sometimes you can't avoid damaging your beads, and you just have to go with it. If the coating is coming off your glass beads and you want to remove it altogether, CLR (a lime remover), Dow Bathroom Cleaner, or chlorine bleach are all ways I've seen mentioned to get it off. *But do not mix these chemicals!* Choose one and put it in a glass jar, then add your beads. Let them sit for a couple days, and the coating should peel off. If one choice doesn't work, rinse the beads and try another.

Pearls are in a class by themselves. Store loose pearls with care. They are especially susceptible to acids, and even body oils and perspiration contain some acids. Wipe pearls with a soft tissue before and after wearing. Don't use any acid-containing substances like detergents, hair spray, or perfume if your pearls are going to lie directly on your skin. And never let pearls come into contact with alcohol, ammonia, bleach, or swimming pool water.

Findings

Want to wear perfume *and* pearls? Consider putting your scent on a cotton ball and tucking it in your bra or putting it behind your ears and on your wrists, but not where the pearls will be. Always apply hair spray before you put on your pearls. Wear pearls over clothing to be safer still.

Don't wear pearls in combination with harder items that can rub against and score them. Use clear, mild, unscented soap and warm (not hot) water to clean your pearls. A pearl cleaning solution works well, too. Dry and polish with a clean, soft dry cloth. Don't store pearls with other jewelry, and have them restrung (or do it yourself) every two years or so with normal wear or once a year if you wear them a great deal.

Pearls can be damaged by cold, especially if they're set on a metal peg. Temperature swings are not good for most soft materials. The care instructions here are also good for mother-of-pearl, conch cameos, and abalone.

Amber is another material that is very sensitive to chemicals and harsh treatment, so beware. Keep it separate from other jewelry. If amber is combined with metal, put a piece of soft cloth around the amber beads to protect them from being abraded by the metal beads.

Opals are another special case. These do not like soaps or detergents at all, but they love water and hate to be dry. Soak your opals in room temperature distilled water or mineral oil now and then. They'll thank you for it. And keep them at even temperatures. They become susceptible to cracking when exposed to extremes of temperature, especially high heat.

Findings

Pearls, opals, and amber like to be worn. They like the natural oils from your skin, just not heavy acid perspiration or chemicals from perfumes, cosmetics, or lotions.

Other natural materials like ivory, horn, and bone like moderate temperatures and humidity. They're not too fond of lots of sunlight, although ivory benefits from some sunlight to keep it from yellowing. Also be aware that bone can absorb odors. Don't immerse these in water, but clean with a damp cloth and wipe dry with another clean, soft cloth.

Metal-Minded

Metals have their own care requirements, and when certain metals are combined with stones or pearls, they present some special challenges. Let's take a look at the most common ones you're likely to encounter.

Sterling Silver

If the item you need to clean is strictly made of silver, you can use the same cleaner you'd use for your silver flatware. Several good ones are on the market, and everyone seems to have his or her favorites. Just be sure you follow the manufacturer's directions.

Knots!

Humidity and heat speed up silver tarnishing. Bleach, acids, salt, and sea air can do damage. Take off your jewelry if you're going in the water, sunbathing, or housecleaning.

You can also whip up some good natural silver cleaners in your kitchen. Try this one: Let your silver set in the water from boiled potatoes for a couple hours and then wipe it dry. You can find more tips like these in many household hints books.

If you're not going to wear your silver for a while, wrap it in an anti-tarnish cloth or bag and then in plastic. But don't put it directly in plastic, as you could trap in moisture and make it tarnish more quickly.

You can wash silver with mild soap or detergent and very hot water. Dry it thoroughly and quickly. Washing with hot water helps clean it and makes it dry faster, according to Cheryl Mendelson, author of *Home Comforts: The Art and Science of Keeping House*. She also recommends consulting the Society of American Silversmiths for any questions concerning silver care. Their website is located at www.silversmithing.com.

Difficulties arise when you combine silver and other materials, as you do in beaded jewelry. Porous gemstones such as lapis lazuli, malachite, turquoise, coral, or pearls cannot be put into silver cleaning solutions.

If you have a combination, try to isolate the silver parts and wipe them with a treated cloth, avoiding the stones altogether. This can be difficult, though. When you can't avoid the stone, use only a cleaning option that is safe for the stone. Just clean with some warm water and polish dry with a soft cloth. Sometimes simple buffing can remove surface tarnish from the silver areas.

Silver Plate

Silver plate can be treated in much the same way as sterling, and the same cleaners are effective, but the same cautions apply to cleaning silver plate coupled with gemstone beads or other natural materials as sterling silver. Warm water and a soft cloth is often all that's needed. Abrasion wears off the plating, so keep this to a minimum, and know that over time the plating will eventually wear off. The best thing you can do is to try to prevent tarnish.

Gold Plate and Gold-Fill

Because gold doesn't really tarnish, some warm water and a clean cloth is usually all you need to keep it clean. Step up to clear soap and water, giving it a good final rinse. Let the other materials combined with the gold or gold fill be your guide when picking cleaning solutions.

Beads in Time: Taking Care of Your Finished Beadwork

Sometimes all you need to do to make something sparkle again is get rid of that outer layer of dust! Blow off dust from fine items using a can of pressurized air you can buy in camera or computer stores. Or simply rub your beaded item lightly with a soft cloth.

Moisture can damage some beading threads over time. Be careful about submerging finished beadwork—especially older beadwork—in water. The same applies to coming in contact with body oils, perspiration, perfume, and lotions.

One of the greatest threats to finished beadwork is the tangles! Keep the clasps fastened, and check them periodically to be sure they're holding fast. Store beads uncoiled. This is especially true with beads strung on flexible wire. If it's stored carelessly, it can kink and stay that way! Don't hang beadwork, either. Gravity will cause it to stretch or sag, and it can break eventually. Lay jewelry flat, and keep it separated in a jewelry box or flat stacking display boxes (available from jewelry supply stores and catalogs; see Appendix B).

Beaded Fabrics

I talked a bit in Chapter 13 about beads on fabric and some precautions to take. The real time to start thinking about care, though, is before you create your beaded item. Before you even apply any beads to fabric, you might want to ask your dry cleaner to run a sample through the cleaning process a few times and compare this with a sample of the original beads and fabric.

Findings

Be sure to choose a dry cleaner who is a member of the International Fabricare Institute (IFI). (Cleaners prominently display membership signs if they are.) Their members are educated in the care of all kinds of fabrics, old and new, and special process items, plus they will stand behind their work.

If you need help finding a good dry cleaner who can handle beaded items, call costume rental shops or theater companies and ask who they use. Any groups who wear period clothing, including living history, museum, and reenactment organizations, will probably know who to send you to. When you find some recommendations, talk to the owner and ask questions. Explain what you plan to do and get his or her reaction. Expect to pay more for expertise and service!

Usually glass beads or those made from semi-precious stones can be dry cleaned, but the finishes or coatings might not survive. Metal beads can change color, and you might have to polish them again after the cleaning process to bring them back—unless you like the more "vintage" patina.

If fabric is machine washable, the beads used are colorfast, and the thread used is machine washable, you can turn the fabric inside out to launder or put in a fabric pouch. You don't want the beads to break against the drum of the washing machine, so you need to cushion the blows. Hand washing will probably be best in most cases. Reshape knitted fabrics by laying out the garment on a thick towel and air drying.

Applying beadwork as an appliqué or removable trim is a smart option. This is often done by good clothiers. In our modern age of Velcro, you can make your beaded decoration so you can remove it or, if it's sewn on, cut the stitches and reattach the piece after cleaning.

Knots!

Be sure a trim is colorfast before applying beading to it and then adding it to fabric. Some dyes are colorfast in water, but not in dry-cleaning solvent. You don't want it to bleed, and if you're not sure, ask your dry cleaner to test it for you.

Always preshrink any trim or fabric you're going to add beadwork to. Be sure your trim and fabric match in the way they need to be cleaned. In other words, don't put "dry clean only" trim on washable fabric or vice versa.

It might seem like there's a lot to know in taking care of beadwork, but it all comes down to some fairly simple rules. Be gentle! Use the least-powerful cleaning methods first and work up. Don't use any chemicals unless you need to and you're sure they're safe. And get yourself a good reference book about gems so you know how to take care of them or refer to various online sources that I've given you in Appendix B. Simple—and your beadwork will be around for years to thank you for it!

The Least You Need to Know

◆ Loose beads can chip or crack if they are not carefully stored, especially if they're going to be jostled while traveling.

◆ A good reference that gives the hardness of gemstones is helpful in determining how to clean them.

◆ Preventing tarnish to silver and silver plate is one way to minimize the risks of damaging stones that are paired with them.

◆ Take care in finding a good dry cleaner to clean your beaded fabrics, and don't expect to pay the lowest prices. Look for one who's a member of the IFI.

◆ Making decorative beadwork removable from fabric is a sure way of prolonging its beauty.

In This Chapter

◆ Surrounding yourself with beaded glitz at home

◆ Making beaded "jewelry" for your car

◆ Gifting friends and family with your beaded creations

◆ Creating bead dreams for the holidays

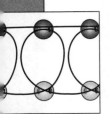
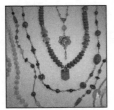

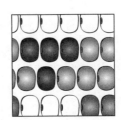

Chapter 18

Beads Everywhere: Decorating With Beadwork

Now that you know how to do so many things with beads, don't you just want to bead the world? One bead artist, Liza Lou, did just that! Well, maybe not the world, but a kitchen and a backyard at least.

If you've never seen Liza's beaded exhibits, you've missed a woman with beads gone wild. Liza takes mundane objects and scenes of suburban domestic bliss and covers them with thousands and thousands of glass seed beads. *The Kitchen* is a 168-square-foot 1950s room in which every surface is covered with glittering glass beads. It took 5 years to complete. *The Backyard*, with more than 250,000 hand-beaded blades of grass, took 2 years after the artist got a grant and could find helpers to do some of the beading for her. In between, Liza beaded the *American Presidents*, an installation containing 42 beaded portraits of our country's leaders.

Even if you don't want to bead the whole world, just your corner of it, in this chapter, we're going to explore a few ideas for letting beads decorate every aspect of your life.

Beads Around the House

Let's put on our beadin' caps and look at our rooms in the beaded way to add glamour, glitz, and color.

Dinner Is Served

Let's start in the dining room. Beads are a natural for gracing your table, whether for special occasions or every day. Beads can make every mealtime special.

◆ **Napkin rings.** Use galvanized wire for your ring—or use memory wire if you want some spring to your ring. You can use an assortment of bead sizes on two or three coils of memory wire or keep the beads all one size for a more tailored look. Make a loop at one end of the wire, add your beads, and make a loop at the other end to secure. If you're not using memory wire, wind the wire around a round object such as a plastic bottle to create as many rows of wired seed beads as you want, then thread fine wire across the rows, much as you learned to do bracing in Chapter 12 on beaded flowers, to secure the loops together.

You can use one of the stretch cords we talked about in Chapters 5 and 6 for your napkin ring. Make it just as you would a stretch bracelet, only smaller.

Then you have the "cheater" method! Just take a smooth-surfaced store-bought napkin ring, cover it with glue, roll it in seed beads, and then let it dry! What could be easier than that?

Or you can make a cloth ring from patterned fabric and accent the pattern with beaded embroidery. You can also use one of your off-loom weaving stitches to create a solid bead-woven ring, or do it on your loom.

Or how about a single beaded flower added to a premade napkin ring or some heavy gauge wire twisted together in a ring? I've seen some beautiful ones that run more than $20 each. Whatever you see in the stores or catalogs, you now have the skill to duplicate it yourself!

Variations on these would be great as favors for a wedding or baby shower, anniversary party, or holiday party. Teach your kids or party helpers one of these easy beading techniques if you have a lot to make.

◆ **Serving wine?** How about adding a beaded cover that fits over the neck of the wine bottle and gracefully hangs down? Let it catch the candlelight and add sparkle to your romantic evening dinner parties. You learned how to do the netting stitch in Chapter 7 on off-loom weaving. Just make your first circle large enough to fit over the neck of the bottle and net out from there. Add some crystal drops to your outer row, and you've got a knock-out table accessory. You can also use this technique to cover perfume bottles in the boudoir or bathroom and glass balls for Christmas ornaments. Think gifts!

◆ **Dining in the great outdoors?** Keep those nasty gnats and flies out of the lemonade with a set of weighted doilies to cover open pitchers and add some old-fashioned homemade appeal to your table. Purchase a premade crocheted doily (or pick up some vintage ones at a thrift or antiques store), sew some sheer fabric on the underside, and weight the edges with some heavier beads in dangles or drops using a needle and thread. These also make great hostess gifts.

In the Bedroom

You can let your imagination go wild in here! I'm lucky to have a husband who leaves the bedroom decorating completely to me. (He gets the family room!) I like romantic Victorian touches in the bedroom, so I can go beady anywhere I like. The same also applies if you're a more modern gal.

◆ **Got a light?** Lampshades offer endless opportunities for beading, from simple beaded touches to all-out beaded Victorian works of art.

You can just add simple beaded touches to any lampshade. Find some trim in your local fabric or crafts store, and add one of the beaded fringes we learned in Chapter 14. Then carefully glue the trim onto your existing lampshade. Add beaded tassels or fiber tassels with beaded embellishment to lamps, fan or shade pulls (I've given you complete instructions for a fan pull in Chapter 19), even a key that resides in a keyhole. How about making a beaded tassel for the doorknob?

This beaded fan pull is easy to make and will add some sparkle to any room.

Findings

If you want to "go for it" and learn how to do Victorian lampshades from scratch, plenty of books and other instructional aids are available to help you. One such book is *The Beaded Lampshade Book* by Wendy Simpson Connor. Wendy's book is a general exploration of these light-catching wonders. If you want to make the fussy Victorian kind, the *How to Make Victorian and Antique Style Lampshades* video will tell you how. Get your supplies, including forms for making fabric-covered and beaded nightlights, books, and videos from www.sugarshades. com or Mainely Shades at 1-800-624-6359 or www.vintageshades.com/.

◆ **Sweet sachets.** Speaking of doorknobs, you can hang sachets embroidered with beads from doorknobs as well, or make a bunch for your drawers. Again, think gift ideas! Know anyone getting married or engaged?

◆ **Pretty pillows.** Pillows with beaded embellishment can empty your wallet faster than a New York minute, even in the discount stores. Instead, why not make your own pillow cover out of a pretty floral or paisley print and embellish both the design and the edges with beads? A simple pattern embroidered on satin makes a smashing pillow for a sumptuous boudoir. (You learned how to do all these in Chapters 13 and 14, remember?)

◆ **Covered with beads.** A purchased throw or lap blanket can also go from ho-hum to wow! with a little added beadwork.

Mirror, Mirror ...

Now, let's move on to the vanity. The possibilities are endless here, too:

◆ **Frame it up!** Use your beading skills to frame a mirror. Embroider a fabric-covered frame, glue beads onto a store-bought one, or make vines of beaded flowers and arrange them around your mirror.

> **Findings**
>
> Peyote stitch is great for covering things (go back to Chapter 7 for a refresher if you need it). You'll need to learn to increase and decrease, and Barbara Grainger's *Peyote at Last* shows you how, plus Barbara's an expert at creating peyote-covered vessels and implements. Check out the bead magazine sites I've given you in Appendix B for lots of articles on the subject.

◆ **Got a (night) light?** Bead a nightlight cover. Just take off the plastic one that came with it, and form wire around it. Some small beaded flowers or one larger one (or how about some leaves?) make a less-than-inspiring everyday item into something really special.

◆ **More bottles.** The beaded bottle covers I mentioned for wine bottles look lovely on bubble bath and bath oil bottles, too.

◆ **Flowers.** Fill a clear vase with loose beads, add water and some fresh flowers— or bead some that last forever.

Beads Where You Live

Next, let's look at the living room. Some of the ideas we used in the bedroom can work here as well. Pillows, lampshades, throws, and pulls can all be embellished with beads for the living room. And a beaded mirror or picture frame takes those objects from just "there" to *there!* Want more ideas?

◆ **Curtains.** Make curtains more interesting and lush with beaded trims and tiebacks.

  Beaded room dividers and curtains are major projects, but not out of your depths when you get some more practice. Attach beads to a curtain rod or wooden dowel and create your own casbah. Think exotic! Add some beaded votive candleholders (see the next bullet), and you've got mood, not just a TV room. You just might forget to turn on the TV!

◆ **Candlelight.** Candles and beads are made for each other. Take a purchased glass candle holder, and glue stringed seed beads around the entire holder or use wire to wrap it instead. Formed wire with beads can also make an interesting holder for a purchased votive candle cup. Wall sconces and candelabra become something more with beaded dangles or floral vines twining around them. If weight is a problem, you can use plastic beads although glass adds the real sparkle.

◆ **Coasting on.** Beaded coasters add beauty to a useful item in any room. Back them with felt or cork to give furniture extra protection. Or embroider directly on the felt using the backstitch you learned in Chapter 13. Or simply use a set of cork coasters as a base, cover one side with glue, and lay still-hanked seed beads in a spiral on the coaster in close rows starting at the center. You can use straight pins to help you. Detailed directions are available on the Martha Stewart Living website at www.marthastewart.com.

Sew What?

The sewing room is an ideal place for some beaded accessories:

◆ **Needle me this.** Cover a needle case with beads in tubular peyote stitch. (The empty wooden needle cases can be purchased from a variety of sources that I've given you in Appendix B. Try Fire Mountain Gems or even your local craft or beads store.)

Findings

There's a book just on beaded needle case patterns. *Beaded Needlecases* by Jeannie Might teaches you how to make 20 real beauties for yourself or to give your favorite needlecrafter.

◆ **Pincushions.** Pincushions embroidered with beads were favorites with nineteenth-century needleworkers, and they've found their way back into our sewing rooms. Many of these were made by Native American beaders and sold to tourists throughout the United States. You can find some antique ones on eBay or from some favorite Victorian tourist spots like Niagara Falls, Chicago, and New York. *Embroidery and Cross Stitch Magazine* has had some lovely patterns for these, so look for back issues.

The instructions are easy: Trace your shape on the wrong side of a piece of scrap velvet, then cut. You'll need two pieces, one for the top and one for the bottom. A high-top shoe, a heart, or a strawberry are all popular shapes. Do your beadwork on the top piece before you construct the cushion. Then sew the edges, right sides together, leaving a small gap large enough to stuff with sawdust, bran, or other filler. Tuck in the raw edges of the opening, and slip-stitch it closed. I've given you even more detailed instructions in Chapter 22. Think gifts, and have fun!

Embroidered pincushions are great to give as gifts—or keep for yourself!

Put On Your Beadin' Cap

Want to get some creative ideas for free? Go shopping! Beaded items are hot right now. You'll surprise yourself when you go to home decorating and accessories stores and look at their expensive beaded items because you know how they did that! Take a few notes, then go home and make your own to suit your décor for far less.

◆ **Cutting edge.** Scissors cases are also another Victorian sewing basket staple. You can make these of anything you like, as long as it's sturdy and decorated with beads. There's a pattern for one in the June/July 2001 issue of *Beadwork* magazine (see Appendix B for information on purchasing back issues), and I've seen some nice kits available online and elsewhere.

◆ **Knit-and-bead.** If you knit or crochet, you can also add beads to those techniques and make beautiful items. There's a pattern for a bead knitted scissors case in Jane Davis's *The Complete Guide to Beading Techniques*.

For the Baby

If you're expecting a baby or know someone who is, why not forego the usual baby quilt or blanket and bead something for baby's room?

◆ **Hanging beads.** How about a dreamcatcher to hang in baby's window or a beaded lampshade? Or make a mobile of bead and wire stars or snowflakes.

◆ **Announcing …** I've seen some adorable baby announcements made with rubber stamps and little alphabet beads with either "Baby" or the baby's name strung on elastic and attached to the card. Check out the www.impressrubberstamps.com to see how it's done.

◆ **Little trims.** A nightlight cover would be great in the nursery, too, or some beaded trims for curtains. Always remember to keep beads out of baby's reach.

You're just getting started, I'm sure. Now that you've covered your house in beads, let's take our act on the road.

Beads on the Road: Car Jewelry

Just because you've got to commute doesn't mean you need to leave your beads at home:

◆ **For your keys.** Bead a key chain for yourself like we did in Chapter 15 using simple macramé knots or, using heavy gauge wire and some chunky beads, just add a dangle to a key ring.

The macramé sample you made in Chapter 15 would work as a key chain. Just add a key ring finding instead of wire.

◆ **Dangling.** Add a sun-catcher to hang from your rear-view mirror. Just be sure it's not distracting, and don't let it impair your vision in any way. String some faceted beads on flexible wire with an old chandelier crystal at the end. Secure with a crimp, and leave a loop large enough to fit over both the mirror and the mirror post or use a clasp to help make it easier to get on and off. Add some charms if you want. I've given you even more detailed instructions for making a sun-catcher in Chapter 19.

A sun-catcher such as this might make sitting in traffic bearable!

Give the Gift of Beads

I've already given you lots of ideas so far for your own house and car that would make a great gift for someone you love. Here are some more!

◆ **For bookworms.** Beaded bookmarks are great for the reader in your family or circle of friends. They can be woven or bead embroidered or made from flattened wire with a bead dangle added to the end. I've given you instructions for making a beaded bookmark using a prefabricated bookmark finding in Chapter 21. They can even be as simple as some satin ribbon with some interesting beads knotted on one end.

Make a fun bookmark for your favorite bookworm.

Findings
Mill Hill Glass has some beautiful counted bead embroidery bookmark kits. Check them out at www.millhill.com. Or just transfer your favorite pattern to your cross-stitch medium of choice and work it on your own.

You can make a quick beaded bookmark with some fancy wide ribbon by adding some beaded fringe to the ends. Just stitch the raw edges of the ribbon under, and use the instructions from Chapter 14 to add some straight or netted fringe. It's quick and easy!

◆ **Jewelry!** Now that you know how to bead, you can make jewelry your favorite folks can't find anywhere else.

Make a birthstone bracelet. See Appendix C for a birthstones chart, or pick beads that are healing or that connect to the chakras if that's your interest.

Make a grandma's bracelet, with beads representing each of the grandchildren's birthdays.

Match your giftee's favorite outfit, or make a wedding ensemble for the bride-to-be.

Findings
Looking for more ideas? There are tons of them—free—on the Internet. Go to Home and Garden Television's website at www.hgtv.com, for example, click on Crafts and search for "beads" or "beaded." You'll get a list a mile long.

Michael's and Ben Franklin store websites also offer lots of ideas. Direct your browser to www.michaels.com and www.benfranklin. com, and you'll have enough projects to check off everyone on your gift list way before the holidays. Think ahead, and when you make one gift, make a few and put them away for a last-minute birthday or get well pick-me-up.

◆ **Put on your beadin' cap!** You made a beaded cap for yourself, now why not make some as gifts? Embroider any design you like, add some charms, and you've got a custom baseball cap that reflects your favorite person's personality. Kids just love these with their hobbies or their names represented on them.

◆ **Beaded boxes.** Boxes lend themselves to beaded decoration. Glue beads on, or cover the box with fabric you've embroidered with your beaded design. Or try your hand at beaded pin embroidery. If you know a tobacconist or someone who smokes cigars, ask him to save his wooden boxes. Some of them are quite nice and would make great foundations for beaded embellishment.

A Beader's Holiday

You've got lots of gift ideas for the holidays, and I can tell you there are lots more out there! We don't want to forget decorating, though, and now that you can bead, this holiday will glitter the absolute most.

◆ **For the tree.** Beaded ornament covers are similar to the netted bottle covers I described earlier and look gorgeous on a tree—or you can purchase special hangers to display your covered ornaments year-round. Just make them so the center ring is big enough to slip over the hangers of the size of glass ball ornaments you've chosen. Clear balls show off the bead-work, and colored ones become part of the design. Bead magazines have more elaborate versions every year, so check the *Bead&Button* and *Beadwork* sites for back issues or articles to download. I've given you detailed instructions for making a netted ornament cover in Chapter 20.

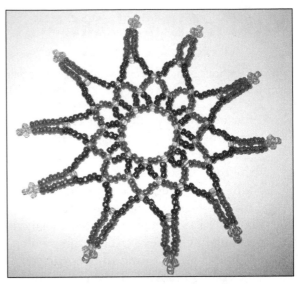

Add some sparkle to your—or your friend's—tree with a beaded ornament cover.

Bead and wire creations are great for the tree as well. Make a beaded poinsettia, angels, or snowflakes (instructions for one version of a beaded snowflake are in Chapter 21) for this year's tree. Kits and instructions are available in books and on a variety of websites. Go surfing for free beaded patterns—there are tons of them!

Let it snow, let it snow, let it snow …

Other types of beaded ornaments are made with Styrofoam balls, straight pins, beads, and sequins. Kits and patterns are available, or you can just experiment on your own. Add pretty trims and ribbons, and you can come up with some spectacular creations.

Knots!

Remember, beads are heavy! My bead tragedy is the story of the red beaded wreath I made using a Styrofoam wreath form as a base. I couldn't find the correct size wreath form the directions called for, so I purchased the next size up. One hundred dollars in red glass beads and two years later, I finally finished my masterpiece—and it was too heavy to hang! My husband was afraid it would rip any hanger off the wall. So we use it as a centerpiece to surround a hurricane candle lamp. Live and learn!

◆ **Holiday dining.** For your Thanksgiving or other holiday table, make beaded napkin holders and place card holders using any of the techniques you've learned.

Opportunities to express yourself in beads are all around you—in your home, in your car, in your wardrobe, and for gift-giving. Don't hold back. Cover your world in beads!

The Least You Need to Know

◆ Decorating with beads gives your home glitz and glamour with a modest price tag. If it's got a surface, you can find a way to bead it!

◆ Even your car can be a showcase for your new-found beading skills.

◆ Beaded gifts that are quick and easy to make are now within your reach using the skills you've learned in this book. Tailor your gifts to the person you're making them for, and when you find an idea you like, make several to put away for unexpected occasions.

◆ Holidays shine with beaded accessories you've made yourself.

In This Part

Part 6

Let's Bead It! Additional Projects for Beginning Beaders

Now that you've gotten a solid background in a variety of basic beadworking skills, these final four chapters will give you a variety of beginner's projects to practice. They will reinforce what you already know, plus show you how you can use your imagination and creativity to design endless variations. There's enough here to keep you busy for a long time, creating jewelry, things for your home, and gifts to give your favorite people. Happy beading!

In This Chapter

- ◆ Stringing a multi-strand bracelet
- ◆ Creating a pair of simple loop earrings
- ◆ Making a crystal sun-catcher to decorate your "wheels"
- ◆ Fashioning a beaded pull to make your ceiling fan fabulous

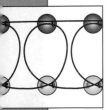
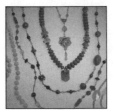

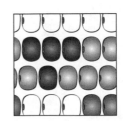

Chapter 19

Stringing Projects

This chapter has four projects to add to your stringing experience—two for yourself, one for your chariot, and one for your home. They're written as "recipes" with tools and supplies first followed by brief instructions.

For complete step-by-step instructions for stringing techniques, refer to Chapter 6. For information on any materials or tools mentioned, check Chapter 5. For color photos of my version of the finished projects, see the color insert.

Multi-Strand Bracelet

Here are two finished multi-strand bracelets.

Supplies:

Soft-Flex or other flexible beading wire, size .014

Sterling silver crimp beads

Toggle clasp

Assorted beads in the color(s) of your choice from 4mm to 8mm

Tools:

Wire cutter

Crimp pliers

Chain-nose pliers

1. Lay out 2 separate strand designs on a bead board or beading cloth, creating a random or repeating design, whatever you wish. The length of each strand should be approximately 7 inches long with the clasp, which is the length of a standard bracelet, so keep the number of beads to the appropriate length. If your wrist is smaller or larger than average, adjust the length to fit.

Knots!

Do consider your placement and spacing, and be careful that your 2 strands will look well together and fit pleasingly when lying side by side. You won't want 2 large beads coming together at the same point, for instance.

2. Cut 2 strands of flexible wire, each approximately 10 inches long. Attach one end of one of the strands to one part of the toggle clasp using a crimp and crimp pliers, the way you learned in Chapter 6. Thread on your first set of beads. Check the length, then connect the other end to the other half of your toggle clasp using a crimp bead and your crimping pliers.

3. Repeat the crimping, stringing, and crimping sequence for the second strand. Trim any wire and tuck ends.

Variations: You can use this same basic recipe to make a beaded watchband. You'll simply be adding a watch face in the center, so you'll be cutting 4 strands and you will need 4 extra crimps for attaching the 2 sets of separate strands to each side of the watch face.

Simple Loop Earrings

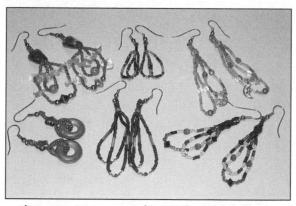

These earrings are simple to make, and the color
possibilities are endless.

Supplies:

Nymo D beading thread

#10 beading needle

Thread conditioner

Pair of earring wires

Size 11° seed beads of your choice

Clear nail polish or glue

Tools:

Scissors

Chain-nose pliers

1. Start by cutting a generous length of
   thread, threading your needle, and condi-
   tioning your thread. Put on 8 seed beads,
   and go around through them to form a
   circle. Tie a knot to secure. Add a dab of
   nail polish or glue to reinforce the knot.

2. Bring your needle and thread out through
   the last bead in the circle and thread on a
   number of seed beads that gives you the
   length loop you want. It can be as long or

as short as you like. You can use all one
color, mix colors, or create a repeating
pattern. You can also make more than
one loop—a long one with a shorter one
is attractive. Be creative.

3. Bring your needle and thread up through
   your 8-bead circle at the top again and all
   the way around. If you have room, bring
   your thread back down through your
   loop(s) again to reinforce them.

4. Knot off, and reinforce your knot with
   polish or glue.

5. Using your chain-nose pliers, open the
   loop in your ear wire and attach your
   looped unit at the 8-bead circle.

6. Repeat steps 1 through 5 for the other
   earring.

Variations: You can use a small (3mm or
4mm) bicone or faceted crystal or any other
bead you desire at the center of your dangling
loop(s). Just be sure you have an even number
of seed beads on either side of your center
bead.

Car Sun-Catcher

Adding a little sparkle to your rear-view mirror doesn't get any easier than this!

Supplies:

Flexible wire in a size appropriate to the size and heaviness of your beads

Crimp beads

Assorted faceted beads of different sizes

Briolette or side-drilled crystal or chandelier crystal

Lobster claw clasp

Tools:

Cutters

Crimping pliers

1. Cut a length of wire that will allow you to make a loop around your mirror, and make a dangle that will be long enough to add some sparkle but not so long that it will hit your windshield (or you!) if you go over a bump. Thread the wire through a crimp bead, the lobster claw clasp and back through the crimp. Close the crimp bead with the crimping pliers.

2. Thread on your beads in whatever order you like, add a crimp bead and put on a drop, dangle, or chandelier crystal at the bottom. I used some seed beads before and after my drop to make a nice compact loop. You can see what I did in the black-and-white photo earlier or, for a better view, see the color photo in the color insert. Also be sure to leave a little space or "play" between your beads so you have a place to fit the lobster claw clasp when you get ready to hang your sun-catcher.

3. Bring the end up through the crimp bead, and close with the crimping pliers forming a loop. Trim the wire closely to the crimp and you're done. Attach your sun-catcher to the mirror of your car by bringing the lobster claw clasp around in a loop and catching the strand between two beads in an appropriate place. By making your sun-catcher with a clasp, you can actually adjust the length so you can take it with you when you get a new car!

Variations: You can make this a multiple-strand project if you'd like. Simply make a wire finding that has three places to attach your strands (a jig might be helpful here), or use a store-bought finding made for adding a clasp to a multiple-strand bracelet or necklace—a "three-to-one" finding. If you'd rather not have your "sun jewelry" in your car, hang your sun-catcher in any sunny window and enjoy it at home.

Fan Pull

A pretty fan pull like this will make you want to look up!

Supplies:

Flexible wire in a size appropriate to the size and weight of you beads

Assorted beads, including 2 size 11° seed beads and 2 (3mm) metal beads

Crimps

Tools:

Cutters

Crimping pliers

1. Cut a length of wire that is long enough that it will hang down from your fan at a height where you can reach up and pull it—but it won't hit anyone in the head as he or she passes under it. Thread on 1 crimp bead, the 3mm metal bead, and 1 size 11° seed. Make a loop and go back through the 3mm metal bead and the crimp bead, then close the crimp. This will keep the rest of your beads on your wire, and this assembly will fit in the ball chain holder at the end of the ball chain that hangs down from your ceiling fan.

The metal bead should fit right into the little "cup" of the holder.

2. Thread on the rest of your beads in a pleasing pattern (you might want to lay out your design on a bead board or cloth first until you create something you like).

3. When you get to the bottom of your pull, use a larger bead to end. But before you put on that bead, put on a crimp, then the ending bead, then the second seed bead. Go back through the ending bead and the crimp, and close the crimp with your crimping pliers. Slide the end with the 3mm metal bead into the ball chain holder, and pull down gently. You're done!

Variations: Use this project idea for a floor lamp or window shade if you don't have a ceiling fan. Just make it shorter and perhaps scale down the proportions to suit the job, using smaller, more delicate beads if you need to. You'll need to devise another way to attach your pull, perhaps using a lobster claw clasp as we did for the sun-catcher.

In This Chapter

◆ Using simple weaving to make a continuous loop daisy-chain necklace

◆ Crafting beautiful hanging earrings using the ladder and brick stitches

◆ Covering a Christmas ornament with lacy beaded netting

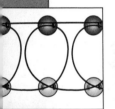 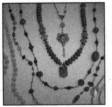   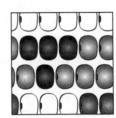 

Chapter 20

Bead Weaving Projects

Practice your weaving skills with the three projects in this chapter.

For complete step-by-step instructions for off-loom weaving stitches, refer to Chapter 7. For color photos of my version of the finished projects, see the color insert.

Daisy-Chain Continuous Loop Necklace

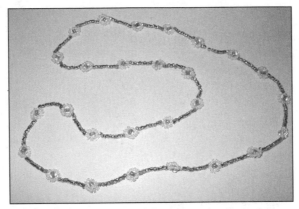

One possible version of the continuous loop daisy-chain necklace.

Supplies:

> Size D Nymo beading thread
>
> Size 10 needle
>
> Size 11° seed beads in 2 colors of your choice; approximately 300 of one and 250 of the contrasting color that will form the daisy
>
> 28 (4mm) round beads that coordinate with your seed beads
>
> Plastic tape
>
> Clear nail polish or glue

Tools:

> Scissors

1. Cut a length of thread about 2 yards long and put some plastic tape at one end. String 10 beads of color #1 and 6 beads of color #2, plus 1 (4mm) bead.

2. Thread the needle through the first #2 bead, then string 4 more #2 beads, and bring the needle through the last #2 bead in the first set of 6 you strung on. This will create a circle with a larger bead in the center—that's your daisy.

3. Continue repeating this pattern until you have a necklace the desired length, approximately 24 inches. It should be long enough that when connected, you can slide it over your head without needing a clasp.

4. Follow the instructions for a continuous loop necklace in Chapter 6. Seal your knots with nail polish or glue.

Variations: If you want to use this pattern for a choker, bracelet, or anklet, just adjust the size and add a clasp. Depending on the colors you choose, this pattern can be dainty enough for a child or sophisticated enough for a grownup. Try alternating the flower colors for more interest. Use metallic or iris beads for a more glamorous look. Use bright primary colors to create a "flower power" rainbow!

Ladder Stitch/Brick Stitch Earrings

As easy as these earrings are to
make, you'll want some in every color.

Supplies:

Beading thread of your choice (I used
Nymo size D.)

Size 10 beading needle

Thread conditioner

Pair of earring wires

Size 11° seed beads

Small bugle beads

Clear nail polish or glue

Tools:

Scissors

1. Make a foundation row of 11 bugle beads
   using the ladder stitch (see Chapter 7).

2. Using the brick stitch (see Chapter 7),
   make your first row of seed beads, which
   should be number 10 seed beads.

3. As you "step up," reduce each row by 1 bead
   until you have 9 seed bead rows altogether.
   Your last row will have 2 seed beads.

4. Come up through the last bead in the
   2-bead row, and add 8 seed beads. Come
   back down the first bead in the 2-bead
   row, and weave through the brick-stitch

triangle you've made, following the existing thread paths. Make a knot somewhere
in your design and reinforce it.

5. Continue weaving down until you reach
   one of the end bugle beads. If you need to
   add more thread, do that, because you'll
   need quite a bit more thread to create the
   fringe.

6. To re-create the fringe on the earring in
   the photograph, add 11 seed beads, 1 bugle,
   6 seed beads, another smaller bugle, and 9
   more seed beads. Bring your needle up
   through the fourth seed bead from the
   needle, forming a little picot at the bottom.

7. Bring the thread up the entire length of
   the fringe you've just made and back
   through that first bugle, then down through
   the second bugle. Continue this process,
   graduating your fringe toward the center
   and making it slightly shorter each time
   by eliminating 1 bead in your first group.
   Your pattern will be 11 seed beads for the
   first fringe, 10 for the second, 9 for the
   third, 8 for the fourth, 7 for the fifth, and 6
   for the center fringe strand. The next row
   you'll start to increase by 1 bead, with 7,
   then 8, then 9, then 10, and finally 11

seed beads on the outermost row on the other side. Otherwise, your pattern sequence remains the same.

8. Weave your thread up through the brick stitch triangle, following the existing thread paths, find a place to knot off, and reinforce the knot. Weave in a little more thread and trim.

9. Using your chain-nose pliers, attach the top 8-bead loop to the loop in one of your

ear wires and close. Now repeat the entire procedure to create a second earring.

Variations: There are many possible variations to this earring. You can create a color pattern within the brick-stitch triangle. You can vary the fringe to come to a V or to be all the same length. The fringe can be longer or shorter, depending on the look you want or the length of your neck. Have fun with this design!

Netted Ornament Cover

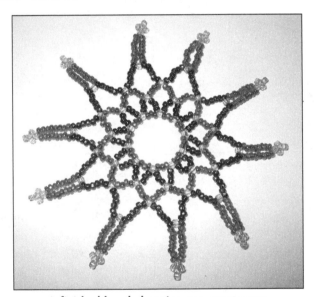

A finished beaded netting ornament cover.

Supplies:

    Beading thread (I used Nymo size D.)

    Size 10 beading needle

    Thread conditioner

    Size 11° seed beads in red, green, and gold

    Glass ball ornament

Tools:

    Scissors

1. Prepare your needle and thread. Give yourself at least 2 yards of thread to start. Put on a stop bead. For round 1, add 3 red beads and 1 gold bead, then repeat 9 times for a total of 40 beads, 30 red and 10 gold. Bring your beads and thread into a circle, make a knot, and go back through the entire circle with your needle and thread, coming out through the last bead, which should be a gold one.

2. For round 2, add 3 green beads, 1 gold bead, and 3 green beads, and go through the next gold bead in round 1. Repeat this sequence, going around the round 1 circle and coming up through the same gold bead you started from.

3. For round 3, go up through the first 3 green beads and 1 gold bead of round 2. Add 4 red beads, 1 gold bead, and 4 red beads, then go through the next round 2 gold bead. You are creating a circular net like we did in Chapter 7. Repeat this sequence until you complete round 3.

4. For round 4, go up through the first 4 red beads and 1 gold bead of round 3. Add 6 green beads, 1 gold bead, and 6 green beads, then go through the next round 3 gold bead. Repeat until you complete the round.

5. You can stop here or add additional rounds, depending on how low you want your ornament cover to drape and how big your glass ball ornament is. You'll need to add beads to the pattern for each round. Just be sure you keep it an odd number with your gold bead in the center. This makes it easy to find the correct bead in the previous round to go through. Tie off, and reinforce your knots.

Variations: You can add pizzazz to this ornament cover in any number of ways. Add drops or fringe to each of the "points" (gold beads) on your last round. (You'll find ideas for different fringes in Chapter 14.) Add drops at various other points within the design. You can also make additional layers of net on top of your base netted ornament cover and even add "ruffles." Substitute bugle beads in the design for some of the seed beads and use bugle beads in your fringe. Adapt this design for bottle or votive candle collars.

Findings

For some gorgeous ornament covers that will keep you beading for holidays to come, check out any of several books with luscious designs. *The Bedecked Ornament, Books 1, 2, 3, and 4* by Laura Jansen is one series full of beautiful patterns. Also, *The Beaded Ornament* by Yvonne Rivero and *Beaded Ornaments* by Jan West and Pamela Hopwood are worth a look. You'll want to display these works of art all year round!

In This Chapter

- ◆ Dazzling chandelier earrings you make yourself
- ◆ Caging a bead
- ◆ Keeping your place with a beaded bookmark
- ◆ Decorating your holidays with beaded wire snowflakes

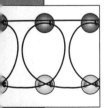 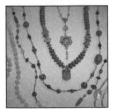   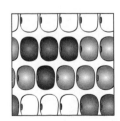 

Chapter 21

Wirework Projects

This chapter has four projects for your wirework library.

For complete step-by-step instructions for wirework techniques, refer to Chapter 11. Chapter 10 should answer your questions on wireworking tools and materials. For color photos of my version of the finished projects, see the color insert.

Chandelier Earrings

These elegant "chandelier" earrings are suited for
any special occasion.

Supplies:

20- or 22-gauge beading wire, your
choice of metal, or 6 head pins of
either gauge

Selection of beads in colors of your
choice (Be sure you have enough of
each type so you can duplicate your
design for both earrings.)

1 pair of matching 3-to-1 findings

1 pair of earring findings

Tools:

Wire cutters

Chain-nose pliers

Round-nose pliers

1. Lay out your design on a beading board
   or cloth. You'll probably want to create a
   symmetrical design of some kind. Some
   possibilities are a center dangle that's
   longer and two matching shorter dangles
   on either side, dangles that graduate in
   length from short to long in either direction, or two longer dangles on the right
   and left with a shorter one in the middle.
   Play with your design until you're happy
   with it.

   Also try different combinations of bead
   sizes, colors, and textures. This is your
   chance to make a pair of custom earrings
   to suit your tastes or to coordinate with
   your favorite outfit. Look at the photograph for some ideas.

2. You can either make your own head pin
   (following the directions in Chapter 11)
   or use a premade head pin to make your
   dangles. To re-create the earrings pictured,
   you'll need 2 longer matching dangles and
   4 matching shorter dangles. You'll also
   need to attach each to the 3-to-1 finding
   as you make the wrapped loop at the top.

3. Attach each finished 3-dangle-and-finding
   unit to an earring finding using your
   chain-nose pliers.

   Variations: Turn your 3-to-1 finding upside
down so the 3 holes are on top and make 3
dangles equal in length for the top of your earring, joining them together by attaching them
to your earring finding, then make one short
dangle to hang down below. See what other
ideas you can come up with!

Caged Bead

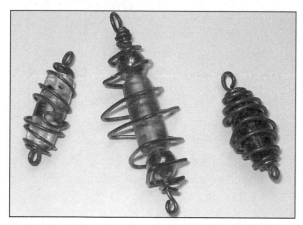

A bead made a focal point by enclosing it in a wire "cage."

Supplies:

>   1 round 10mm bead
>   20-gauge wire in metal of your choice

Tools:

>   Wire cutters
>   Chain-nose pliers
>   Round-nose pliers

1. Cut about 12 inches of wire. Make a tiny loop at one end, and close it.

2. Grasp the loop flat between the jaws of your chain-nose pliers, and make a coil (refer to Chapter 11 if you don't remember how to do this). Keep coiling until you have a coiled circle about the diameter of your bead.

3. Cut the remaining wire so you have approximately the same amount of wire left that you just used to make your first coil. Make a loop at the end going in the opposite direction of your first loop, and coil the remaining wire. You should have a figure eight made out of 2 equal size coils.

4. Lay your bead on one of the coils and push down, making your coil look more like a cup. With your chain-nose pliers, bend the wire where the two coils meet so the second coil now lays over the top of the bead. Push it down over the bead, forming another cup. Use a head pin, an eye pin, or your own connectors made out of wire to incorporate your caged bead into a design.

Variations: Instead of making a round coil, make a triangle. Start by bending the ends of your wire at 45-degree angles with your chain-nose pliers and then coiling the wire at the same angles until you reach the desired diameter. You can also do a square. Use different shape beads to put in your "cages."

Wire Bookmark

A beaded bookmark made using a purchased book-mark finding.

Supplies:

Flat metal bookmark finding in metal of your choice

Beads of your choice

20-gauge wire or head pin to match bookmark finding

Tools:

Wire cutters

Round-nose pliers

Chain-nose pliers

1. Make a head pin or use a premade head pin.
2. Make a dangle, and attach it using closed circuit wirework to the bookmark finding.

Now that was easy!

Variations: You can also make your own wire form for your bookmark. Hammer it flat so it doesn't make a crease in your book. Add more than one dangle or a dangle and some charms. Have fun with your own designs.

Beaded Snowflake

Make a bunch of these easy snowflakes for your tree or anywhere you want to add a bit of holiday sparkle.

Supplies:

4mm glass beads in white, clear, and gold

10 6mm fire-polished glass beads

22-gauge wire

Tools:

Wire cutters

Chain-nose pliers

Round pencil or pen

Findings

This pattern is adapted from one created by Ruth Danielle for Interweave Press. Hers uses smaller beads and has a more intricate design. If you'd like to try it, you can find it at www.interweave.com.

1. Cut about 18 inches of wire and then 4 pieces of wire each about 12 inches long. Thread 10 gold 4mm beads onto the wire 18-inch piece, bring the beads to the center, then go through the circle of beads a second time, making a circle. Twist the two ends of the wire together once, and separate the two ends to make a V.

2. Skip 2 beads on the circle from the V you just made, and take 1 of the 12-inch pieces you cut, cross the wires between the gold beads, and twist with your pliers if necessary, keeping everything tight. Separate the ends of this wire to make another V.

3. Repeat step 2 until you've got 5 V shapes around the circle.

4. Thread 6 clear beads on the left leg of one V shape and 6 clear beads on the right leg of nearest side the nearest V shape, and put the ends of both wires through a 6mm crystal bead. Add 2 white 4mm beads and 1 gold 4mm bead to the two ends above the 6mm bead. Bend the ends down toward the back and through the second white bead. Pull snug and trim the wires. Use the pen or pencil to open the spaces between the clear beads.

5. Repeat around with all the other wires in the same manner. Shape your snowflake, and add a ribbon hanger if you wish.

Variations: Try different patterns adding sections with your wire and beads. Vary colors. Use different sizes of beads.

In This Chapter

◆ Sewing a sachet or pincushion embroidered with beads

◆ Making an embroidered cabochon barrette

◆ Knotting a hemp and bead bracelet

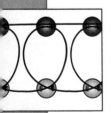    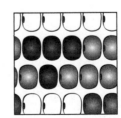 

Fiber and Fabric Projects

To give you some more practice combining beads with fiber and fabric, here are three fun projects for you to have fun with.

For information on beading on fabric, refer to Chapters 13 and 14. For step-by-step instructions on macramé, see Chapter 15. For color photos of my version of the finished projects, see the color insert.

Beaded Pincushion or Sachet

Dainty bead-embroidered sachet and pin cushion.

Supplies:

Scraps of satin or velvet, color of your choice

Scrap of coordinating organza or other tightly woven sheer material for sachet

Assorted size 11° seed beads, colors of your choice

Embroidery thread

Needle with sharp point that will fit through seed beads

Card stock

Sawdust or other filler for your pincushion

Potpourri mix or other scented filler of your choice for the sachet

Scented oil (optional for the sachet)

Tools:

Embroidery hoop (optional)

Sharp scissors

Pencil

1. Decide on a design for your pincushion or sachet. A heart makes a nice design for either one, as does an old-fashioned high-button shoe, or you could just make it a square or rectangle. Draw your design onto your card stock, then cut it out with scissors. This is your design template. Remember, because you'll need a seam allowance, make the size of your design approximately ¼ inch bigger then you want your final pincushion or sachet.

2. Using tailor's chalk or a temporary fabric marker in a contrasting color, trace your design on the right side of your fabric using the template you made in step 1. If you're making a pincushion, you'll need to cut 2 of the same fabric—either satin or velvet. If you're making a sachet, you will cut one from your satin or velvet and one from the organza. This will give you a porous side that will allow the scent to waft through. *Do not* cut out the top piece for your pincushion or sachet yet. Just mark it. You may cut out the bottom piece.

3. Using your chalk or temporary fabric marker, draw a design onto the top piece of your fabric on the right side that you can embroider with beads, keeping in mind the stitches you learned in Chapter 13 or any new stitches you've learned. Stay within the boundaries of the outside edges of your overall design, leaving a ¼-inch area around the edges free of any embroidery. Put your fabric into your embroidery hoop if you like, and embroider your design. You can use the design in the photo as a guide or create your own.

4. Remove your finished embroidered fabric, and cut out your top piece. Putting right sides together, hand or machine stitch the top and bottom pieces together, leaving a small opening to allow you to turn it right side out and to put in your filling.

5. Turn your pincushion or sachet right side out, and stuff with the filling you've chosen. Slip-stitch the opening closed, and you're done!

Variation: Add a beaded picot edge or other trim using the directions in Chapter 14.

Beaded Barrette

What your completed barrette might look like.

Supplies:

Barrette finding

Stabilizer foundation for embroidery. (Choose from card stock, EaZy Felt, Pellon or any of the other materials you learned about in Chapters 13 and 14.)

Seed beads in the colors of your choice

4 (6mm) crystals or glass druk beads to coordinate with your choice of seed beads

1 (12mm×18mm) cabochon

Soft leather or ultrasuede to coordinate with your beads

Embroidery thread

Sharp needle small enough to go through your beads

Glue

Tools:

Scissors

1. Copy the pattern in the following figure onto your foundation making it actual size. Glue on the cabochon in the center using Hypo cement or other adhesive. Then attach the 4 (6mm) crystal or druk beads using needle and thread and going through each several times to secure them.

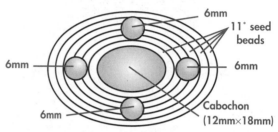

My pattern for the beaded barette you see in the photo. Feel free to design your own!

2. Using the backstitch and starting close to the cabochon, work your design around it and outward in concentric circles. When you come to the 6mm beads, go under the bead and continue your circle of seed beads on the other side. Repeat until you have filled in your design.

3. Glue the leather or ultrasuede to the back of your foundation so the wrong sides are together. Trim to fit, being careful not to cut any of your stitches. Let dry.

4. Bead a picot edge around your beaded piece, going through both the foundation and your backing material. Glue the finished piece to the top of the barrette back and let dry.

Variations: Use this piece as a brooch by adding a pin back instead of a barrette finding. Add a beaded chain on each side and a fringe on the bottom, and wear it as a neckpiece.

Macramé Hemp and Bead Bracelet

Natural hemp and bead macramé bracelet.

Supplies:

Fine hemp cord, 20# test is good

1 focal bead of your choice (Be sure 2 strands of hemp can pass easily through the bead's hole.)

Tools:

Scissors

Chair (optional)

1. Cut 2 pieces of hemp, each 30 inches long. Fold in half equally and, putting the folded edges together, make an overhand knot leaving a small loop (about ½ inch) between the end and the knot. Cut a holding cord and thread through the end loop; then tie it to the rung or back of a chair or other object you can pull against.

Findings
If your wrist is larger or smaller than 7 inches, you might have to adjust your proportions, so be sure you decide this before you do step 2.

2. Make a half square knot with your 4 working cords, and repeat until you have knotted approximately 3 to 3½ inches. Thread your focal bead on the 2 center working cords, and continue making half square knots until you have an equal amount knotted on the other side of the focal bead.

3. When your bracelet is the length you want it, make an overhand knot at the end. This will be the ball that fits through the loop you made at the other end. If you wish, you can thread a bead onto the end of your working cords and then make an overhand knot. The bead will have to have a large enough hole to accommodate all 4 cords or at least the center 2 working cords. You can then make an overhand knot and trim all 4 working cords to finish.

Variations: Try adding beads at regular intervals for a different look.

Glossary

° Indicates the size of the bead, such as 24° and 6°. The higher the number, the smaller the bead.

anneal The process of heating glass or metal to a predetermined temperature for a set period of time, then cooling it slowly to make it harder and less brittle. Small pieces can be heated with a torch. A kiln or an annealing oven is needed for larger pieces.

asymmetrical design Design that is not identical on both sides of a central line or looks off center.

bead The word bead is derived from the Anglo-Saxon *bidden*, which means "to pray," and *bede*, which means "prayer." It is anything that has a hole and can be strung to make jewelry or other decorative items.

bezel That part of a ring, bracelet, etc. to which gems are attached; a grooved ring or rim holding a gem, watch crystal, etc. in its setting.

buckram A cloth made from cotton or linen, usually the former, and closely woven, occasionally with a double warp. It is used most often in book-binding and hat-making and is filled or coated and pressed between rollers to give it a smooth finish, which blocks well and is reasonably durable.

bullion Also called French wire, this is a tight coil of very thin wire used to finish and reinforce the thread that loops through a clasp when stringing beads.

cabochon A smooth, domed gem, polished but not faceted.

calyx A green "cup" or separate small green leaves that sit at the base of a flower. Study a flower to see all its parts if you intend to replicate them in beads, or check out pattern books, which do this for you.

double overhand knot   A type of overhand knot made by simply bringing the tail through the knot twice instead of once.

faience   A type of ceramic developed by the Egyptians, also called "Egyptian paste," made with quartz sand and a colored glaze. Faience is thought to be the forerunner of true glass. You can still buy faience beads today in Cairo and even on the Internet.

finding   Any one of various manufactured pieces other than beads, usually made of metal, that are used to make jewelry or other beaded items.

gold-filled   Also called "rolled gold," this is wire made of a core of metal such as copper, brass, or sterling silver, with a coating of 14-karat gold. Its quality is determined by a number ratio: 14/20 means $\frac{1}{20}$ of the weight of the overall wire is 14-karat gold heated and bonded to the outside of a core of another metal.

hank   Strands of beads tied together and sold as a unit.

Mohs hardness scale   A comparison scale of how a mineral reacts when scratched with a pointed testing object. This scale of scratch hardness, ranging from 1 (softest) to 10 (hardest) was introduced by Viennese mineralogist Friedrich Mohs (1773–1839). The softest on the scale is talc, which can be scratched with a fingernail. The hardest is the diamond.

mounting cord   In macramé, the cord that remains fixed and is used to hold additional cords (working cords) for making knots.

peyote stitch   The term commonly used to describe the gourd stitch, a highly versatile bead weaving stitch common in Native American beadwork. Peyote is actually a small, wooly, buttonlike cactus with hallucinogenic properties that is used as part of a sacred ceremony by a wide variety of Mexican and North American Indian tribes. Peyote beadwork is that beadwork specifically used to decorate some of the ritual objects used in the peyote ceremony.

polymer clay   The generic term for a family of manmade modeling compounds that remain pliable until baked in a typical home oven (at temperatures from 215 to 275°F, depending on the manufacturer). It is actually a plastic called polyvinyl chloride (PVC) mixed with a plasticizer for flexibility and any number of pigments for color. The clay can then be shaped by hand and molded prior to baking. Once hardened, pieces can be wet-sanded, drilled, carved, buffed, glued, and painted.

sepals   Individual green leaves that sit at the base of a flower, at the calyx. Study a flower to see all its parts if you intend to replicate them in beads, or check out pattern books, which do this for you.

soutache   A flat, narrow braid in a herringbone pattern, used for trimming and embroidery.

symmetrical design   Design characterized by arranging parts on opposite sides of a line or point as equally or regularly proportioned, even identical.

texture   The visual and especially the tactile quality of a surface.

warp threads   The set of threads that run lengthwise on a loom.

weft threads   The crosswise thread that forms the woven beaded fabric, under and over the warp threads.

working cords   The cords attached to the mounting cord used to create knots in macramé.

Resources

As you progress in your beadwork, you'll undoubtedly be looking for more specialized or detailed resources than you can find in your local community. This chapter gives you books, magazines, videos, suppliers, shows, and anything else I could think of that has been useful to me or other beaders I know. With what you've learned in this book, what's listed here, and your own imagination, the sky's the limit!

General Beading Information

The following resources will add to your basic knowledge and beading skill.

Books

The Bead Book: A Step-by-Step Guide to the Creative Art of Beading by Victoria Dutton, 1996. (ISBN 0-7651-9943-2)

The Bead Jewelry Book by Stefany Tomalin, 1998. (ISBN 0-8092-2933-1)

Beaded Adornment: Six Beadwork Techniques to Create 23 Necklace and Earring Sets by Jeanette Shanigan, 1998. (ISBN 0-87341-585-X)

Beads: An Exploration of Bead Traditions Around the World by Janet Coles and Robert Budwig, 1997. (ISBN 0-684-83462-6)

Beads! Make Your Own Unique Jewellery [*sic*] by Stefany Tomalin, 1988. (ISBN 0-7153-9839-5)

Beautiful Beads: How to Create Beautiful, Original Gifts and Jewelry for Every Occasion by Alexandra Kidd, 1994. (ISBN 0-8019-8629-X)

The Best Little Beading Book by Wendy Simpson-Conner, 1995. (ISBN 0-96459-570-2)

The Book of Beads: A Practical and Inspirational Guide to Beads and Jewelry Making by Janet Coles and Robert Budwig, 1990. (ISBN 0-671-70525-3)

Findings and Finishings by Sharon Bateman, 2003 (ISBN 1-931499-40-3).

Gemstones of the World by Walter Schumann, 2000. (ISBN 0806994614)

The History of Beads: From 30,000 B.C. to the Present by Lois Sherr Dubin, 1995. (ISBM 0-8109-8178-5)

The Irresistible Bead: Designing and Creating Exquisite Beadwork Jewelry by Linda Fry Kenzle, 1996. (ISBN 0-8019-8843-8)

Magazines

Bead&Button
BeadStyle
Kalmbach Publishing Company
PO Box 1612
Waukesha, WI 53187-1612
www.beadandbutton.com or
www.beadstylemag.com

Beadwork
Interweave Press
201 E. Fourth Street
Loveland, CO 80537-5655
www.beadworkmagazine.com

Lapidary Journal
60 Chestnut Avenue, Suite 201
Devon, PA 19333-1312
www.lapidaryjournal.com

Step-by-Step Beads
60 Chestnut Avenue, Suite 201
Devon, PA 19333-1312
www.stepbystepbeads.com

Supplies and Equipment

You'll definitely want to get out your phone book and check for bead stores in your area. Look in the Yellow Pages under "beads" and also try general "crafts" stores such as Michael's and Ben Franklin.

Some mail-order and online suppliers you'll want to know about include the following:

Fire Mountain Gems and Beads
One Fire Mountain Way
Grants Pass, OR 97526-2373
1-800-423-2319
www.firemountaingems.com

Rings and Things
PO Box 450
Spokane, WA 99210-0450
1-800-366-2156
www.rings-things.com

Rio Grande
7500 Bluewater Road NW
Albuquerque, NM 87121-1962
1-800-545-6566
www.riogrande.com

Shipwreck Beads
8560 Commerce Place Drive NE
Lacey, WA 98516
1-800-950-4232
www.shipwreckbeads.com

Bead Museums

The Bead Museum
5754 W. Glenn Drive
Glendale, AZ 85301
623-931-2737
www.thebeadmuseum.com

The Bead Museum of Washington, D.C.
400 Seventh Street NW
Washington, DC 20004
202-624-4500
www.beadmuseumdc.org

Bead Shows

Bead show organizers have shows all over the country. To see if there's one near you, check their websites for current locations and dates.

The Bead Renaissance Shows
www.beadshow.com

The Whole Bead Show
www.wholebead.com

Intergalactic Bead Shows
www.beadshows.com

These shows are held at specific times of the year:

Bead&Button Show (June)
www.beadandbuttonshow.com

Tucson Gem and Mineral Show (January through February)
www.tucsonshowguide.com

Miscellaneous

Roseanne Andreas's Beaded Phoenix Bead and String Reference Chart Poster and Booklet Set
Beaded Phoenix
PO Box 1053
Warwick, NY 10990
www.beadedphoenix.com

Making Your Own Beads

Handcrafting your own beads makes your work unique. If you can't find just what you want, you can make it!

Books

The Bead Maker: Projects for Creating Hand-Crafted Beads by Mary Maguire, 2002. (ISBN 1581803044)

Beadwork Creates Beaded Beads, edited by Jean Campbell, 2003. (ISBN 1931499276)

Chinese Knots for Beaded Jewelery [sic] by Suzen Millodot, 2003. (ISBN: 0-80483-399-0)

Chinese Knotting by Lydia Chen, 2003. (ISBN 0-80483-399-0)

Creative Clay Jewelry: Designs to Make from Polymer Clay by Leslie Dierks, 1994. (ISBN 0937274747)

Herbs & Things by Jeanne Rose, 2001. (ISBN 0-86719-525-8)

Making Polymer Clay Jewellery [*sic*] by Sue Heaser, 1997. (ISBN 0304350303)

Temari: How to Make Japanese Thread Balls by Diana Vandervoort, 1992. (ISBN 0-87040-881-X)

Videos

There are many videos on making polymer clay beads and jewelry. To see a list from several different artists and video production companies, go to www.polymerclayexpress.com/videos.html.

Also check out the polymer and precious metal clay videos at:

abba dabba Productions
713 Blake Hill Road
New Hampton, NH 03256-4428
1-877-744-0002
www.abbadabbavideo.com
Temari: How to Make Japanese Thread Balls with Diana Vandervoort
www.temari.com

Supplies and Equipment

American Art Clay Company, Inc.
4717 W. Sixteenth Street
Indianapolis, IN 46222-2598
www.amaco.com
Manufacturers of Fimo polymer clay and a variety of hardening and nonhardening clays.

Polyform Products Company
1901 Estes
Elk Grove Village, IL 60007
www.sculpey.com
Manufacturers of Sculpey polymer clay. Lots of projects and information on this site.

Clay Factory of Escondido
PO Box 460598
Escondido, CA 92046-0598
1-877-728-5739
www.clayfactoryinc.com
Suppliers of Premo, Sculpey, Super Sculpey, SculpeyIII, Super Flex, "THE AMAZING Eraser Clay," Granitex, Elasticlay, and Cernit. Also on the site: videos, tools, and equipment.

Online Resources

www.polymerclaycentral.com
An online supplier and polymer clay community.

www.temari.com
Diana Vandervoort's site for Japanese woven embroidery, which can be used to make beads.

www.knottingartist.com
Yvonne Chang's Chinese knotting site.

Organizations

The National Polymer Clay Guild
1350 Beverly Road, Suite 115-345
McLean, VA 22101
www.npcg.org

Bead Stringing and Off-Loom Weaving

The following resources are intended to supplement the instructions given in this book and take you as far as you want to go.

Books

The Magic of Beaded Spherical Nets: Techniques and Projects by Merry Makela, 1996. (ISBN 1-57472-201-8)

Creative Bead Weaving: A Contemporary Guide to Off-Loom Stitches by Carol Wilcox Wells, 1996. (ISBN 1-57990-080-1)

Magazines

Beadwork Magazine Presents Stringing
Interweave Press
201 E. Fourth Street
Loveland, CO 80537-5655
www.beadworkmagazine.com

Videos

Pearl and Bead Stringing with Henrietta
This is Henrietta Virchick's step-by-step instructions for bead and pearl stringing with individual knots. There's an accompanying book as well. It's available from www.blessedbeads.com as well as other online sources.

Pearl Knotting like a Pro and **Step-by-Step Stringing Techniques**
The Bead Shop
158 University Avenue
Palo Alto, CA 94301
650-328-7925
www.beadshop.com

Beadweaving—Peyote Stitch with Carol Perrenoud
Beadcats
PO Box 2840
Wilsonville, OR 97070-2840
503-625-2323
www.beadcats.com

Basic Brick Stitch, Basic Netting, Basic Square Stitch, Basic Right Angle Weave, Basic Peyote (Round Stitch), Basic Peyote (Flat Stitch), Basic N-Dbele (Round and Flat), and **Basic Huichol**
Art Gems, Inc.
3850 E. Baseline Road, Suite 119
Mesa, AZ 85206
480-545-6009
www.artgemsinc.com

Supplies and Equipment

Soft Flex Company
PO Box 80
Sonoma, CA 95476
707-938-3539
www.softflexcompany.com
Manufacturers of Soft Flex flexible stringing wire.

Adam Beadworks
PO Box 2476
Guerneville, CA 95446-9742
707-869-2556
www.threadheaven.com
Manufacturers of Thread Heaven Thread Conditioner and Protectant.

Software

Beadscape (for Macintosh)
Gigagraphica
1265 Allen Avenue
Erie, CO 80516
303-828-1375
www.gigagraphica.com/beadscape/
beadscape.html

AutoBead and **The Bead Pattern Designer**
(for PC)
The Virtual Bead Works
228 Dry Brook Road
Owego, NY 13827-2813
607-687-2793
www.beadville.com

BeadCreator (for PC)
2530 Mitten Lane
Ramona, CA 92065
760-788-1288
www.beadcreator.com/?=bead-patterns

The Bead Cellar Pattern Designer (for PC)
6305 Westfield Avenue
Pennsauken, NJ 08110
856-665-4744
www.beadcellar.com

BeadWizard (for PC)
www.beadwizard.com/
info@beadwizard.com

Bead Painter (for PC)
www.beadpainter.org
This is free software available for downloading
from their website.

Loom Work

Have loom, will travel to new worlds! Here are
some resources to make you even more of a
loom-a-tic.

Books

American Indian Beadwork by W. Ben. Hunt
and J. F. Burshears, 1951.

How to Do Bead Work by Mary White, 1904
(Dover, 1972). (ISBN 0-486-20697-1)

Those Bad Bad Beads by Virginia L. Blakelock,
1990. (Available from Beadcats, PO Box
2840, Wilsonville, OR 97070-2840,
503-625-2323, www.beadcats.com.)

Videos

Bead Woven Necklaces with **Virginia Blakelock**
Beadcats
PO Box 2840
Wilsonville, OR 97070-2840
503-625-2323
www.beadcats.com
Also available with a kit to make the necklace
in the video.

Basic Bead Loom Weaving
Art Gems, Inc.
3850 E. Baseline Road, Suite 119
Mesa, AZ 85206
480-545-6009
www.artgemsinc.com

Bead Weaving Featuring The Mirrix Loom
with **Claudia Chase**
abba dabba Productions
713 Blake Hill Road
New Hampton, NH 03256-4428
1-877-744-0002
www.abbadabbavideo.com

Supplies and Equipment

Mirrix Tapestry and Bead Looms
1097 Bible Hill Road
Francestown, NH 03043
603-547-6278
www.mirrixlooms.com

Crazy Acres Wolf Ranch
Spokane, WA
509-327-9927
www.crazyacreswolfranch.com
They make another loom I like. It's beautifully made, sturdy, comes in a variety of sizes, is reasonable, *and* by buying one, you help the wolves.

Online Resources

rogue.northwest.com/~ahawley/loom.htm
Good site for instructions on making your own loom.

shala.addr.com/beads/resources/ graphpaper/index.html
Graph paper website.

Several sites offer free loom beading designs, such as:

> users.easystreet.com/sequoia/ patterns.html
>
> members.tripod.com/~beadnik/ patdex.html
>
> home.flash.net/~mjtafoya/ patterns.htm
>
> www.nfobase.com/html/ loom_patterns.html

If you're looking for purse frames for woven beaded bags:

> www.baglady.com
>
> www.catspawonline.com
>
> www.victoriancottagetreasures.com

Wirework

Getting wired is just the beginning. These resources will take you over the top.

Books

All Wired Up by Mark Lareau, Interweave Press, 2000. (ISBN 1-883010-73-X)

Basic Wire Work for Bead Jewelry by Kate Drew-Wilkinson, 1994. (ISBN 1884648002)

The Complete Metalsmith: An Illustrated Handbook by Tim McCreight, 1991. (ISBN 0-87192-240-1)

The Wire Bending Book by Wendy Simpson Connor, 1998. (ISBN 0-9645957-9-60)

Videos

Wild About Wire
The Bead Shop
158 University Avenue
Palo Alto, CA 94301
650-328-7925
www.beadshop.com

Basic Wire Work
Art Gems, Inc.
3850 E. Baseline Road, Suite 119
Mesa, AZ 85206
480-545-6009
www.artgemsinc.com

Basic Wire Work for Bead Jewelry
This is the companion video to Kate Drew-Wilkinson's book. It's available from Kate Drew-Wilkinson Designs at: personal.riverusers.com/~beads/newsite/.

Supplies and Equipment

Kate Drew-Wilkinson Designs
PO Box 1803
Bisbee, AZ 85603
520-432-7818
personal.riverusers.com/~beads/newsite/
Get Kate Drew-Wilkinson's earring jig here.

Online

www.wire-sculpture.com
Preston Reuther's wire sculpture site.

The Science Company
www.coscosci.com/patinas/patinasintro.htm
Offers information on wire finishes.

Beaded Flowers

I've given you lots of sources in this section for flower patterns, plus that great video I promised and where to get a bead spinner (or make one yourself, if you're so inclined). And there are plenty of places online to hang out with bead gardeners, as well.

Books

The Art of French Beaded Flowers: Creative Techniques for Making 30 Beautiful Blooms by Carol Benner Doelp, 2004. (ISBN 1-57990-426-2)

Beaded Flowers, Bouquets and Garlands by Suzanne McNeill, 2001. (ISBN 1-57421-804-2)

Beads in Bloom: The Art of Making French Beaded Flowers by Arlene Baker, 2002. (ISBN 1-93149-906-3)

French Beaded Flowers I: A Guide for Beginners by Helen McCall, 1993. (ISBN 0-932255-04-3)

French-Beaded Flowers: New Millennium Collection by Dalene Kelly, 2001. (ISBN 0-87349-357-5)

Making Bead Flowers and Bouquets by Virginia Nathanson, 1967. (ISBN 0-486-42246-1)

More French Beaded Flowers: 38 Patterns for Making Blossoms, Leaves, Insects, and More by Dalene Kelly, 2004. (ISBN 0-87349-734-1)

New Patterns for Bead Flowers and Decorations by Virginia Nathanson, 2004. (ISBN 0-48643-297-1)

Videos

www.geocities.com/roetopol/
Rosemary Topol, an accomplished beaded flower artist, has a homemade beginner's video for sale at her website. You can also see her beautiful work and order patterns there.

Supplies and Equipment

Beadwrangler
7echoes.com/beadspinner/spinner-pak.htm
This is a good source for bead spinners. (A good bead store might have a decent bead spinner, but they're not that easy to find.) The Beaded Garden, mentioned later, also carries bead spinners.

kimberlychapman.com/crafts/beadspinner.html
This site has instructions on making your own bead spinner from inexpensive materials, which might suit you for a while.

Online Resources

www.groups.yahoo.com
Beaded flowers is an excellent beaded flower e-mail list on Yahoo! Dalene Kelly, Carol Doelp, and Rosemary Topol can all be seen there sharing their expertise.

www.beadedgarden.com
Both French and Victorian technique beaded flowers as well as patterns, tools, instruction, and supplies are available here.

www.beadedflowerpatterns.com
This is Dalene Kelly's site. She has patterns and books for sale.

Embroidery and Embellishment

Expand your beading world, and learn more about the unlimited ways to put beads and fabric together.

Books

The Art of Silk Ribbon Embroidery by Judith Baker Montano, 1993. (ISBN 0-91488-155-8)

Bead Embroidery by Valerie Campbell-Harding and Pamela Watts, 1993. (ISBN 0-7134-8606-6)

Beaded Cords, Chains, Straps and Fringe by Jean Campbell, 2001. (ISBN 1-93149-901-2)

Beaded Embellishment: Techniques and Designs for Embroidering on Cloth by Amy C. Clarke and Robin Atkins, 2002. (ISBN 1-931499-12-8)

The Beading on Fabric Book by Wendy Simpson Conner, 1999. (ISBN 0-9645957-8-8)

Beadpoint by Ann Benson, 2003. (ISBN 0-80698-939-4)

Beautiful Beading: A Beginner's Guide by Ruth Wilson, 1995. (ISBN 1-86351-147-4)

The Crazy Quilt Handbook by Judith Montano, 1986. (ISBN 0-914881-05-1)

Crazy Quilt Odyssey: Adventures in Victorian Needlework by Judith Montano, 1991. (ISBN 0-914881-41-8)

Crazy Quilt Stitches by Dorothy Bond, 1981. (ISBN 0-9606086-0-5)

Dimensional Flowers, Leaves and Vines by Barbara Grainger, 2000. (ISBN 0967983320)

Elegant Stitches: An Illustrated Stitch Guide and Source Book of Inspiration by Judith Baker Montano, 1995. (ISBN 0-91488-185-X)

Embellishing With Beads by Nancy Nehring, 2003. (ISBN 1-40270-059-8)

Embroidery Beading: Designs and Techniques by Maisie Jarratt, 1992. (ISBN 0-86417-720-8)

Haute Couture Embroidery by Palmer White, 1988. (ASIN: 0865650942)

How to Bead: French Embroidery Beading by Maisie Jarratt, 1993. (ASIN 0-86417-372-5)

Pin Beading by Victoria Waller, 1999. (ISBN 1-57421-754-2)

Dover Publications
31 East 2nd Street
Mineola, NY 11501-3852
www.doverpublications.com

Magazines

Belle Armoire
Stampington and Company
22992 Mill Creek, Suite B
Laguna Hills, CA 92653
949-380-7318
www.bellearmoire.com

Threads magazine
The Taunton Press
PO Box 5506
Newtown, CT 06470
www.tauntonpress.com

Videos

Bead Embroidery Techniques with Carol
Perrenoud
Yarn Barn
PO Box 334
Lawrence, KS 66044
(ISBN 1-892206-58-7)

Judith Baker Montano's Crazy Quilting
C&T Publishing
PO Box 1456-V
Lafayette, CA 94549
1-800-284-1114
(ISBN 1-57120-013-4)

Judith Baker Montano's Embellishments
C&T Publishing
PO Box 1456-V
Lafayette, CA 94549
1-800-284-1114
(ISBN 1-57120-036-3)

Supplies and Equipment

Lacis
3163 Adeline Street
Berkeley, CA 94703
510-843-7178
staff@lacis.com
www.lacis.com

www.nedastarrdesigns.com
Neda Starr Designs
Get Timtex interfacing here.

Happy Jack's Inc.
PO Box 2646
Rosewell, NM 88202-2646
505-623-1544
www.lacysstiffstuff.com
This is the place for Lacy's Stiff Stuff.

Online Resources

CQembellishers@yahoogroups.com
If you want to share supplier secrets and embroidery tips, this is the place to hang out. There's
plenty of sharing via websites and photos of
some stunning work, as well.

CQ Magazine Online
www.cqmagonline.com/

Vintage Vogue
www.vintagevogue.com/
Supplies, books, patterns, and kits.

Bead Creative with Nancy Eha
www.beadcreative.com
Supplies, gallery, and kits.

Beads and Macramé

Books

Hemp It Up with Beads by Janie Ray for Suzanne McNeill Originals, 1998. (ISBN 1-57421-147-1)

Hemp Masters: Ancient Hippie Secrets for Knotting Hip Hemp Jewelry by Max Lunger, 1998. (ISBN 0-94360-457-5)

The "Knotty" Macrame & Beading Book by Wendy Simpson Conner, 1997. (ISBN 0-96459-574-5)

Online Resources

Macramé Superstore
www.macramesuperstore.com
Books, supplies, and free projects.

Miscellaneous

International Guild of Knot Tyers [*sic*]
www.igkt.net/

Decorating With Beads

We only scratched the surface of the many ways to cover your world with beads in Chapter 18. Here are the resources to help you "kick it up a notch."

Books

The Beaded Lampshade Book by Wendy Simpson Connor, 1996. (ISBN 0964595710)

Beaded Needlecases by Jennie Might, 1998. (ISBN 0966585305)

The Complete Guide to Beading Techniques by Jane Davis, 2003. (ISBN 0873419677)

Inspirations: Decorating With Beads by Lisa Brown, 1998. (ISBN 1-85967-749-5)

Videos

How to Make Victorian and Antique Style Lamp Shades
This 100-minute video will tell you how. The video, plus two others, supplies, and kits are available from:

Heart Enterprises
PO Box 532
Roseville, CA 95678
916-783-4802 or 1-800-398-4981
www.victorianlampshadesupply.com

Online Resources

www.marthastewart.com
The Martha Stewart Living website offers lots of ideas for decorating with beads.

www.hgtv.com
More ideas from Home and Garden Television.

There are also some great free ideas at the Michael's and Ben Franklin store websites:

www.michaels.com
www.benfranklin.com

www.vintageshades.com
Offers beaded lampshade supplies.

www.sugarshades.com
Find forms for making fabric-covered and beaded nightlights here.

www.impressrubberstamps.com
Find out how to make birth announcements with beads here.

Mill Hill Glass
www.millhill.com
Kits and supplies for bookmarks and other decorative items and gifts.

Supplies and Equipment

Mainely Shades
100 Gray Road
Falmouth, ME 04105
207-797-7568 or 1-800-624-6359
Lampshade forms and supplies.

Safety, Care, and Maintenance

Working safe and keeping the clutter at bay, then taking good care of the fruits of your love's labor—here are the resources to help you keep it all together.

Books

The Complete Idiot's Guide to Organizing Your Life by Georgene Lockwood, 2002. (ISBN 0-02-864318-6)

Home Comforts: The Art and Science of Keeping House by Cheryl Mendelson, 1999. (ISBN 0-68481-465-X)

It's Not Carpal Tunnel Syndrome! RSI Theory and Therapy for Computer Professionals by Suparna Damany and Jack Bellis, 2001. (ISBN 0-96551-099-9)

Online Resources

www.ott-lite.com
Ott Lite.

www.gelighting.com/na/reveal/media_faqs.html
Information about General Electric Reveal bulbs.

msds.pdc.cornell.edu/msdssrch.asp
Cornell University's free MSDS (Materials Safety Data Sheet) site.

eeshop.unl.edu/rsi.html
Information about Repetitive Strain Injury.

www.silversmithing.com
Society of American Silversmiths

Appendix C

Some Useful Charts

A little math goes a long way! With the charts I've given you here, you won't have to do too much calculating. I've also provided you with some other charts to make your beadwork just that much more meaningful. Have fun!

Note: All conversions are approximate and are to be used as a guide.

Millimeters to Inches

Millimeters	Inches
2	slightly over $\frac{1}{16}$
3	$\frac{1}{8}$
4	$\frac{5}{35}$
5	$\frac{3}{16}$
6	$\frac{1}{4}$
8	$\frac{5}{16}$
10	$\frac{3}{8}$
13	$\frac{1}{2}$
16	$\frac{5}{8}$
19	$\frac{3}{4}$
22	$\frac{7}{8}$
25	1

Number of Seed Beads Per Inch

Size	Beads per Inch
16/0	28
11/0	18
8/0	11.5
5/0	7.5

Approximate Number of Round Beads in a Strand

Bead Size	16 Inches	18 Inches	24 Inches
2mm	200	225	300
3mm	132	144	200
4mm	100	112	153
5mm	82	90	124
6mm	68	76	100
7mm	57	63	85
8mm	50	56	76
10mm	40	45	61

Note: These numbers are for beads on a strand without knots between beads. If you are using a clasp, subtract the number of beads that approximate the length of your clasp.

Number Uniform Round Beads on a Strand Per Inch

Size	Beads per Inch
2mm	13
4mm	7
8mm	3.25
10mm	2.5
12mm	2

Bead Size Chart

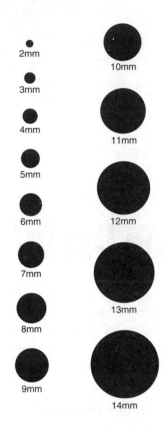

Common Chain Styles

Cable

Charm

Curb

Figaro

Long and short cable

Rollo

Mariner

Krinkle link

Number of Feet of 14k Gold-Filled Wire per Ounce

Gauge	Inches	Millimeters	Round Foot/Ounce	Square Foot/Ounce	Half-Round Foot/Ounce
24	0.0201	0.511	55.50	41.87	n/a
22	0.0253	0.643	35.50	25.89	71.0
20	0.032	0.813	21.68	15.95	42.87
18	0.0403	1.02	13.80	11.1	27.6
16	0.0508	1.29	8.75	6.76	17.82

Adapted from www.jewelry-tools.com.

Number of Feet of Sterling Silver Wire per Ounce

Gauge	Inches	Millimeters	Round Foot/Ounce	Square Foot/Ounce
24	0.0201	0.511	48	36
22	0.0253	0.643	31	22
20	0.032	0.813	19	14
18	0.0403	1.02	12	9.50

Adapted from www.jewelry-tools.com.

Some Helpful Measurements and Weights

1 gross (gr)	144 pieces, 12 dozen, or 72 pair
1 inch	25.4 millimeters or 2.54 centimeters
1 ounce (oz.)	28.35 grams
1 millimeter (mm)	$\frac{1}{25}$ inch
1 kilogram (K)	1,000 grams, 2.2 pounds, or 35.27 ounces
1 gram (g)	.035 ounces

Adapted from www.bobbybead.com.

Seed Bead Sizes

Seed Bead Size	Size in Millimeters
6°	3.3
7°	2.9
8°	2.5
9°	2.2
10°	2.0
11°	1.8
12°	1.7
13°	1.5
14°	1.4
15°	1.3

Adapted from www.2bead.com.

Birthstones

Month	Stone(s)
January	Garnet
February	Amethyst
March	Aquamarine, bloodstone
April	Diamond, quartz
May	Emerald, chrysoprase, beryl
June	Pearl, moonstone, alexandrite
July	Ruby, carnelian
August	Peridot, jade
September	Sapphire, lapis lazuli
October	Opal, tourmaline
November	Yellow topaz, citrine
December	Blue topaz, turquoise

Zodiac Stones

Sign	Dates	Stones
Capricorn	December 22 to January 19	Ruby, agate, garnet
Aquarius	January 20 to February 18	Garnet, moss agate, opal, amethyst
Pisces	February 19 to March 20	Rock crystal, sapphire, amethyst, bloodstone
Aries	March 21 to April 19	Bloodstone, diamond
Taurus	April 20 to May 20	Sapphire, turquoise, amber, blood, coral, emerald
Gemini	May 21 to June 20	Agate, chrysoprase, pearl
Cancer	June 21 to July 22	Emerald, moonstone, pearl, ruby
Leo	July 23 to August 22	Tourmaline, sardonyx, onyx
Virgo	August 23 to September 22	Jasper, carnelian, jade, sapphire
Libra	September 23 to October 22	Opal, lapis lazuli, peridot
Scorpio	October 23 to November 21	Aquamarine, topaz
Sagittarius	November 22 to December 21	Sapphire, amethyst, turquoise, topaz

Chakra Stones

Chakra	Stones and Colors
7th, Crown	Clear quartz, white howlite, white marble, moonstone, and amethyst (clear, white, and purple stones)
6th, 3rd Eye	Lapis lazuli, amethyst, lepidolite, sugilite, iolite, selenite, and moonstone (clear, white, and purple stones)
5th, Throat	Blue lace agate, lapis lazuli, sodalite, turquoise, aquamarine, sapphire, iolite, and blue topaz (blue, blue-green, and blue-purple stones)
4th, Heart	Green aventurine, jade, amazonite, moldavite, pink quartz, rhodonite, rhodachrosite, and kunzite (pink and green stones)
3rd, Solar Plexus	Citrine, yellow jasper, yellow calcite, sunstone, tiger's eye, golden topaz, peridot, and serpentine (yellow and yellow-green stones)
2nd, Sacral	Red and orange carnelian, red jasper, and orange jasper (red and orange stones)
1st, Base	Obsidian, onyx, blue-black sunstone, hematite, black tourmaline, red jasper, red carnelian, and red garnet (black and red stones)

Adapted from www.crystal-life.com.

Index

pearl cotton, 175
pearls, 8
pellon, 162
pendants, 39
perforated disks, 38
perle, 175
pet safety, 189-190
peyote stitches, 80
    bezels, 164
    flat even count peyote, 80-83
    tubular, 84
picot edging, 167
pillows, 207
pin backs, 38
pin beading, 158
pincushions, 209, 236
plastic beads, 13
pliers
    chain-nose, 40, 115
    crimping, 41
    flat-nose, 41
    nylon-jawed, 137
    round-nose, 40, 115
    split-ring, 41, 117
    wirework, 114-116
PMC (Precious Metals Clay), 27
polymer clays, 25-26
pony beads, 14
positioning looms, 100
pound beads, 12
powercords, 60
prayer beads, 6
Precious Metals Clay (PMC), 27
pressed glass beads, 12
primary colors, 50
primitive cultures, 6
primitive styles, 51
princess length necklaces, 49
protecting beads, 195-196
purse frames, 38

R

random designs, 48
rattail, 175
rattail satin cords, 60
reamers, 41
recycled materials, 10
repeating patterns, 48
Reveal light bulbs, 187
rice beads, 15
right-angle stitches, 86-87
ritual offerings, 6
rocaille beads, 12
rolled gold wire, 112
Romantic styles, 52
rondelle beads, 16
rope necklaces, 49
rosettes, 169-170
round beads, 15
round-nose pliers, 40, 115
RSI, 188
rulers, 40

S

S clasps, 37, 130-131
sachets, 207, 236
safety
    children, 189-190
    eyes, 185-188
    lungs, 189
    pets, 189-190
    RSI, 188
sanding blocks, 117
satin beads, 12
satin cords, 60
scales, 16
scallops, 167
scatter stitches, 157-158
The Science Company website, 118
scissors, 40, 210

secondary colors, 50
seed beads, 12, 137
self-hardening clays, 25
semi-precious stones, 8-9
setting cabochons, 163-166
sewing rooms, 209-210
shapes, 14
    bicone, 14
    briolette, 14
    cabochon, 14
    cameo, 14
    chevron, 14
    corrugated, 14
    crow, 14
    designs, 47
    disk, 14
    donut, 15
    double-drilled, 15
    drop, 15
    druk, 15
    eye, 15
    fetish, 15
    heishi, 15
    lantern, 14-15
    melon, 15
    oval, 15
    rice, 15
    rondelle, 16
    side-drilled, 16
    slant-drilled, 16
    tube, 16
    wire, 110
side wire cutters, 40
side-drilled beads, 16
silamide, 59
silk, 58
silk threads, 175
silkon, 59
silver
    plates, 200
    wire, 112
silver-lined beads, 13
single fringe, 168

X–Y–Z